COLLECTOR'S BOOK OF CHILDREN'S BOOKS

THE COLLECTOR'S BOOK OF CHILDREN'S BOOKS

Eric Quayle

Photographs by Gabriel Monro

Studio Vista

Produced by November Books Limited, 23–29 Emerald Street, London, WC1N 3QL.

Published by Studio Vista Publishers, Blue Star House, Highgate Hill, London, N19.

Text filmset by Yendall & Company Limited, 22–25 Red Lion Court, Fleet Street, London, EC4.

Printed by Compton Printing Limited, Pembroke Road, Stocklake, Aylesbury, Bucks.

Bound by Webb Son & Co. Ltd., 303 Chase Road, Southgate, London, N14.

© Eric Quayle and November Books Limited 1971.

SBN 289.70203.8

Designed by Tom Carter.
House Editor: Frances Kennett.

TO

Percival Hinton

IN MEMORY OF OUR TUESDAY EVENINGS

BY THE SAME AUTHOR
Ballantyne the Brave, 1967
The Ruin of Sir Walter Scott, 1968
R. M. Ballantyne: A Bibliography of First Editions, 1968
The Collector's Book of Books, 1971

155,929

Outer back jacket
First issued as 'penny dreadfuls', the boy's 'bloods' of the period 1885–1900 are difficult to find as complete tales in their original pictorial paper-wrappers, published at six-pence, ninepence, or one shilling a copy.

B/9428

Contents

The Author's Choice

Being a selection of the best 100 works to form the basis of a representative library devoted to the history of children's books.

A.B.C. for Children
Aesop's Fables
Alice's Adventures in Wonderland
Adventures of Baron Munchausen
Andersen's Fairy Tales
Basket of Flowers
Black Beauty
Books for the Bairns
Boy's Country Book
Boy's Own Annual
Butterfly's Ball
Children of the New Forest
Child's Garden of Verses
Christie's Old Organ
Christopher Robin books
Coral Island
Daisy Chain
Elementarwerke für die Jugend und ihre Freunde
Emil and the Detectives
Eric or Little by Little
Fabulous Histories
Fairy Books, by Andrew Lang
Girl of the Limberlost
Girl's Own Annual
Golliwogg books
Goody Two-Shoes
Grimm's Fairy Tales
Gulliver's Travels
Helen's Babies
Histoires ou Contes de Temps Passé
Historical Account of the most celebrated Voyages
History of Babar
History of Little Henry
History of Sandford and Merton
History of the Earth, and Animated Nature
History of the Fairchild Family
Holiday House
Home Treasury of Books
Huckleberry Finn
Hymns for Infant Minds
In Fairyland
Island Home
Jack Harkaway Stories
Jessica's First Prayer
Jungle Books
Just William
King of the Golden River
Kunst und Lehrbüchlein
L'ami des Enfans
Leather-Stocking Tales

Life and Perambulations of a Mouse
Little Lord Fauntleroy
Little Master's Miscellany
Little Pretty Pocket-Book
Little Women
Looking-Glass for Children
Martin Rattler
Masterman Ready
Ministering Children
Minor Morals for Young People
Moonfleet
Mopsa the Fairy
Only Toys
Orbis Sensualium Pictus
Original Poems, for Infant Minds
Out on the Pampas
Parent's Assistant
Peacock "at home"
Pentamerone
Peter and Wendy
Peter Parley annuals
Peter the Whaler
Pilgrim's Progress
Peter Rabbit books
Queechy
Railway Children
Rambles of a Rat
Renowned History of Giles Gingerbread
Rollo stories
Sandford and Merton
Secret Garden
Stalky & Co.
Story of Little Black Sambo
Story of Little Henry
Story of the Treasure Seekers
Swallows and Amazons
Swiss Family Robinson
Tarzan of the Apes
Through the Looking Glass
Tom Brown's School Days
Tommy Thumb's Pretty Song Book
Tom Sawyer
Treasure Island
Uncle Tom's Cabin
Under the Window
Voyages of Dr Dolittle
Water Babies
Wide, Wide World
Wind in the Willows
Wizard of Oz

Introduction

Long after the novels and romances of adult life have faded and been forgotten, the simple stories and tales we read in childhood live on in our hearts. Who ever forgets *The Story of the Three Bears*, the tale of *Jack the Giant Killer*, or the plots of *Rumplestiltzkin, Cinderella*, or *The Wizard of Oz*? The nursery rhymes and fairy-tales we first heard in the tucked-up-in-bed security of early youth continue to exert a fascination throughout life, the words and phrases etching themselves in the memory for instant recall at any time or place. They colour our literary consciousness, and are repeated as fables to the eager young listeners who re-create the image of ourselves so many years ago. Just to hear again the magic words 'Once upon a time . . .' with all the breath-taking anticipation they inspire, is to crowd the mind with the lost delights of childhood and conjure up a picture of a never-never land of make-believe and fantasy. Once, a long time ago, all of us lived there and believed it to be true. This is the story of the little books that made us believe; and probably brought us more happiness and peace of mind than anything we have ever read since.

To embark on a history of children's books will take us back into the 16th century, to the days when Shakespeare was still a boy, carrying not only his satchel 'unwillingly to school', but more than likely a battered and well-worn horn-book, used as a primer during lessons, but pressed into service in the school-yard as a short-handled bat for ball games. Books for the amusement of children in those days were few and far between, but were not entirely absent, as will be seen in the next chapter. The scope of this work allows us to study their evolution, through the days of Queen Elizabeth I; the early 'courtesy books' and the Puritan aids to youthful piety; the mid-18th-century world of John Newbery in London and the early American publishers in Boston and Philadelphia; the Victorian world of the 19th century with its classical titles, such as *Alice in Wonderland* or *Huckleberry Finn*; to the adventure stories and larger-than-life fiction of the present literary cavalcade. The little volumes in which our great-great-grandparents first spelled out the story of *Goody Two-Shoes, The Butterfly's Ball, The Tales of Peter Parley*, or of the brothers Grimm, have an unfailing attraction for specialist book-collectors all over the world. Since the days when I first began collecting books, I have been unable to resist purchasing each and every volume I could (or could not) afford. In fact, these ephemeral and so often elusive little books, with their hand-coloured frontispieces and woodcut and copperplate engravings, brightly printed boards or floral Dutch-paper bindings, have brought me more pleasure as a collector of literature than any of the massive folios and important looking quartos that line the bottom shelves of my study walls.

Many of the books described here can still be bought for a few shillings; although the tardy realisation of the important part literature for children and young people plays in moulding the outlook of youth has caused reassessments of the work of several neglected authors. The rarer and better known early and first editions will now cost the present-day collector many pounds to acquire; and if he or she reaches for the high-spots in juvenilia they will soon be into the three- or even four-figure bracket, with only a handful of volumes to show for it. The earlier you retreat in time the higher the cost will mount; but this present work will, I trust, allow the reader to avoid many of the pitfalls and mistakes that trap the unwary.

Early children's books, and neglected items of once treasured juvenilia, can

An illustration by E. Caldwell for *The Diverting History of Three Blind Mice*, published by Marcus Ward, *c.* 1900.

Size of plate: 10.8 cm × 13.5 cm.

still be discovered in attics and junk-rooms where the faded playthings of youthful readers have been hidden away after spring-cleans. The once proudly exhibited school prize can as easily be a first as a fourteenth edition. At least we can be reasonably certain that it started life brand new in the possession of the highly commended young owner whose name sometimes appears on a pasted-in ornamental label. I have volumes dated as early as the first quarter of the 19th century that are still as bright and untarnished as the day the original owner opened their covers for the first time. Some youthful bibliophile had seen to it that they were paper-wrapped and protected from that day forth. But these are exceptional cases. Usually, the condition of those works whose popularity had led them to pass through the loving fingers of several generations of sometimes grubby hands leaves much to be desired. Nevertheless, any collector who wishes to earn respect in the world of books will seek out and acquire only volumes whose condition, both as regards binding and internal make-up, will add lustre to his shelves. Those of the Edwardian and Victorian eras must be sought in complete and unsullied state in their original bindings, with all their tipped-in plates, which are so often missing. The further back you step in time, the less likely are you to find fine copies of stories and picture-books once cherished by juvenile owners. This observation applies, of course, to all classes of literature – the older the book the less likely it is to have survived intact – but to children's books, especially popular and well-loved titles, it refers with special force. Those produced in the 18th century are often known only by a single, surviving, imperfect copy. It is surprising how many have, in fact, withstood the ravages of time, and a glance at the accompanying illustrations will reveal a varied cross-section of happy survivors, the earliest dating from 1580.

The gradual acquisition of a well-chosen selection of early children's books, dating from the days of one's own childhood as far back as luck and your financial resources allow you to go, soon becomes a rewarding hobby. As your library grows, so will the fascination the painstakingly acquired little volumes exert over you. Mine stand in serrated rows of talls and shorts, some stout and important looking or elegantly thin, some plain and unadorned in their original grey-paper boards, others blazoned with gold-blocking and gay in a spectrum of blind-stamped cloth bindings. Some hide in miniature slip-cases less than two inches tall, while the late 19th-century annuals tower over their shelf-mates and announce their volume numbers by the stars on their spines. The oldest stand erect and aloof in glass-fronted mahogany cabinets jointly occupied by a disdainful array of Eng. Lit. high-spots and rare first editions. The most extravagantly dressed are the crowded spines on the shelves devoted to the collections of boys' adventure stories; the titles by Fenimore Cooper, R. M. Ballantyne, G. A. Henty, Gordon Stables, W. H. G. Kingston, Herbert Strang, and others. They are a gaily chattering concourse of similar-sized octavos, bright with gold-blocking and a rainbow-hue of pictorial cloth bindings. I find it difficult to resist their appeal, and that of their as yet unacquired companions in the pages of antiquarian booksellers' and auctioneers' catalogues. I have never regretted buying a book, but I mourn for several that hesitation allowed to fall into other hands.

The means by which first editions are identified, the points and pitfalls to watch, and the technical terms used by antiquarian booksellers, auctioneers, and experienced book-collectors, have all been fully explained in *The Collector's Book of Books*, a companion volume to this present work. I would also like to make clear that, as with the previous volume, I have used only books that are in my own collection as illustrations, thus giving an indication of the possibilities that are still open to present-day collectors of early children's books.

Almost from the start of my book-collecting career, I reserved a few shelves for early children's books. Let me say at once that, viewed from the financial aspect, the hobby is most rewarding. The prices I paid a few years ago are mouth-watering when compared with the sums asked today for other works in the same field.* This is a fortuitous state of affairs that is likely to increase in emphasis during the coming decades. No one, whether he is a millionaire collector with unlimited funds, or an impoverished seeker-out of trifles in book-shop back rooms, can command the appearance of an 1865 *Alice*, much less a copy of a 1765 *Goody Two-Shoes*. Undoubtedly, the longer the purse, the more expediently a specialist library covering any sphere of human endeavour can be acquired. But, especially in the field of early children's books, there are 'high-spots', such as the two quoted above, that just cannot be bought for love or money and are as likely to be stumbled on in a Liverpool cellar as at a London auction. With minor authors and neglected or forgotten titles that no self-respecting antiquarian bookseller has bothered to retain, a collector of moderate means is on an almost equal footing with his wealthier rival. Finding the book is more important than the ability to pay for it.

My own collection of juvenilia and books specially produced for children and young people has expanded to a size that demands a room of its own. I am constantly adding to it and hope to continue to do so for as long as I am fit enough to open a bookshop door. The pleasure is in the collecting. Despite the keenness of present-day competition, there is still plenty of scope for the old campaigner and room enough for the novice collector. A love and understanding of the little volumes that brought so much pleasure to countless children of past ages is a prime requisite. Much of the rest you can learn by a diligent perusal of this present work.

* All prices quoted with US equivalents are given at the current UK/USA exchange rates prevalent at the time of writing.

If the date given after the title of any work quoted here is enclosed in parentheses, this bibliographical device indicates that it was published in that year but appeared without a date of issue on its title-page or elsewhere in the book.

A coloured illustration from *A Sketch-Book of R. Caldecott's* (1883), engraved by Edmund Evans, published by George Routledge & Sons.

Size of plate: 20 cm × 15 cm.

Juvenile
Incunabula

To those collectors who appreciate the rarity of children's books published as late as the latter half of the 18th century, it will come as a surprise to learn that examples have survived that can be dated some 200 years earlier. Printing as we know it today, by means of moveable metal type, was invented by Johann Gensfleisch zum Gutenberg (*c.* 1400–68), a German craftsman from Strasbourg. For some 20 years he worked in his native town on the perfection of his printing-press, later moving to Mainz. It was here his one-time partner Johann Fust, with the help of his son-in-law Peter Schoeffer, supervised the printing of the first book, as we know books today. The result was the magnificent and noble masterpiece the Gutenberg *Bible*, published in 1456.

The Latin word *incunabula*, used as a heading for this chapter, can be translated in a literal sense into the old biblical term of 'swaddling-clothes'. The

The title-page of the earliest known picture-book for children, *Kunst und Lehrbüchlein*, 1580, the first part of the translation reading: 'A Book of Art and Instruction for young people, wherein may be discovered all manner of merry and agreeable drawings . . .'

Size of page: 16.5 cm × 13 cm.

term incunabula has come to be accepted by bibliographers as denoting books printed during the infancy of the art, usually any book printed before the arbitrary but convenient date of 1500. The '42-line' Gutenberg *Bible* appeared in 1456; but we must wait well over another hundred years before the appearance of the first book specially published for children and young people. Juvenile incunabula must be allowed a more generous time-scale than their adult counterparts in the world of literature. I have suggested 1700 as a date before which any book produced for the amusement or instruction of children in particular, or young people in general, can be accorded the distinction of belonging to a select handful of volumes known as juvenile incunabula. They are undoubtedly far rarer than their mature predecessors, the 'fifteeners' as the Victorians called them, with a familiarity bred of a frequent meeting with pre-1500 folios and quartos offered for sale in antiquarian booksellers' catalogues. Books published for young people before 1700 are of an absolute rarity; such examples that have survived are treasured by a dwindling band of private collectors and the majority have long since found their ultimate resting place in the archives of museums and national libraries.

It is only within the last few years that the first picture-book for children was recognised. Its discovery, in a glass-fronted case in the backroom of a small bookseller's shop within a mile of the British Museum, is a story of bibliographical detection that must one day form a chapter in the memoirs of a bibliophile's secret life. The tale itself must wait; but the book is here revealed.

Kunst und Lehrbüchlein was first published in Germany in 1578, although it was then composed of a hotch-potch of illustrations culled from a variety of books which the publisher, Sigmund Feyerabend (1528–90), had issued during the previous decade. *Book of Art and Instruction for Young People*, to give the work its English title, was re-issued in 1580 as a book specially prepared for the youth of the day. The finely-executed full-page woodcut illustrations, of which several are displayed here, were the work of Jost Amman (1539–91), who lived the early part of his life in Zurich, Switzerland. He had designed and drawn the pictures with an eye to their appeal to the younger members of the family, and in this he appears to have eminently succeeded, for the work passed through a number of editions, the last dated as late as 1669. 'These (illustrations) have been published for the benefit of all who wish to profit by them, and it is my sincere hope that this book will confer particular benefits upon the young,' wrote Sigmund Feyerabend in the preface. He was a pioneer in book production, a forward thinking man and the head of a profession of printers and publishers that was to make the name of the city of Frankfurt world-famous as a centre of book production. The fact that the present-day Frankfurt Book Fair is held annually in the city is a tribute to Feyerabend's independence of thought and business initiative. He can now be awarded the laurels for publishing the first picture-book ever produced for juveniles, and possibly the first children's book ever printed. 'We have a duty to our children, no matter what our standing or profession,' he told his readers, addressing his remarks to the parents, relatives, or friends of the young people for whom the book was primarily intended. No child of the age could have afforded to purchase on its own account any printed work, much less a lavishly illustrated quarto such as *Kunst und Lehrbüchlein*. 'The setting and publishing of books during these years has not been accomplished without incurring considerable expense . . .' Feyerabend added, in mitigation of the price he was forced to charge. A glance at the magnificent series of woodcut illustrations, depicting almost every aspect of European everyday life, some ten years before the Spanish Armada set sail for Flanders, makes one appreciate that perhaps this statement was not just part of a 16th-century book publisher's prepared speech to stimulate sales. Those collectors and experts in the field of early illustrated books who have examined the copy shown are unanimous in their praise of the quality of the woodcuts, the design and general format of work. As the first book aimed at the unexplored juvenile market it set a standard that Feyerabend's competitors must have found extremely difficult to meet.

The full importance of *Kunst und Lehrbüchlein* was appreciated even before it was known that the work contained the first printed pictures of a young scholar using a horn-book, and also of a child holding a doll. Both these illustrations, reproduced in this present work, are outstanding examples of Jost Amman's observant attention to detail and a tribute to his masterful skill as

Left and right
Illustrations by Jost Amman for *Kunst und Lehrbüchlein*, 1580, showing (*left*) the first printed picture of a child using a horn-book.
Size of page: 16.5 cm × 13 cm.

both artist and draughtsman. Horn-books such as the one which the young man is so diligently using, consisted of a piece of paper or parchment let into a recess in a tablet of wood, leather, or, in rarer cases, metal or bone. There may have been ivory examples, but I know of none which have survived. No two examples seem to be identical and a child starting school may have had one carved specially for his use. Girls in those days received what education was thought fit for them from their mothers or aunts or other knowledgeable female members of the household. A slice of thin transparent horn covered the paper of the young man's horn-book, thus protecting it from the grubby fingers of its owner, rather in the manner in which a slip of plastic sheeting might be used today. On the sheet of paper or parchment there was either printed or written the Lord's Prayer, the alphabet, and perhaps a set of Roman numerals. These were then studied in the manner in which the boy in Amman's picture is applying himself. Of particular interest is the way the lad is using his horn-book: in his right hand he has a metal rod, which has a hook at one end, from which it hangs from his belt when not in use. At the other end is a ring to circle individual letters as they are read out. The handles of the earliest horn-books, such as the one shown here, had a hole bored through the projection at the top so that they could be attached to the scholar's belt by a loop of string. They are believed to have first come into use in the 16th century and it was only in later years that the projection gradually became more elongated. Some ended with handles of a length sufficient to enable scholars to wield them as makeshift bats in the playground; a forerunner of the bat and ball games that finally resulted in the evolution of the English game of cricket.

The little girl with the doll represents a figure familiar in children's literature from that time onwards; but the illustration depicts the first known printed picture of a doll or puppet of any sort. The child herself is shown by Amman dressed in the identical clothing worn by her mother and other grown-up female relatives, just as the little doll is itself wearing a dress in the same style as its young mistress. It is sometimes forgotten that children as late as the first quarter of the 19th century invariably wore scaled-down versions of the dresses and clothes used by their elders. Clothes specially designed for children were a late innovation, a fact that will quickly become apparent if illustrated books and pictures produced before the 1830s are studied. The rest of the woodcuts in *Kunst und Lehrbüchlein*, totalling in all 94 full-page illustrations, provide an intimate picture of the late 16th-century society in which Jost Amman lived,

as well as a rich store of legends, fables and folk-tales popular with children
of that time. It seems more than likely that budding young artists used the
book as an aid to draughtsmanship, as Sigmund Feyerabend primarily
intended that they should. The figures were probably traced over, coloured,
cut out for scrap-books, disfigured by rude and humorous alterations, stiffened
with backing and used for cardboard soldiers and citizens of model towns, and,
in the final stages of the little volume's disintegration, carefully folded for boats
and paper darts. Children, from the time of Amman onwards, have committed affectionate outrages on the picture books that have brought them the
greatest pleasure, rating the book's value only in direct proportion to the
practical enjoyment it brings them. It is tolerably certain that the children
of the 16th and 17th centuries made use of Feyerabend's *Book of Art and
Instruction for Young People* in similar fashion and its mortality in the first fifty
or so years of its life must have been very high. By the 18th century, it was
already a collector's piece and copies that had managed to survive that far in
time had more than a sporting chance of lasting to the present day. But damp
walls and the perils of fire, shipwreck and war, no doubt went on taking their
toll. The copy illustrated is one of the few that have lasted; but a finely produced collotype facsimile of this landmark in the annals of children's books has
recently been published in a limited edition by the Eugrammia Press, London.

Picture-books provide one of the most fruitful ways in which a child can
increase his knowledge of the world and extend his vocabulary to include a
diverse and exotic mixture of places and things to which he would otherwise
remain a stranger. John Locke, in *Some Thoughts concerning Education*, 1693,
believed that pictures riveted the attention of the young in a way that could
be exploited for their own good. 'As soon as he begins to spell, as many pictures
of animals should be got him as can be found, with the printed names to them,
which at the same time will invite him to read, and afford him matter of
enquiry and knowledge.' But Locke was by no means the first with this idea.
Johannes Amos Comenius (1592–1671), a philosopher as well as an educationalist, had compiled and illustrated his instructional picture-book for
children as early as 1657. *Orbis Sensualium Pictus*, was published in Nuremberg,
Germany, the author expressing the hope in his preface that his little book
might 'entice knowledgeable children . . . to read more easily than hitherto.'
In 1658, within a few months of the work's first appearance, an English translation by Charles Hoole was published over a London imprint. *'Visible World;
or, A nomenclature, and pictures, of all the chief things that are in the world, and of
men's employments therein; in above 150 cuts . . .'* as the translator entitled it, and

new editions continued to be called for until well after the end of the 18th century. Comenius (more correctly Jan Komensky) was at one time Bishop of Leszno, Poland, and a leading member of the Moravian Brethren. His educational books became so well known that he was invited by Parliament to assist in reforming the English educational system, only to see his plans frustrated by the outbreak of the Civil War. He was one of the first to seek to make learning more attractive to children. 'Boyhood is distracted for years with precepts of grammar, infinitely prolix, perplexed and obscure,' he justly complained. 'For children, pictures are the most easily assimilated form of learning they can look upon.' He put his theories into practice when he published his *Orbis Sensualium Pictus*, with the primary purpose of instilling a knowledge of Latin into youthful heads, this international language taking pride of place over the High Dutch version which accompanied it. The pictures themselves set out to depict practically every aspect of life of the time that could be considered fit for the eyes of youth, from 'God' to 'crawling vermin'. Sports and pastimes were not forgotten, and typical of the vernacular text which stood beside the Latin version, in this case against the picture entitled *Ludus Pilæ*, or 'Tennis-Play', is the English version of Charles Hoole: 'In a Tennis-Court they play with a Ball, which one throweth, and another taketh, and sendeth it back with a Racket: and that is the sport of Noble-men to stir their body.' The crudely-drawn miniature woodcut illustrations accompanying Comenius's text measured less than 5 cm × 4 cm in the earliest editions, not much bigger than some modern postage stamps. The artistic ability and technical merit so fluently displayed in Jost Amman's woodcuts eighty years earlier is totally absent and it seems more than likely that the drawings were originally made by Comenius himself. Nevertheless, a fresh start had been made in an attempt to amuse children while teaching them how to read. Like Sigmund Feyerabend in an earlier century, John Comenius had recognised that an

Typical of the religious works produced during the 17th century in a style that made them attractive to children and young people is this example translated from the French of L. E. du Pin. It contains six full-page copperplate engravings, and a simple but comprehensive index.

Size of title-page:
17.4 cm × 11.2 cm.

element of enjoyment was a desirable factor in endeavouring to reach into the minds of the young. Both men were far ahead of their time, pioneers in a puritanical age when books were written at children rather than for them, and sought to terrify into docile obedience with threats of everlasting hell-fire all those youngsters who obstinately persisted in enjoying their leisure hours.

For most of the rest of their reading, it was necessary for children to rely on the permitted books they could openly peruse with freshly washed hands and due regard for decorum. These were the heavy brigade of 'suitable' works brought out on Sunday afternoons by well-meaning adults. They were opened in respectful silence in the hope of an English, rather than a Latin, text and perhaps the chance of a picture or two; then consumed in leaf-turning boredom in a gloom deepened by the thoughts of the 'now let us observe how much you have learned' catechism that would probably follow. The more fortunate child might on occasion be allowed to choose his or her own book from the family library, in which case the delights of John Foxe's *Actes and Monuments*, 1563, affectionately known as the *Book of Martyrs*, would be sought, filled with a crackling inferno of full-page copperplate engravings of dead and dying Christians that delighted the youth of the 16th century onwards as much as an 'X'-certificate wide-screen presentation of the present day. There was a genuine affection for at least one of the works of John Bunyan (1628–88): not perhaps for such titles as *A Few Sighs from Hell, or the Groans of a Damned Soul*, 1658; or, *The Strait Gate, or, Great Difficulty in Going to Heaven*, 1676. These brought a pleasant sense of mortification to the more pious of their elders, but a glance at the title-pages of many of Bunyan's well-meaning tracts would have been enough to dismay the most stout-hearted juvenile. *The Pilgrim's Progress*, 1678, a work remarkable for the beauty and almost childish simplicity of its language, permeated with the author's insight into nature and evident sense of humour, was a work young people quickly discovered and took to their

A work 'exemplifying the Power of Religion in a Dying Hour' by Jabez Burns, published by Milner & Sowerby, Halifax, 1857. A collection of 100 death-bed tales for children, calculated, one would think, to chill the blood of the stoutest hearted.

Size of title-page:
12.6 cm × 7.8 cm.

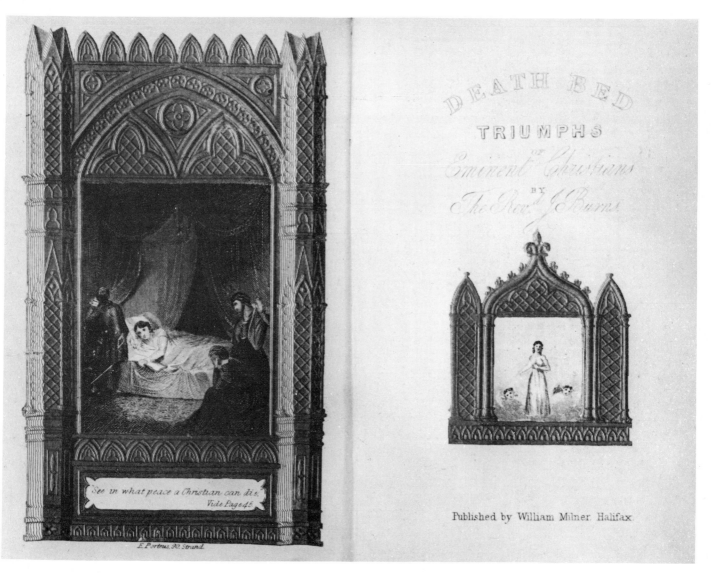

See in what peace a Christian can die.
Vide Page 45.

E. Porteus, 90, Strand.

DEATH BED TRIUMPHS
of Eminent Christians
BY
The Rev J Burns

Published by William Milner Halifax

hearts. The many luridly illustrated editions that continually appeared in the following years, and still appear in more muted tones in the present day, had a particular appeal for children, and there could have been few nursery shelves that were unable to boast of at least one drastically abbreviated, but excitingly illustrated, well-worn copy. It was a work that every literate child in the English-speaking world knew in the late 17th century, and more especially the 18th century, and most would have been able to recite the plot by heart. The author had not intended it for a juvenile audience, any more than Defoe with *Robinson Crusoe* or Swift with *Gulliver's Travels*, but children took to it with a surety of instinct that led each succeeding generation to endorse their choice. In essence it is an adventure story, a romance bristling with dangerous escapades and peopled with giants, ogres and fabulous monsters; a world through which the hero threads his perilous way to the happiest of all endings. What more could any child require? Yet when the author purposely addressed himself to the young he failed to make an impact. Lured by an attractive title, many must have opened the work expectantly; but very few could have ploughed their way through the morass of pious platitudes and moral precepts in which Bunyan clothed his finger-shaking lines. *A Book for Boys and Girls; or, Country Rhimes for Children*, first appeared in 1686, priced at sixpence; then in 1701 with an altered sub-title; and again in 1724, but this time with cuts to illustrate the text and with the title altered to read *Divine Emblems; or, Temporal Things Spiritualized*. A facsimile of the first edition of 1686 was published in 1889. Bunyan made no pretence of having written the work for the amusement of children: he was determined to save their souls by whiffing brimstone through the nursery and rooting out every thoughtless pleasure indulged in by the young. He stated plainly that he was setting out to show them:

> . . . how each fingle-fangle,
> On which they doting are, their souls entangle.

Unfortunately, he was by no means the only inspired divine of his time soul-saving in the play-grounds and schoolrooms, nor was he by any means the most fearsome of the moralising oppressors of youthful spirits who stalked the pages of juvenile literature in the 17th and early 18th century. James Janeway (1636?–74), helped set the trend with his *A Token for Children: being an Exact Account of the Conversion, Holy and Exemplary Lives, and Joyful Deaths of several young Children* (c. 1671); followed a few years later by his equally menacing *Token for Youth*. To stand any chance of being considered for a place in Heaven, he tells his young readers, they must live lives of religious ecstasy, before dying joyfully with their Saviour's name on their lips. Satan

BLANDIMAN, DISARMING THE ARCH PRIEST, WHO OFFERED VIOLENCE TO THE EMPRESS BELLISANT.

THE HISTORY of Valentine and Orson A NEW EDITION Embellished with Six New Designs Illustrative of the most interesting Subjects REVISED & CORRECTED, from the ORIGINAL QUARTO EDITION.

LONDON
Published by H. Ireton, Cold Bath Square.
1810.

This early French romance, first printed in 1495 at Lyons, was translated and embellished by Henry Watson, and printed in quarto form by William Copland about 1565. It became a favourite story, in mutilated form; with chapmen and ballad-mongers; but the edition shown is the first that was revised with reference to Copland's original printed text.
Size of title-page:
18.2 cm × 11 cm.

was very active and their task a hard one; but the author set down a chapter full of rules that would allow them a chance of redemption. Toys of all shapes and forms were strictly forbidden; whipping tops in the playground only brought the Devil another recruit; secular enjoyment in any guise was only for the hell-bent; they must do their best to prevent their playmates enjoying themselves and have the courage to rebuke all frivolity, while constantly reminding themselves of their own inherent tendency to live sinful lives. 'I would fain do what I can possibly to keep thee from falling into everlasting Fire,' he informed them, and promised that God would reward the pious with a joyful death at an age too early to have allowed them time for more than a modicum of sin. He was an earnest man, hardworking and faithful to his cause. His books give us an example of morbid and gloating piety and the preoccupation with death of a consumptive fanatic. His works for children appeared when his own health was undermined by the disease that killed him 'in the 38 yeare of his age . . .' and at a time when he probably knew he was doomed to an early, and let us hope joyful, death.

A Looking-Glass for Children, 1672, by Abraham Chear, was a pleasant sounding title from a pleasant sounding author, but any young hopeful who picked the book up in the expectation of a light-hearted discourse about nature and the world around him was due for a frowning disappointment.

> What a pity such a pretty maid
> As I should go to Hell

muses a little girl, as she gazes at her own reflection in that snare for the unwary – a looking-glass. Nor was Thomas White's *A Little Book for Little Children* (*c.* 1670) much of a comfort with its exhortations against singing ballads or reading other than strictly religious works. But another work with the same title, published at the turn of the century, contains an early printing of *A was an Archer, and shot at a Frog*, and the rest of the alphabet in rhyme. The version *A was an Apple-pie* was recited by children as early as 1650, although the first printed reference (and that a parody) did not appear until 1671 in John Eachard's pamphlet about the clergy. In America, the rhyme was printed at Boston in 1761.

'Courtesy' books, and works of instruction on how young people ought to behave in polite society, were popular presents, at least with parents, for boys and girls in their late 'teens. Francis Hawkins' *Youth's Behaviour, or Decency in Conversation amongst Men*, 1636, was followed by a second part by Robert Codrington in 1664, entitled *Youth's Behaviour, or Decency in Conversation Amongst Women*; reissued in 1680 as *The Education of Young Ladies and Gentlewomen*. Such works were commonplace in the late 17th century. *A Cap of Gray Hairs for a Green Head: or, the Fathers Counsel to his Son, An Apprentice in London*, 1671, by 'Caleb Trenchfield, Gent.', was one of the many similar titles in this field of manners and deportment. All were didactic and of serious intent, and most must have been studied with the same attention given to the grammars and schoolbooks of earlier years. Those wishing to improve their social etiquette were left in no doubt of the basic rules of courtly conduct, as in this hint to newly-weds, taken from the last named work: 'Women can with no patience endure to be mew'd up till Mid-night, while you are clubbing it at a Tavern; and you cannot think it a wonder, if at such times they sport with your Servants at home . . . How long is Love like to last, where the blundering Husband comes home like a sous'd Hogshead, with a steam of Smoke and Drink, would almost choak a Greenlander who had been fed with Blubber.' Blunt advice to a boy about to make his own way in the wicked world.

The late 17th-century child could have found few books to entertain him, and even fewer that contained pictures. An exception was the edition of *Aesop's Fables* produced by John Ogilby in 1651, 'paraphras'd in Verse'. An edition in English had been printed by Caxton at his press in Westminster as early as 1484, and Latin editions containing crude little woodcuts had been in circulation throughout the 16th century. The Plantin Press, Antwerp, published an edition under the title *Fabellae Aliquot Aesopicae* in 1566, illustrated with 37 woodcuts, and similar productions were issued by other publishing houses throughout the rest of the century. But they were not primarily intended for the amusement or instruction of children, and a glance at their close-packed black-letter Latin texts reveals that it would have been a formidable

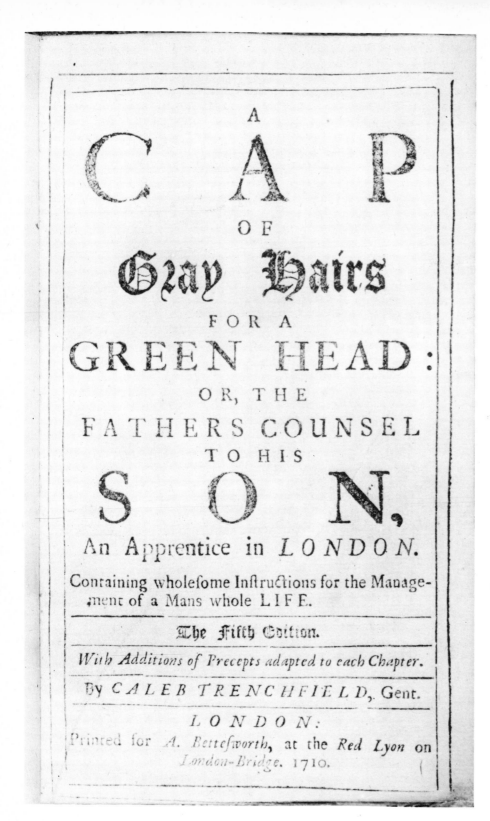

First published in 1671, this courtesy book by Caleb Trenchfield was in print almost to the end of the 18th century. It was one of many similar titles in the field of manners and deportment.

Size of title-page:
17 cm × 10.5 cm.

A

C A P

OF

Gray Hairs

FOR A

GREEN HEAD:

OR, THE

FATHERS COUNSEL

TO HIS

S O N,

An Apprentice in *LONDON*.

Containing wholefome Inftructions for the Management of a Mans whole L I F E.

The Fifth Edition.

With Additions of Precepts adapted to each Chapter.

By *CALEB TRENCHFIELD,* Gent.

L O N D O N:

Printed for *A. Bettefworth*, at the *Red Lyon* on *London-Bridge.* 1710.

academic exercise for any juvenile to attempt a translation of the fables for his own amusement. Children liked looking at the pictures and knew the legend of the fox and the grapes and the rest of the tales from oral tradition since their nursery days. Ogilby's edition of 1651 was intended for the adult market, but it would not have taken the children of the house long to discover the volume and hug it to their hearts. Young people were starved of interesting books that they could read with enjoyment. Only slowly did the printers and publishers come to realise the vast potential of the juvenile market, and it was to be left to John Newbery, nearly a century later, to exploit this potential by revolutionising the methods and outworn ideas associated with what the adult world considered suitable books for the young. '. . .'tis hoped the whole will seem rather an Amusement than a Task,' he wrote in the preface to one of his earliest works for the young. That sentence contains the key that opened the gates.

18th-Century Children's Books

EMBLEMS

OF

MORTALITY;

REPRESENTING,

IN UPWARDS OF FIFTY CUTS,

DEATH

SEIZING ALL RANKS AND DEGREES
OF PEOPLE;

Imitated from a Painting in the Cemetery of the
Dominican Church at BASIL, in *Switzerland:*

With an APOSTROPHE to each, tranflated from the
Latin and French.

Intended as well for the Information of the CURIOUS,
as the Inftruction and Entertainment of YOUTH.

TO WHICH IS PREFIXED

A copious PREFACE, containing an hiftorical Account
of the above, and other Paintings on this Subject,
now or lately exifting in divers Parts of Europe.

LONDON:

Printed for T. HODGSON, in George's-Court,
St. John's-Lane, Clerkenwell.

MDCCLXXXIX.

A rare edition of a version of the 'Dance of Death', intended for 'the Instruction and Entertainment of Youth'. Published in 1789, this is one of the rarest and finest examples of the woodcut illustrations of Thomas Bewick. Most of the edition was destroyed in a fire at Hodgson's in London.

Size of title-page: 18 cm × 11 cm.

Until almost the middle of the 18th century, young people had little to read except adult books they had adopted as their own, and these personal possessions were nearly always in the form of debased, chapbook versions of well-known prose tales, or doggerel verses with a moral to swallow. For light relief there was the *Arabian Nights*, first introduced into England early in the 18th century from a translation made from the French of Antoine Galland, who in his turn had them from the mouth of a Syrian friend, for no manuscript was then known in existence. Stories from this collection were soon circulating in chapbooks, as were the fairy tales of Charles Perrault. These, and other fairy and folk tales are dealt with more fully in the appropriate chapter.

The chapmen and pedlars carried what literature there was for children in the form of little pamphlets, usually no more than sixteen pages in length, illustrated with crude woodcuts and selling at anything from a halfpenny to as much as sixpence a copy. Here young people could read the Arthurian legends, and of the princesses and ogres and the brave-hearted knights of the Middle Ages. These 18th-century tales were often coarsely told, full of strange oaths and the groans of the fallen, the clunk of head-severing strokes or the thud of a cloth-yard arrow, stories as violent and as earthy as the hawkers who sold them. With nothing better to read for their own amusement, children of all ages loved each and every one of them, the older members of the family spelling out the adventures of *Guy of Warwick, Tom Thumb, Springheel Jack, Tom Hickathrift, Friar Bacon, Robin Hood*, and a host of other heroes, both real and mythical, to a mute and attentive circle of round young eyes and ears. These, and a hundred others, were the titles the pedlars kept in string-tied bundles in their crowded packs. They were beneath the dignity of regular booksellers, these penny-plain, twopenny-coloured little booklets, but young people devoured the stories like modern children read comics. Here they could live out their dreams, fighting their playground battles dubbed with the names of the indigenous heroes of a Britain long ago. Early 18th-century examples are very hard to find, and any titles issued before the last few years of the century command prices that put them beyond the reach of most collectors of juvenilia. They were printed on the cheapest and coarsest of untrimmed paper, the sheet folded to make its eight, sixteen or twenty-four page gathering, but usually with the leaves unopened, to await the knife or ruler-edge of the first owner. There was always a woodcut illustration to top the tale, lurid

and dramatic in content and invariably badly drawn and crudely printed. Yet these stories, and the ballad sheets that accompanied them in the pedlar's pack, sold by the thousand to both young and old throughout the length and breadth of the British Isles. The stories they told and the songs they brought helped to satisfy a deep-seated longing amongst the grossly underprivileged poor, who composed seven-eighths of the population, for news and entertainment brought in from the outside world, especially in the remote hamlets and villages where the travelling chapmen did most of their trade.

These little chapbooks and ballad sheets were the only form of reading matter the vast majority of people could possibly afford to own, and they probably did more to spread the art of reading amongst the children of the poor than any other event up to the enforcement of the Education Acts of 1870 and after. The pictures they carried, often seeming to have little or no connection with the text, were studied with eager attention by the illiterate circle gathered around the one fortunate enough to be able to act as reader of the verses or story the chapbook contained. As early as 1648, the news-sheet *Mercurius Britanicus Alive Again* was asking its more sophisticated readers 'How many Ballads would sell without a formal wood cut?' and the same comment applied to the chapbooks and children's romances and fairy-tales that kept them company. By the end of the 18th century, an empire of cheap printing was thriving in the Seven Dials area of St Giles-in-the-Fields, London, devoted to supplying the needs of the chapmen and colporteurs for ballad sheets, tracts, legends, fairy stories, last-dying-speeches, and a host of other unbound and unprotected printed ephemera that the walking booksellers stuffed in bundles of a hundred copies a time into their sailcloth packs. Such names as William Thackeray; William Dicey, who founded the great wholesale houses in Bow

One of the earliest books of children's verse to have survived, shown here in the third edition, 1750. Interspersed with anecdotes in prose and moral fables, the poems and songs were specially written for the work. The editor has not been identified.

Size of title-page:
15 cm × 9 cm.

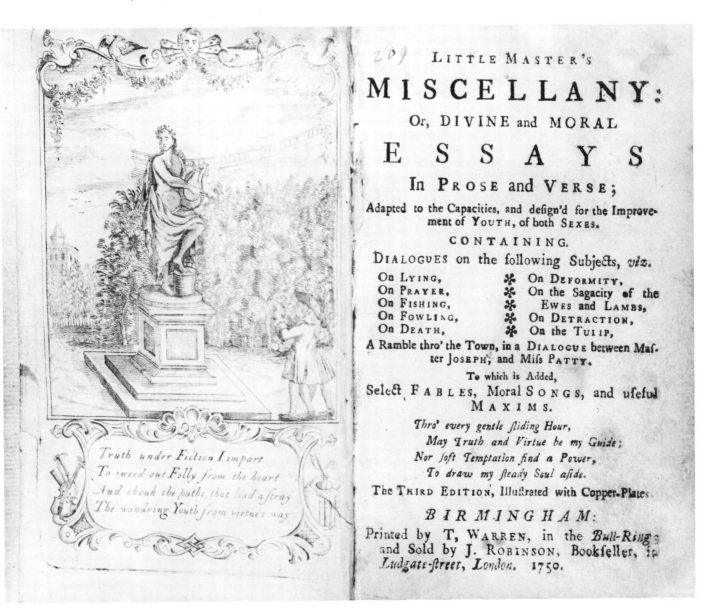

Truth under Fiction I impart
To weed out Folly from the heart
And choak the paths, that lead astray
The wandring Youth from virtue's way

LITTLE MASTER's
MISCELLANY:
Or, DIVINE and MORAL
ESSAYS
In PROSE and VERSE;
Adapted to the Capacities, and design'd for the Improvement of YOUTH, of both SEXES.
CONTAINING.
DIALOGUES on the following Subjects, *viz.*

On LYING,   ❋ On DEFORMITY,
On PRAYER,   ❋ On the Sagacity of the
On FISHING,   Ewes and Lambs,
On FOWLING,   ❋ On DETRACTION,
On DEATH,   ❋ On the TULIP,

A Ramble thro' the Town, in a DIALOGUE between Master JOSEPH, and Miss PATTY.

To which is Added,
Select FABLES, Moral SONGS, and useful
MAXIMS.

Thro' every gentle sliding Hour,
May Truth and Virtue be my Guide;
Nor soft Temptation find a Power,
To draw my steady Soul aside.

The THIRD EDITION, Illustrated with Copper-Plates

BIRMINGHAM:
Printed by T. WARREN, in the *Bull-Ring*; and Sold by J. ROBINSON, Bookseller, in *Ludgate-street, London.* 1750.

Church Yard and Aldermary Church Yard, London, in the 18th century, and issued lists containing over twenty different versions of Robin Hood's adventures; Robert Powell, of Stonecutter Street; John Marshall, who expanded his business in the 1780s and issued hardbacked versions of many hundreds of children's books, some of which are shown in the illustrations; John Pitts (1765–1844); and the great James Catnach (1792–1841), will always be associated with the ballad and chapbook market that for two centuries provided reading matter for the poor.

Songs and nursery rhymes produced in book form specially for children appeared during the first half of the 18th century; an appreciable advance on the unbound chapbooks and ballad sheets that had been used before. *Tommy Thumb's Pretty Song Book* was an early example, being published in two miniature volumes about 1744. This date, and the existence of volume one is only conjectural, for only an undated copy of volume two is known to have survived, and it is now in the British Museum. An early specimen of songs and verses specially written for children in my collection is represented by a copy of *Little Master's Miscellany*, 1750, published in Birmingham. This is undoubtedly one of the earliest, if not *the* earliest, poetical and prose miscellanies produced for young people, the first edition having been published in 1743. Any collector of early children's books would be pleased to possess a copy of the third edition illustrated here, for examples of books for the young dating from as early as the reign of George II are extremely rare. Any fragment of any children's book of this period or earlier is well worth keeping, for in too many cases titles have completely disappeared, and their existence is known only through the medium of advertisements contained in other works.

It was John Newbery (1713–67) who first realised that there was a vast market for specially produced children's books, and an even greater potential sale if these could be displayed in a format that made them attractive and desirable possessions in the eyes of young people. Friends and business associates who knew him personally described him as restless, with nervous energy, a commercial dynamo who no sooner had one enterprise running successfully than he was off to start another. 'A red-faced, good-natured little man who was always in a hurry', to quote the words of Oliver Goldsmith in *The Vicar of Wakefield*, 1766. 'He had no sooner alighted, than he was in haste to be gone, for he was ever on business of the utmost importance.'

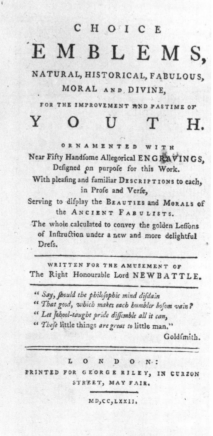

Written by John H. Wynne (1743–88), the frontispiece of this first edition, dated 1772, is by Samuel Wale, librarian to the Royal Academy.

Size of title-page:
15.3 cm × 9 cm.

Newbery had started in business on his own account in Reading in 1740, moving to London four years later to establish a thriving book publishing business. He soon branched out, widening his commercial activities to include several newspaper and magazine enterprises, and then to manufacture patent medicines on a large scale, including the famous 'Dr. James's Fever Powder'. He is remembered today as the first bookseller (a term at that time synonymous with publisher) to appreciate the desire of young people for books of an amusing and entertaining nature, rather than the didactic and morally uplifting works they had been forced to yawn their way through in the past. From his newly opened shop at the sign of the 'Bible and Sun', 65 St Paul's Churchyard, London, an address soon famous with the younger members of the reading public, he started to issue the tiny volumes of his *Juvenile Library*. Each was bound in the brightly-gilt, embossed and coloured paper, designed in a flowered pattern, which came to be called 'Dutch paper', but the secret of its manufacture was lost and never rediscovered. He personally designed the format of his juvenile books, and almost certainly supplied the text for several of the most popular stories.

The first book he published for children was issued from his earliest London address at the 'Bible and Crown', near Devereaux Court, Temple Bar, from whence he moved to St Paul's Churchyard in July 1745. To stimulate sales he inserted an advertisement in the *Penny Morning Post* on 13 June 1744:

A Little Pretty Pocket-Book, intended for the instruction of Little Master Tommy and Pretty Miss Polly, with an agreeable Letter to read from Jack the Giant Killer; as also a Ball and Pincushion, the use of which will infallibly make Tommy a good Boy, and Polly a Good Girl.

Even with this first of his long run of children's titles, Newbery was exploring the possibility of extra inducements to increase turnover: the price of the book alone was sixpence, but with a choice of ball or pincushion, only eightpence. *A Little Pretty Pocket-Book* eventually became one of his longest-selling titles, still appearing in the lists of his business successors some forty years later. In the text he was at pains to include 'a letter on education humbly addressed to all Parents, Guardians, Governesses, &c., wherein rules are laid down for making their children, strong, healthy, virtuous, wise and happy . . .'

It was not long before he had invented an exciting string of fictitious characters whose adventures children came to anticipate in much the same manner that the modern child follows the escapes and uncertainties of present-day heroes and heroines: Primrose Prettyface, Toby Ticklepitcher, Nurse Truelove, Woglog the Giant, Giles Gingerbread, Tommy Trip, Peter Puzzlewell, and R. Goodwill, the reputed secretary of the Lilliputian Society, who, young readers were told, kindly produced *The Lilliputian Magazine*. There was also, of course, Margery Meanwell, alias Goody Two-Shoes:

> Who from a State of Rags and Care,
> And having Shoes but half a Pair;
> Their Fortune and their Fame would fix,
> And gallop in a Coach and Six.

as described by the author, Oliver Goldsmith, and placed on the title-page of the first edition of 1765. *The History of Little Goody Two-Shoes* is now familiar to modern children only through the name of the heroine, but late in the 18th century it was a well loved best-seller amongst the young, the 'philanthropic publisher of St Paul's Churchyard', as Goldsmith called his employer, doing much to instil a love of reading in thousands of children in nearly every walk of life. There were many who, in later years, acknowledged their debt to John Newbery, and who looked back with nostalgia on the days when they first learned to decipher the stories and romances in the little books he published. Robert Southey, a future Poet Laureate, was sent twenty different titles direct from the publishers, such as '*Goody Two-Shoes, Giles Gingerbread*, and other delectable histories, in sixpenny books for children, splendidly bound in the flowered and gilt Dutch paper of former days . . . and laid the foundation of a love of books which grew with the child's growth'. As late as 1802, Charles Lamb wrote to S. T. Coleridge:

Goody Two Shoes is almost out of print. Mrs Barbauld's stuff has banished all the old classics of the nursery, and the shopman at Newbery's hardly deigned to reach them off an old exploded corner of a shelf, when Mary asked for them. Mrs Barbauld's and Mrs Trimmer's nonsense lay in piles about . . . Science has succeeded to poetry no less in the little walks of children than with men. Is there no possibility of averting this sore evil? Think what you would have been now, if instead of being fed with tales and old wives' fables in child-hood, you had been crammed with geography and history!

There can be little doubt that it was Oliver Goldsmith (1730?–74) who sup-plied the text for *Goody Two-Shoes*, published during a period when he was working almost full-time for Newbery, and living quite close to him at Islington, where the publisher paid for his board and lodging and much else besides. Modern scholarship confirms this attribution, made by many literary figures and critics of the past, including Charlotte Yonge (1823–1901), who was the first to point to the similarity of style and content of parts of *Goody Two-Shoes* and Goldsmith's later *The Deserted Village*, 1770. His dry humour is evident in the reference he makes to his employer's patent medicine in the opening paragraph of the story:

Care and Discontent shortened the Days of Margery's father. He was forced from his Family, and seized with a violent fever in a place where Dr James's Powder was not to be had, and where he died miserably.

Goldsmith's hand is less evident in many other works issued by the publish-ing house about this time, including *The Renowned History of Giles Gingerbread*, 1764, *The Easter Gift; or, The Way to be Good*, 1765, *The Whitsuntide Gift; or, The Way to be Happy*, 1765, and several other titles, most of which could equally have been written by John Newbery himself or even a joint literary production between the two. The facts of the matter are uncertain; but *An History of England in a Series of Letters from a Nobleman to his Son*, 2 vols. 1764, issued under the Newbery imprint is certainly by Goldsmith, as were a number of other instructional works, including *Dr Goldsmith's Roman History. Abridged by him-self for the Use of Schools*, 1772. *The Lilliputian Magazine*, believed to have been first issued in monthly parts during 1751 (although no copies of the part issue are known to have survived) is most certainly *not* by Goldsmith, although attributed to him in the British Museum catalogue and elsewhere, but it is possibly by Christopher Smart (1722–71). This magazine is the first periodical specially produced for children, and was later issued in book form with an engraved frontispiece, four woodcuts and twelve other engraved leaves. Gold-smith's *An History of the Earth, and Animated Nature*, 8 vols. 1774 (with 'tygers' in Canada), was amongst the last of his works, which later went through edition after edition, many of which were embellished with delightful series of hand-coloured plates of animals and birds. It remained a favourite with children until late into the second half of the 19th century.

Where Newbery led, his rivals were quick to follow, and by the 1790s the trade in books for juveniles had increased to a degree that had at least six other publishing houses specialising in the production of children's books in England alone. Much the same situation existed in Europe, and, to a lesser degree in America, for there, with no language problem, they were able to import the productions of the London booksellers. L. F. Gedike, a German schoolmaster, quoted by Percy Muir in his *English Children's Books*, 1954, was an annual visitor to the Leipzig Book Fairs during the second half of the 18th century, and wrote in 1787:

No other form of literary manufactory is so active as book-making for young people of all grades and classes. Every Leipzig Summer and Winter Fair throws up a countless number of books of this kind like a flooding tide. And see how young and old rush to buy – there are few pearls and little amber, but much mud, and, at the best, painted snail-shells. They take all kinds of names and forms: almanacks for children, newspapers for children, journals for children, collections for children, stories for children, comedies for children, dramas for children, geography for children, history for children, physics for children, logic for children, catechisms for children, travels for chil-

A children's tract of 1796, with the text in verse by Miss Hannah More (1745–1833), a friend of Garrick, Burke, Horace Walpole, Dr Johnson, Mrs Montagu and the other ladies of the Blue Stocking coterie.

Size of page: 19.5 cm × 12.8 cm.

dren, morals for children, grammars for children, and reading books for children in all languages without number, poetry for children, sermons for children, letters for children, talks for children, and unlimited variations on the same theme, so that the literary doll-shops are crammed all the year round with them but especially at the time when loving parents and aunts and uncles may be attracted by the appositeness of the notice 'Christmas Gifts for good children'.

To ignore for a moment the chronological sequence of this chapter, in order to complete the somewhat complicated history of the firm of John Newbery, will enable the collector of early children's books to identify with a degree of certainty the various imprints and initials he will meet with in the period 1745–1810. The business was started by the John Newbery discussed above. He was born in 1713 at Waltham St Lawrence, Berkshire, the son of a farmer whose few acres were insufficient to supply the needs of a growing family. John left home before he was sixteen in order to find work in nearby Reading. Here he eventually managed to obtain a place in the office of William Carnan, the proprietor and editor of one of the earliest provincial newspapers, the *Reading Mercury*. The only education Newbery had received was at his village school at Waltham, but his love of reading and of English literature in general, coupled with a diligent and untiring pursuit of knowledge in every sphere of the arts and sciences, soon made him an invaluable asset to Carnan and his publishing business. Seven years after he joined the firm, his employer died, leaving most of his property to his one-time assistant, at that time twenty-four years of age. John, perhaps to consolidate his position still further, promptly proposed to his late employer's widow, some six years his senior. By 1740, he was established as a book publisher and newspaper proprietor in Reading, moving his head-office to London in 1744 and eventually settling near the 'Bible and Sun', St Paul's Churchyard. The troubles of '45 and the trade depression that followed all but bankrupted him; but after this precarious start the business thrived to an extent that made him one of the most successful men in his profession. He was a friend to most of the leading literary figures of his day, a great many of whom contributed to his newspapers and periodicals. One final picture of John Newbery comes from the pen of Dr Johnson, who had gently satirized the mercurial little publisher in the *Idler*, dubbing him 'Jack Whirler'; Johnson told his readers:

When he enters a house, his first declaration is that he cannot sit down, and so short are his visits that he seldom appears to have come for any other reason but to say he must go.

Oliver Goldsmith thought the world of him, and wrote the epitaph in which the clues to his friend's name are hidden:

> What we say of a thing that has just come in fashion,
> And that which we do with the dead,
> Is the name of the honestest man in the nation:
> What more of a man can be said?

John Newbery died on 22 December 1767, at his house in St Paul's Churchyard, leaving his publishing business to his son, Francis, who promptly entered into partnership with his step-brother Thomas Carnan (the son of John Newbery's wife by her first marriage). Carnan had been publishing on his own account since 1750, sometimes as nominee of his step-father, and was an enterprising man of business and a pioneer in several respects. It was Carnan who first offered his young readers a choice of binding styles. For an extra penny a copy they could have their books bound with vellum spines (frequently stained green) on which were paper labels giving the title and volume number. The boards were usually covered with a glazed blue paper contrasting vividly with the spines. Children were thus able to have their own library of volumes bound in a style that was tough enough to withstand years of handling, whereas the earlier paper-covered spines usually parted company with their boards after a few months of wear and tear. Young people were seldom able to persuade their parents to go to the expense of rebinding favourite texts, whereas the boarded books bought by adults for their own libraries were usually sent to the binder after their initial reading for clothing in calf or morocco in the owner's favourite style. Examples of Carnan's green spines and blue boards are now sought by collectors of publishers' binding styles, as well as those of early children's books, and command quite high prices in any edition.

Francis Newbery (1743–1818) remained in uneasy partnership with Carnan until the latter's death in 1788, but spent much of his time managing the patent medicine side of the business. He married Mary, the sister of Robert Raikes, the founder of Sunday Schools for children. Described by a contemporary as 'a scholar and a poet, and a lover of music', Francis Newbery must be distinguished from his cousin of the same name, with whom he and Carnan quarrelled violently. Francis Newbery (the nephew of old John Newbery) had been intimately connected with his uncle's publishing business during the latter's lifetime, but seems to have been forced out of the firm soon after his uncle's death, setting up on his own account at 20 St Paul's Churchyard (the rival business was at 65). He died in 1780 and from that time onwards his widow, Elizabeth Newbery (1746–1821), carried on the business, employing as manager Abraham Badcock, who died in 1797, and then a craftsman whose name will always be associated with children's books, John Harris. He succeeded to the business on Elizabeth's retirement in 1801.

I have gone into the details of the Newbery family tree at some length, as the name is one of the most important in the annals of children's books, and the confusion of imprints caused by rival businesses trading under similar names has led to many bibliographical errors in the past. Mysteries still remain, and it is still not clear which of the two Francis Newberys, son or nephew, were designated by their uncle or father to publish the first edition of *The Vicar of Wakefield*, 1766. The row between the two reached such a pitch of intensity after John Newbery's death that Thomas Carnan and Francis Newbery (the son) regularly had printed on their title-pages:

Printed for T. Carnan and F. Newbery, junior, at No. 65, in St. Paul's Church Yard, (but not for F. Newbery, at the Corner of Ludgate street, who has no share in the late Mr. John Newbery's Books for Children.)

Although the Newberys and their business associates were the leading figures in the field of book publishing for children and young people during the second half of the 18th century, they had many rivals in trade and never dominated the market. Even John Newbery, the innovator and pioneer, owed much to his predecessors, and to those whose identities are remembered only by their names on the little volumes they sponsored and exhibited for sale in the bow-fronted bull's-eyed glass windows of their bookshops. A glance at my own shelves reveals a host of forgotten titles and publishers, all dating from the time when John Newbery was begrudging himself a full night's sleep above his warehouse within the shadow of the dome of St Paul's. The majority are grammars and schoolbooks, for which there was a constant and ever increasing demand; but stories and picture books for the amusement and entertainment of children were published in rapidly increasing numbers as the century entered its final quarter.

As early as 1713, one of the masters of Charterhouse School, Andrew Tooke (1673–1732), a Fellow of the Royal Society, translated and published on behalf of his scholars *The Pantheon, representing the Fabulous Histories of the Heathen Gods*, a work which passed through over thirty editions before the end of the 18th century. My copy, of the 17th edition, dated 1750, contains a series of 28 full-page copperplate engravings of the more dramatic adventures of the old-time gods and goddesses, with the text posed in a series of questions and answers, a method commonly employed by writers for children at this period:

Q. Who are those two handsome, beautiful, young Men that ride upon White Horses?

A. They are the Twin-Brothers, the sons of *Jupiter* and *Leda*; their Names are *Castor* and *Pollux*.

The work appears here as a translation by Tooke from the original edition of *Pantheum Mythicum*, by Francois Antoine Pomey (1618–73). It established itself as one of the favourite picture books with young people until better and more exciting productions became available from 1750 onwards.

In the meantime, many versions of *The Life, and Strange Surprizing Adventures of Robinson Crusoe; of York, Mariner*, by Daniel Defoe (1661?–1731), appeared in abbreviated form, 'embellished with cuts', for the use of children. It was a work that quickly established itself as a firm favourite with young people of all ages, and one that has never ceased to be in print since its first appearance in 1719. Two further volumes, entitled *Further Adventures of Robinson Crusoe*, 1719, and *Serious Reflections . . . of Robinson Crusoe*, 1720, followed almost immediately, in the first of which Crusoe revisits his island with Man Friday, is attacked by a fleet of canoes on his departure, and loses his faithful companion in the encounter. A set of the three first editions in contemporary bindings would now be worth well over £4,000 ($9,600). Eighteenth-century juvenile versions, of which there must have been well over a hundred different editions, are eagerly sought by collectors, those of the Newbery period, adorned with wood-cuts and in the original floral Dutch paper-covered boards, changing hands at up to £100 ($240) a copy. Much depends on the condition of the volume, and its date; but any version printed before the turn of the century is a prize to be sought.

The first issue of the first edition of *Travels into Several Remote Nations of the World, by Lemuel Gulliver*, appeared on 28 October 1726, and 10,000 copies of the work are said to have been sold in three weeks. The first edition was issued by Benjamin Motte, London, in two volumes. The author was Jonathan Swift (1667–1745), and all those who had been captivated by the realism and cliff-hanging expectancy of *Robinson Crusoe* were almost equally fascinated with the sustained logic of his satirical fable of Gulliver, a giant towering high over the Lilliputians, and a minikin crouching amongst the massive feet of the Brobdingnagians. The work, in abridged form, had an instant appeal to the young as a believable tale of fantastical travels in far distant unexplored lands, in the same way that planetary tales of science-fiction exert a fascination over much of present-day youth. The first of the many shortened versions for children was an unauthorised edition of 1727, published by J. Stone and R. King. The later chapbook editions, usually containing only the story of Lilliput, started to appear about the middle of the century and continued for at least sixty years.

The themes of these two books have served as plots for a multitude of romances and novels ever since, by no means all of which have been intended for the juvenile market. Crusoe's desire to escape from humanity, and the idealised notion of fending for oneself in a patch of territory safe from the rest of the world, whether it is a warm and benevolent desert island, a clearing in the jungle, or even a remote cottage in the country, lurks within most of us. Eighteenth-century children delighted in the story of *Robinson Crusoe* and its many imitations, the first of which appeared from the pen of J. H. Campe (1746–1818), a German author. *Robinson Crusoe der Jüngere* was first published in two volumes, in Hamburg in 1779, the author translating it into French the same year and into English in 1781 as *Robinson the younger*. But the most popular edition of Campe's original text was issued by John Stockdale in four volumes in 1788, complete with a total of 32 woodcut illustrations, all by John Bewick, the younger brother of the famous Thomas Bewick. Mention can also be made here of *The Swiss Family Robinson*, by Johann David Wyss (1743–1818), a Swiss army chaplain, who wrote the story for his four sons in 1792. The work was left in manuscript, and the first edition of the German text appeared in book form in two parts in Zurich in 1812–3, the author's son, Johann Rudolf Wyss (1781–1830), having prepared the work for the press. The first English edition appeared as *The Family Robinson Crusoe: or, Journal of a father shipwrecked with his wife and children, on an uninhabited Island*, 1814, and was translated by William Godwin (1756–1836), the father of the wife of the poet Shelley. There are four plates engraved by Springsguth after Henry Corbould, and the work would not be overpriced at anything less than £200 ($500). The first edition in French, *Le Robinson Suisse*, 1814, was published in Paris and has 12 engraved plates. Any edition, in any language, dated before 1830, is now sought avidly by collectors, as are the various versions of the book that inspired the story. One of the best of these is shown in the illustration, and was issued in boards with uncut leaf edges by Cadell & Davies, London, in two volumes in 1820. The fine series of plates are engraved by Charles Heath after designs by Thomas Stothard, the sheets being reissued in the 1830s in a cloth binding at two guineas ($5.04) a copy, with the date on the title-pages remaining the same.

Book publishing began to develop in a way we recognise today with the appearance of sophisticated and worldly-wise fiction for adults and books of amusement and entertainment for children. Both these phenomena occurred in the 1740s, the former with the appearance of the first 'true' novel in English, *Pamela; or, Virtue Rewarded,* 4 vols. 1741–2, by Samuel Richardson (1689–1761), a book discussed in the companion volume to this present work; and the latter with the publication by John Newbery of his first book for children in 1744. Brief mention must be made of Thomas Boreman, a publisher of children's books, who sold them from his shop at the 'Boot and Crown', and from a temporary stall erected with those of other traders within the Guildhall, London. *A Description of a Great Variety of Animals, and Vegetables . . . especially for the Entertainment of Youth,* 1736, and *The Gigantick History of the two famous Giants . . . in Guildhall,* 2 vols. 1740, shows that he was publishing books for children before Newbery came into the field. Thomas Warren, who had a printing business and bookshop in the Bull Ring, Birmingham, as early as 1740, was one of the earliest provincial publishers of books for children. He sent many of his finished products by road to the booksellers gathered in and around Ludgate Hill in London, at that time the centre of the publishing trade in the capital.

In the 1770s, elaborate picture books for children were being produced in Europe, with Leipzig and Frankfurt as the main centres of the book publishing trade. Foremost amongst these was J. D. Basedow's *Elementarwerke für die Jugend und ihre Freunde,* 1774, which was accompanied by a separate volume in the form of an oblong quarto containing 100 full-page copperplate engravings after designs by Daniel Chodowiecki (1726–1801), often referred to as the German Hogarth because of his truthful presentation of middle-class everyday life. Johann Bernhard Basedow (1723–90), was a German educational reformer who had been strongly influenced by Rousseau's *Émile.* His illustrated schoolbook, paid for by contributions from influential and wealthy people, set out to instruct the youth of his day in the ways of the world by a series of textual and pictorial illustrations that covered almost every aspect of human endeavour. The few illustrations I have been able to show give little indication of the breadth and scope of Basedow's monumental work, and the quality of Chodowiecki's finely executed series of copperplate engravings make the work one of the cornerstones of my collection of early children's books. About thirty different children's games are pictured (including, for teenage youth, one of the earliest printed illustrations of a game of billiards in progress, on what appears to be a full-sized slate-bedded table). The book also contains one of the finest series of pictures on the circus that we know of up to that time, as well as illustrations of all the trades, arts and crafts, and domestic offices which the artist could manage to include. The eight full-page maps, some hand-coloured, of countries of Europe and the rest of the world, are amongst the best to be included in a work intended for a juvenile readership.

Meanwhile in England the same year 1774 saw the publication of the two massive quarto volumes of Chesterfield's *Letters to his Son,* issued on behalf of Eugenia Stanhope from the originals in her possession. Philip Stanhope, fourth Earl of Chesterfield (1694–1773), compiled a voluminous correspondence to his son and godson. These private letters, instructional in character, warning the two young men of the perils they might well encounter, make fascinating reading. They were quickly discovered by the parents and guardians of the young people of their day and put into the hands of teenage youth as a work they should read, learn from, and enjoy. Chesterfield's *Miscellaneous Works,* 2 vols. 1777, with 'Volume the Third' (really a separate, and much rarer, work), 1778, are sometimes found bound as a matching set with his *Letters.* The latter well deserve a place in any collection of books devoted to children, giving an intimate glimpse of the perils and frustrations which a fond parent thought confronted those about to make their own way in the world of the mid-18th century.

An illustration from J. B. Basedow's *Elementar-werke für die Jugend und ihre Freunde,* 1774. The first edition, shown here, is extremely rare, and consists of an oblong folio of 100 full-page copperplate engravings by, or after, D. Chodowiecki (often called the German Hogarth).

Size of plate: 20.5 cm wide × 15 cm.

Daniel Chodowiecki (1726–1801), a Polish painter and engraver, depicted German middle-class life in a fashion unequalled by his contemporaries. This series of children's games is taken from *Elementar-werke für die Jugend und ihre Freunde,* 1774.

Size of total engraved surface: 21.7 cm × 16.7 cm.

Another great admirer of Rousseau was Thomas Day (1748–89), the author of a classic example of 18th-century children's literature, *The History of Sandford and Merton*, published in three volumes, dated variously 1783, 1786, and 1789. The first volume is much the rarest of the three to find in first edition form, and complete sets dated as above are seldom encountered. It was originally Day's intention to write a short story for inclusion in Richard Lovell Edgeworth's *Practical Education: or, the History of Harry and Lucy*, a work which was being prepared for publication as early as 1780. But once having started to write the tale, he became so absorbed with his characters that his efforts resulted in a full-length book. Written without the least sense of humour, it tells the story of the rich young prig, Tommy Merton, who is contrasted with the hard-working and too-good-to-be-true Harry Sandford, the moral being drawn by the Revd. Mr Barlow, their tutor. Day wished to emphasise that virtue ultimately pays off, and that man can be converted from his evil ways by an appeal to his humanity and reason. *Sandford and Merton* quickly became an 18th-century best-seller, and was translated into several foreign languages

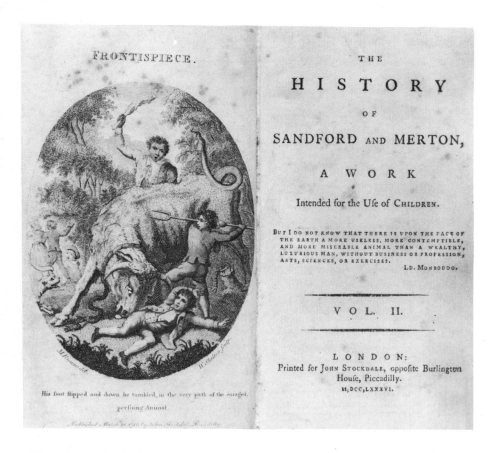

Written without the slightest trace of humour, *The History of Sandford and Merton*, by Thomas Day, was nevertheless one of the most widely read of the late 18th-century story-books for children. Volume I appeared in 1783, volume II in 1786, and volume III in 1789.

Size of title-page: 16.6 cm × 10 cm.

before the end of the century. A parody, *The New History of Sandford and Merton*, 1872, by F. C. Burnand, was illustrated in characteristic fashion by Linley Sambourne. Day also published *The History of Little Jack, who was suckled by a Goat*, 1788; and in 1798, *The Grateful Turk*, one of the series *Moral Tales, by Esteemed Writers*. This latter story had been extracted from the first volume of *Sandford and Merton*.

In the 1780s, an increasing number of women writers were published, many apparently with the avowed intention of making a puritanical onslaught on the literate youth of the day. Anna Laetitia Barbauld (1743–1825) produced her *Hymns in Prose for Children*, 1781, in the preface to which the authoress discusses the necessity of preventing children from reading verse. Her *Lessons for Children, from two to three Years old*, was published in 1778 (parts two and three following in 1794 and 1803 respectively), because, as she put it, no book adapted to the comprehension of little children, printed in large type and easy to read, could as yet be found. The work was printed on good quality paper, with generous margins and widely spaced lines, all innovations in juvenile book production. It proved to be an example for many imitators who copied the style and format of the little volume. Mrs Barbauld was the sister of John Aikin (1747–1822), with whom she wrote *Evenings at Home; or, The*

Juvenile Budget Opened, 6 vols. 1792–6, a companionable and homely collection of miscellaneous pieces 'designed to provide entertainment for thirty evenings'.

Hannah More (1745–1833), was next in the field with her *Sacred Dramas: Chiefly intended for Young Persons*, 1782, published by Thomas Cadell (1742–1802), in which the authoress relates in verse the histories of Moses, David and Goliath, Daniel, etc. 'A laudable and useful work' as Mrs Trimmer described it, with none of the 'perverted Scripture history' produced by Madame de Genlis in her own version of *Sacred Dramas*. Comtesse de Stéphanie de Genlis (1746–1830), had published her *Théâtre de l'éducation* in France in 1779–80; followed by *Les veillées du Chateau*, 1784; the two being published in English translation as *Theatre of Education*, 4 vols. 1781, and *Tales of the Castle*, 5 vols. 1785, under London imprints. The Comtesse had been governess to Louis-Philippe, and was considerably in advance of her time as an educationalist, being one of the first to illustrate her lessons by means of lantern slides, and teaching botany to her pupils when out on nature walks. Thomas Cadell, mentioned above, who published English versions of many of her works, as well as a varied assortment of children's books in the period 1780–93, was eventually succeeded by his son, also Thomas Cadell (1773–1836), of the famous publishing firm of Cadell & Davies, an imprint seen on many juvenile works.

Lady Eleanor Fenn (1743–1813) wrote her books for children under a bewildering collection of pseudonyms; 'Solomon Lovechild', 'Mrs Teachwell', and 'Mrs Lovechild' are those that can be associated with her with certainty. She was the wife of the antiquary Sir John Fenn, the first editor of the Paston letters, and fully shared his literary zeal, writing over a score of books for children although she had none of her own. 'May God preserve you blameless amidst a crooked and perverse generation', she told her young readers in the dedicatory letter prefacing her *School Dialogues, for Boys*, 2 vols. (1783). *School Occurrences: Supposed to have arisen among a set of Young Ladies*, 1782, was followed by her most famous title, *Cobwebs to Catch Flies*, 2 vols. 1783.

Dorothy Kilner (1755–1836) can be identified by the pseudonym 'M.P.', the initials of Maryland Point, the village in Essex in which she and her sister Mary lived. Later, at the request of her publisher, she adopted the pseudonym 'Mary Pelham' using the same initials. An illustration is given of one of her most famous titles, *The Life and Perambulation of a Mouse* (1783), in which she relates the story of a country house party for children and young people at Meadow Hall:

After the more serious employment of reading each morning was concluded, we danced, we sung, we played blind-man's buff, battledoor and shuttlecock, and many other games equally diverting and innocent. And when we tired of them, we drew our seats round the fire, whilst each in turn, told some merry story to divert the company.

Their young hostess set each child the task of relating to the assembled company the story of his or her life, two days being allowed for writing down the facts and incidents of their respective careers. The young lady who narrates the tale is unable to write a word of her memoirs:

The adventures of my life (though deeply interesting to myself) will be insipid and unentertaining to others, especially to my young hearers: I cannot therefore attempt it: nor will I disgrace myself by endeavouring to transcribe my own stupid life.– 'Then write mine, which may be more diverting', said a little squeaking voice, that sounded as if close to me . . .

And there, of course, sat Nimble, the mouse, who promptly proceeds to tell his own life-story and that of his three brothers, Longtail, Softdown, and Brighteyes. Dorothy Kilner was one of the first authors of children's books to employ the literary device of having an animal, bird, or even an inanimate object, to act as narrator of the tale, and there have been a host of imitators ever since. She herself used the method more than once, notably in *The Rational Brutes: or, Talking Animals*, 1799, published by Vernon & Hood. Her sister Mary Jane Kilner, used the same device in *The Adventures of a Pincushion*

Frontispiece of *The Life and Perambulation of A Mouse*. This first edition was published undated in 1783, and is still in its original binding of boards covered with brightly coloured Dutch flowered paper. Written by Dorothy Kilner (1755–1836).

FRONTISPIECE.

Page xii.

(1783), and *Memoirs of a Peg-Top* (1784), both published by John Marshall (1755?–1828). This publisher, who had previously issued *The Life and Perambulations of a Mouse*, was a deadly rival in trade of Elizabeth Newbery. He had been quick to copy the Newbery binding style for his children's books, and procured a close imitation of their flowered and gilt Dutch paper for his little volumes. He dated few if any of his books at this period of his career, thus causing generations of bibliographers a great deal of exasperation and hours of often fruitless research. The children's books he issued so generously in the latter quarter of the 18th century can eventually be dated with a fair degree of certainty by a time-consuming process of elimination. By cataloguing the many dated inscriptions, the comparison of dated advertisements in other works, and attention to the clues and dates sometimes given in the dedications and prefaces, I have been able to date a large proportion of books containing his imprint, as shown above. The apportioning of the unsigned titles of the stories for children from the pen of either Dorothy or Mary Kilner has been carried out by a similar process, and one with which every collector of early children's books will eventually have to make himself familiar. *Anecdotes of a Boarding-School; or, an Antidote to the Vices of those Useful Seminaries*, 2 vols. (1781), also published by Marshall, was Dorothy Kilner's first book that we know of; while *A Course of Lectures for Sunday Evenings* (1783), was written by her sister, who used the pseudonym 'S.S', or, more rarely, 'Sarah Slinn'.

Little is known of the life of that enterprising young lady Miss Lucy Peacock, who later set up in business on her own account in Oxford Street, London, after writing several books at her private address in Lambeth. Her first work, written when she was still in her early teens, is notable for the fact that she stood in attendance at Mr A. Perfetti's shop at 91, Wimpole Street, and personally signed all the copies that were sold there. *The Adventures of the Six Princesses of Babylon, in their Travels to the Temple of Virtue*, 1785 (second edition, also often bearing the signature of the authoress, dated 1786), is unusual because it was published in quarto size (approximately 25 cm high × 19 cm in uncut copies) as well as by having a most impressive 16-page list of aristocratic

One of the woodcut illustrations from the first edition of *The Holyday Present* (1783), by Dorothy Kilner. The running title was changed to 'The Holiday Present'.

Size of page: 11.8 cm × 7.8 cm.

The initials 'M.P.' stand for 'Mary Pelham', itself a pseudonym for the writer Dorothy Kilner (1755–1836): this two-volume work is her earliest production, published undated in 1781.

Size of title-page: 15 cm × 9.5 cm.

Right
Scrap-books were favourite presents for children throughout the latter half of the 19th century and the one shown dates from 1892. The coloured cut-outs were mostly printed in Germany, as was this magnificent Santa Claus standing nearly 40 cm high.

and wealthy-sounding subscribers amounting in all to over 1,250 names. The work is dedicated, by gracious permission, to H.R.H. the Princess Mary, and seems to have been something of a literary best-seller in its day, despite the fact that it sold for 3*s*. 6*d*. (42 cents) a copy. The usual price for the children's story books issued by E. Newbery, John Marshall, and other publishers of the

B.B. Nº 195.

LITTLE MISSES.

FROM A PICTURE BY KATE GREENAWAY.

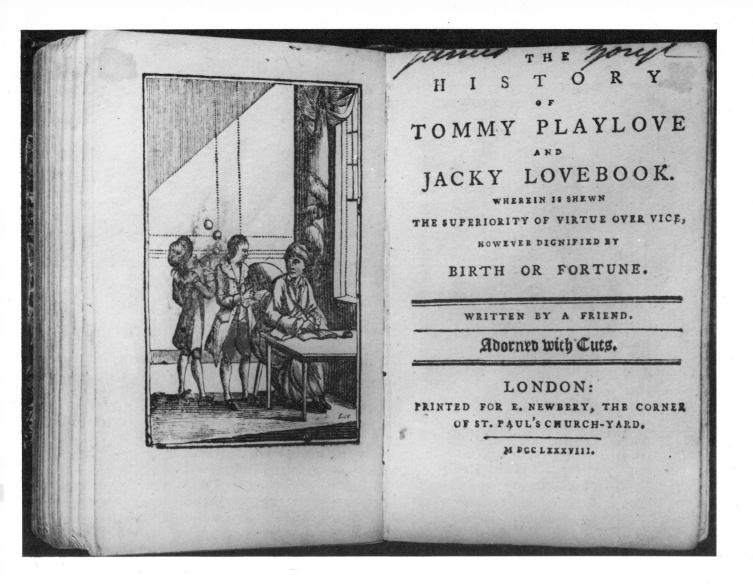

Above
A story by Stephen Jones (1763–1827) first published in 1783, the copy shown being the second edition. The author states that he will 'make bold to tell my little friends, that those among them who will not take my physic, can certainly have no claim to the sweetmeats with which it is accompanied . . .' The woodcut illustrations are by John Lee.

Size of title-page:
11 cm × 7.2 cm.

A frontispiece by Kate Greenaway for the annual *Little Wide-Awake*, 1888, an illustrated magazine for children edited by Mrs Sale Barker. The monthly magazine ran from 1875 to 1892.

period was sixpence (6 cents) a copy, 'bound and gilt'. Lucy Peacock's allegorical romance of the six princesses is modelled, as the young authoress freely admits in her preface, on Edmund Spenser's *The Faerie Queene*. Amongst her other works for children were *The Rambles of Fancy*, 2 vols. 1786; *The Knight of the Rose*, 1793; *The Visit for a Week; or, Hints for the Improvement of Time*, 1794; and *The Little Emigrant*, 1802. She is also remembered as the editor of one of the first periodicals ever produced for children, *The Juvenile Magazine*, which appeared in a series of twelve monthly parts during 1788, and was later published in book form as a two-volume work.

Literature for the instruction and amusement of children, with the emphasis very much on the former, was dominated for a period of almost twenty years by a solid phalanx of didactic females. This heavy brigade of formidable matrons seemed determined to root out any tendency on the part of the young to read solely for their own entertainment and amusement, especially such frivolous fiction as fairy tales and other pernicious rubbish. The superiority of virtue over vice 'however dignified by birth or fortune' was their reiterated theme; and vice was usually designated by these belligerent moralists as the type of conduct we should today class as merely youthful naughtiness or boisterous high spirits.

In the vanguard of this 'Monstrous Regiment of Women', as Percy Muir dubbed them, no doubt with a backward glance over his shoulder at John Knox, were several I have named above, reinforced by their contemporaries listed below. Mrs Pinchard contributed *The Blind Child, or Anecdotes of the Wyndham family*, 1791, saying that her aim was 'to repress that excessive softness of heart, which too frequently involves its possessor in a train of evils'. Her *Dramatic Dialogues, for the use of Young Persons*, 1792, was published in two volumes by E. Newbery, who two years later issued *The Two Cousins, a Moral Story*, a tale of a self-righteous young lady who sets out to reform her easygoing cousin by precept and example. Mary Pilkington (1766–1839), the wife

of a naval surgeon, wrote over sixty books for children. *Tales of the Hermitage;*
Written for the Instruction and Amusement of the Rising Generation, 1798, was probably her most successful work, written after two of her earliest books, *Edward*
Barnard; or, Merit Exalted, 1797, and *Obedience Rewarded and Prejudice Conquered*,
1797. Her other works include: *A Mirror for the Female Sex*, 1798, *The Spoiled*
Child, 1799, *Biography for Girls*, 1799, and its companion volume *Biography*
for Boys, 1799. All were severely moral and instructional in character. Priscilla
Wakefield (1751–1832) contributed several juvenile works of natural history
as well as a number of travel books. *Mental Improvement; or, The Beauties of and*
Wonders of Nature and Art, 2 vols. 1794, *Juvenile Anecdotes*, 2 vols. 1795–8,
Excursions in North America, 1806, and *The Traveller in Africa*, 1814, are typical
of her titles. Elizabeth Helme, who died in 1816, had written in much the same
vein, and her *Instructive Rambles in London, and the adjacent villages*, 2 vols. 1798,
was followed by a sequel entitled *Instructive Rambles extended in London, and the*
adjacent villages, 2 vols. 1800.

The century drew to a close with the appearance of *The Parent's Assistant;*
or, Stories for Children, 3 vols. 1795, published anonymously. This first edition
of the first work for children by Maria Edgeworth (1767–1849), does not
appear to have survived in records in any private or public library, and
copies of the two-volume second edition of 1796 can be counted on a single
hand. This famous collection of short stories for young people was written to
exemplify the principles later expounded in *Practical Education*, 2 vols. 1798,
written in conjunction with her father, Richard Lovell Edgeworth (1744–
1817). *The Parent's Assistant* contains the stories of *The Little Dog Trusty, The*
False Key, The Purple Jar, The Bracelets, The Birthday Present, and *The Mimic*,
amongst several others, *The Barring Out* not being added until the appearance
of the second edition. The work was reissued in six volumes in 1800, this
time with Maria Edgeworth's name on the title-page. To this edition she
added eight new stories and omitted three, transferring these to *Early Lessons*,
which was at first issued under the title of *Harry and Lucy*, 1801. Most of the
stories in this latter work were by her father and Mrs Honora Edgeworth.

A full list of the works of the Edgeworths and other authors of whom I have
been able to make only brief mention will be found in the specialist bibliographies of the period. The critical works of the redoubtable Mrs Sarah
Trimmer (1741–1810) are discussed later; but no treatise on 18th-century
books written for children can ignore her most famous work, a book that has
continued in print until the present day. *Fabulous Histories. Designed for the*
Instruction of children, respecting their treatment of animals, 1786 (second edition the
same year), was a landmark in the annals of children's literature. Under its
later title, *The History of the Robins*, numerous generations of children have
delighted in the adventures and hair's-breadth escapes of the daring little
birds Robin, Dicky, Flapsy, and Pecksy, whose names she seems to have culled
from the works of John Newbery. Between writing her many educational tracts
and religious works, Mrs Trimmer found time to have no less than twelve
children of her own, and was a tireless advocate of the necessity for Sunday
schools in every town and village in the land.

Arnaud Berquin (1749–91) published his *L'Ami des Enfans* in Paris in a
series of 24 monthly parts beginning on 1 January 1782. The French
Academy awarded him 'a Prize for usefulness', and his work was acclaimed
as the finest book for children of the period. As *The Children's Friend* it quickly
established itself as a firm favourite with the children of Britain, appearing in
five volumes, 1783–4, and thereafter in a variety of formats and selections.
Another popular translation in the latter half of the 18th century (other than
fairy stories, discussed separately) was *Paul et Virginie*, 1788, by Jacques Henri
Bernardin de Saint-Pierre (1737–1814), issued in England as *Paul and Mary*,
an Indian Story, 2 vols. 1789. A later translation by Helen Maria Williams was
entitled *Paul and Virginia*, 1795, the name by which the work is usually known
on this side of the Channel.

One final title known to every child and annexed by the youth of the day
within a few months of its first appearance was *The Diverting History of John*
Gilpin, by William Cowper (1731–1800), first printed in *The Public Advertiser*,
14 November 1782, and later in book form as the final item in *The Task, A*
Poem in Six Books, 1785, issued as a companion volume to his *Poems*, 1782.
Children of the late 18th century learned most of the sixty-three verses by

Right, top
First published in Paris in 1782, under the
title of *L'ami des Enfans*, this translation by
Lucas Williams contains 33 of Arnaud Berquin's stories and first appeared in 1788.
Size of title-page:
17 cm × 10 cm.

Right, bottom
In her introduction Mrs Sarah Trimmer
states that her object in writing these stories
of birds and animals was to show children the
wrong they did in 'tormenting inferior
creatures, before they are conscious of giving
them pain; or fall into the contrary habit of
immoderate tenderness to them'. The first
edition appeared the same year as this second
edition, and the work was later issued under
the less forbidding title of *The History of the*
Robins.
Size of title-page:
17.5 cm × 10.2 cm.

Below
Mrs Mary Pilkington (1766–1839) started
writing children's books when her husband
left to commence a career in the Navy, and
this first edition is the fifth of her sixty or
more titles to appear. Despite the forbidding
title this is a quick-moving tale full of unconscious humour.
Size of title-page:
13.3 cm × 8.8 cm.

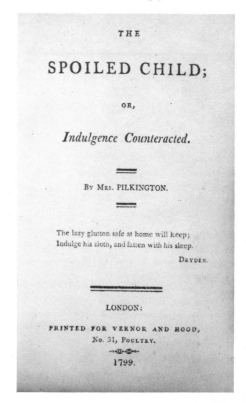

THE

SPOILED CHILD;

OR,

Indulgence Counteracted.

By Mrs. PILKINGTON.

The lazy glutton safe at home will keep;
Indulge his sloth, and fatten with his sleep.
DRYDEN.

LONDON:
PRINTED FOR VERNOR AND HOOD,
No. 31, POULTRY.
1799.

Eat there, said Claribell to him, it is all that I have left to give you. You are the Father of this Child, and if you do not devour him, Famine and Misery shortly will. ———

THE
CHILDREN's FRIEND.

BEING

A SELECTION

FROM THE

WORKS of M. BERQUIN.

CITO NEQUITIA SUBREPIT; VIRTUS DIFFICILIS INVENTU EST, RECTOREM DUCEMQUE DESIDERAT. ETIAM SINE MAGISTRO VITIA DISCUNTUR.   SEN.

A NEW EDITION.

LONDON:

PRINTED FOR A. MILLAR, W. LAW, AND R. CATER, AND WILSON, SPENCE, AND MAWMAN, YORK.

M,DCC,XCVI.

FABULOUS
HISTORIES.

DESIGNED FOR THE

INSTRUCTION

OF

CHILDREN,

RESPECTING THEIR

TREATMENT OF ANIMALS.

By Mrs. TRIMMER.

SECOND EDITION.

LONDON.

PRINTED FOR T. LONGMAN, AND G. G. J. AND J. ROBINSON, PATER-NOSTER-ROW; AND J. JOHNSON, ST. PAUL'S CHURCH-YARD.

M DCC LXXXVI.

---

heart, and the fact that prose, illustrated, abridged, parodied, chapbook, moveable, and innumerable imitative versions have since appeared aimed at the juvenile market has persuaded me to include it here. The final stanza has been shouted in chorus in schools and nurseries through the length and breadth of the English-speaking world for close on two hundred years:

> Now let us sing, long live the king,
> And Gilpin long live he,
> And when he next doth ride abroad,
> May I be there to see!

35

Fairy, Folk Tales and Fantasia

Children have never ceased to enjoy reading fairy tales since the first collection of them appeared in print early in the 17th century. They were the first literature for children to escape from the stifling toils of didacticism and were attacked and condemned by the puritanical writers for precisely this reason. The battle between the strait-laced juvenile tract and the fairy stories that children delighted to read extended until well into the 1830s. By the age of Victoria, they had been grudgingly accepted by the parents, guardians and governesses of even the most strictly regulated children, and well-thumbed collections of the best known tales were to be found on nursery shelves everywhere.

Stories about fairies and supernatural beings exist in the mythology and folklore of all nations. The first collection to appear in print was a book of peasant fairy stories in the Neapolitan dialect, collected and transcribed by Giambattista Basile, and published posthumously in 1637. *Il Pentamerone*, also known under its popular name of *Lo Cunto de li Cunti*, was divided by the author into five days each containing ten tales, a fact which explains the name. *The Pentamerone, or The Story of Stories*, first appeared in English as a translation from the Neapolitan by John Edward Taylor, and was published by David Bogue, London, dated 1848. The work contains a delightful series of copper-plate illustrations by George Cruikshank, some of which are equal to the best of his work. The first edition of this translation ranks with the most difficult children's books of the 19th century to find in acceptable condition in the original cloth binding. It is a heavy, almost square octavo, of some 404 pages, plus the bulk of 12 full-page engravings printed on thick paper. Once dropped, or even read and handled a number of times, is enough to strain the hinges of the cloth binding, spring the text, and eventually to see the interior of the book part company with its covers. *The Pentamerone* is a key book in the annals of children's literature and a milestone in the history of fairy stories. It is also of priceless interest to folklorists, retaining as it does all the freshness of the original tales as heard from the lips of the Italian peasants by Giambattista Basile. The best of the editions in the original tongue is that by G. Croce, *Giambattista Basile ed il Cunto de li Cunti*, 1891. The first English edition, quoted above, is deserving of greater recognition and appreciation than scholars and literary historians have so far accorded it, for the prose style is as earthy and as robust as one could wish; surprisingly so when one remembers the mood of the age in which the translation was made. Tales such as *Peruonto*, in which the mother of the hero describes her son as not being worth 'a dog's mess', and in which princesses are struck down suddenly with phantom pregnancies, may have made early 19th-century publishers pause, for few editions of this first collection of fairy and folk tales appeared during the ensuing decades. The first edition in a language other than Italian was a German translation by Felix Liebrecht, published in 1844. Thomas Keightley (1789–1872) wrote *The Fairy Mythology*, 2 vols. 1828, and *Tales and Popular Fictions: their Resemblance and Transmission*, 1834, both of which contain extracts from Basile's collection of tales, but these works were intended for an adult readership.

France contributed much to the development of children's books in general and to the spread of interest in fairy tales and traditional folklore stories in particular. Some of these old tales remembered by the countryfolk, and the delightful *contes* of Charles Perrault (1628–1703), were first translated into

English by Robert Samber in about 1730. Perrault was a member of the French Academy, and is supposed to have first been introduced to the stories by his own little son – who may well have heard them from the lips of his nurse. He entitled his collection *Histoires ou Contes du Temps Passé*, and they were first published in Paris in 1697, some sixty years after the first appearance of *Il Pentamerone*. The frontispiece had the legend, *Contes de ma Mere l'Oye*, and from this title grew the familiar name of *Tales of Mother Goose*. Who the original old French woman may have been (one somehow always thinks of her as a gnarled old crone with a tender heart) we shall never know. Many of the tales were probably invented by unrelated individuals, to be collected later in the memory of others, who passed them on to generations of young children, although a common authorship can be traced by some scholars in certain groups of Perrault's collection. Whoever was originally responsible for their invention and subsequent preservation in embellished form, we know that from the 1730s onwards, children took to their hearts the stories of *Red Riding Hood*, *Cinderella*, *Blue-beard*, *The Sleeping Beauty*, *Puss-in-Boots*, and the rest of the tales told by Mother Goose. Young people have kept them there ever since and they have remained in print throughout the subsequent 270 or more years since their first appearance in Paris. Samber's original English edition of about 1730, whose existence is only known through the medium of advertisements in other works, was reissued in 1764 as *Tales of Passed Times, by Mother Goose*, and again in 1785, this time in two volumes, as *The Histories of Passed Times*. All 18th-century editions are extremely rare and extremely valuable; the earlier examples would be priced at well over £1,000 ($2,400) if they came on the market.

Jacob Ludwig Carl Grimm (1785–1863), and Wilhelm Carl Grimm (1786–1859), were brothers born at Hanau, Germany. Both became professors of linguistic studies, first at Göttingen and later at Berlin University, and they collaborated in collecting from the mouths of countryfolk and literary sources as many of the old folk tales and fairy stories as they could find. *Kinder- und Hausmärchen*, was published in 2 vols. 1812–5, and has ever since been known by the affectionate title of *Grimms' Fairy Tales*. The first English edition is a rarity eagerly sought after by collectors of early children's books, for the first issue is distinguished by lacking the *umlaut* marks in the word Märchen. This

Probably the most difficult of all collections of fairy stories to find as a first (English) edition in the original cloth binding. This earliest collection of European fairy tales was published posthumously in 1637. The edition of 1848 was the first to appear in English. The book is of priceless interest to folklorists.

Size of title-page:
17.8 cm × 13 cm.

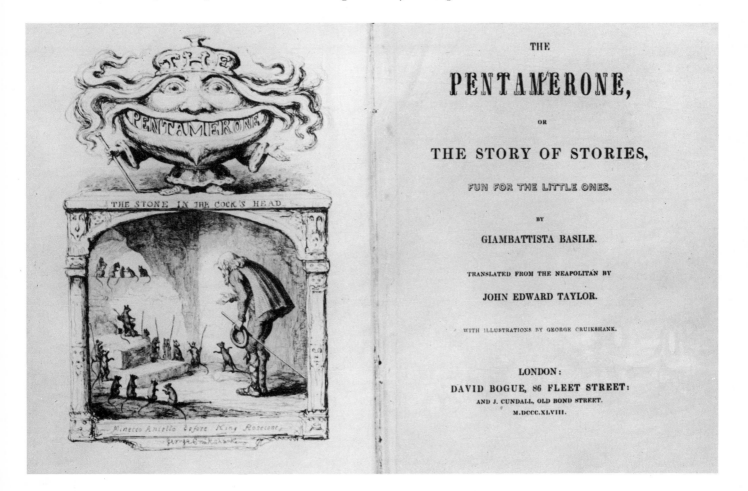

English edition appeared as *German Popular Stories, Translated from the Kinder und Haus Marchen*, 2 vols. 1823–6, the first volume being issued by C. Baldwyn, in a binding of pictorially-printed paper-covered boards with uncut leaf edges, and the second, three years later, by James Robins & Co., in a binding of pink paper-covered boards with the leaf edges again left uncut. Later issues of the first edition of volume one had the *umlauts* inserted. The imprint of James Robins & Co. appeared on both volumes with the second edition of volume one in 1825. George Cruikshank (1792–1878) supplied a series of 22 full-page engravings to illustrate the work, and it has been a favourite subject with artists and book-illustrators ever since. Arthur Rackham (1867–1939) was famous for his interpretations of fairyland and the books illustrated by him, especially in the form of the limited editions in which his publishers delighted, are now collector's pieces in their own right and fetch high prices at auction. His *Grimm's Fairy Tales*, 1909, in the special binding of parchment spine with linen ties, is now regularly catalogued at over £100 ($240), the ordinary trade edition being worth only a tenth of that amount. Another title illustrated by the same artist, *Little Brother and Sister*, 1917, a story extracted from the collection made by the brothers Grimm, is now priced at about £60 ($144) in the limited edition binding.

This ever popular collection of fairy tales has since been translated into nearly every language. The first French edition, *Vieux Contes pour l'Amusement des Grands et des Petits Enfans* (1824), was published in Paris by Auguste Boulland, George Cruikshank's illustrations being re-engraved by Ambroise Tardieu from the 1823 English edition. Extracts, and the printing of individual stories or short collections has continued without interruption since the early 1830s. *Hans in Luck*, *The Fisherman and his Wife*, *Tom Thumb*, *The Adventures of Chanti-*

A George Cruikshank illustration for *Hop-O'My-Thumb and The Seven-League Boots*, 1853, the first of four booklets he edited in the series *George Cruikshank's Fairy Library* published by David Bogue.

cleer and Partlet, *Snow-Drop* (now immortalised as *Snow White and the Seven Dwarfs*), *The Elves and the Shoemaker*, *The Golden Goose*, *Hansel and Grettel*, *The Frog-Prince*, *Rumpel-Stilts-Kin*, *The Goose-Girl*, *Hans in Love*, *Cat-Skin*, *The Juniper Tree*, and a dozen or more other stories whose titles have since become household words, all appeared in this collection of German fairy stories, folk tales and legends that the brothers Grimm preserved for posterity by establishing the texts in the early years of the 19th century.

It was after reading the first edition of *Kinder- und Hausmärchen* that Thomas Crofton Croker (1798–1854), determined to make a collection of *Fairy Legends and Traditions of the South of Ireland*, later published by John Murray, London, in 1825, illustrated by a series of vignettes from designs made by W. H. Brooke. The work was translated into German by Jacob and Wilhelm Grimm as *Irische Elfenmärchen*. Two further volumes of Croker's *Fairy Legends* appeared in 1828, the last of which was dedicated to Wilhelm Grimm. A collected edition, edited by T. Wright, was published in 1882.

Brief mention must be made here of a few early collections of fairy tales that perhaps lack many of the best loved stories in original form, but were nevertheless the forerunners of the well-known selections that followed. *The Fairy Spectator; or, the Invisible Monitor*, 1789, by Mrs Teachwell (i.e. Lady Eleanor Fenn), was published by J. Marshall & Co., London. A more important early collection appeared as *Temple of the Fairies*, 2 vols. 1804, to be reissued as *The Court of Oberon: or, Temple of the Fairies*, 1823, and again, under a Glasgow imprint, as *Fairy Tales, or The Court of Oberon* (1824). Most of the stories are culled from Charles Perrault's *contes*, although *Cinderella* is missing, and we have such tales as *Jack and the Beanstalk*, a fairy story whose origins are lost in the mists of time and which appears to have been known to the North American Indians as well as to the native tribes of South Africa before the coming of the white man. *The White Cat*, *Prince Fatal and Prince Fortune*, *The Invisible Prince*, and *The Fair One with the Golden Locks*, are included in the thirteen tales. The last title mentioned has no connection with the favourite nursery tale of *Goldilocks and the Three Bears*, although the name of the heroine may well have suggested to later publishers of the story a pleasing title for their own heroine. *The Story of the Three Bears* was an English nursery story; the first manuscript giving the text that we know of can be dated September 1831, and was written and illustrated by Eleanor Mure, who could already describe it at that early date as 'The celebrated nursery tale of the Three Bears. . . .' It first appeared in print in volume four of *The Doctor*, 1837, by Robert Southey. *The Three Bears and their Stories*, with a dedication signed and dated 'G.N.' July 1837, appeared in time for Christmas that year, and was subsequently reissued by Wright & Co., in 1841. Any text of the story dated before 1850 is a rare and desirable possession for the collector of children's books.

The Renowned Tales of Mother Goose as Originally Related, was one of the first collections of fairy stories issued under the imprint of John Harris, who had succeeded to the business of Elizabeth Newbery in 1801. It was published undated about 1818, in a binding of marbled paper-covered boards with the usual red roan-spine crossed in horizontal gold lines, which Harris had established as his standard binding for nearly all his vast output of children's books. The lithographed frontispiece of the 'Discreet Princess' was one of the earliest examples of this newly introduced printing process to appear in a children's book, but Harris reverted to the use of his usual copperplate engravings and woodcuts soon after this initial experiment. All the early editions of the *Tales of Mother Goose* seem to have been read to death by the generations of children who first possessed them, for examples dating from the first few decades of the 19th century are scarcely ever found, while 18th-century examples seem to have completely disappeared.

The story of the best-known and best-loved puppet-play, that children have known as *Punch and Judy* since its first appearance in England in 1662, has formed the subject of many tales for the young since the 1830s onwards. Most had brightly coloured plates, or plates purposely left in outline to be brightly coloured by the young owner of the book. Although some historians have classed the little drama that we have all seen as children at the seaside or on city streets (now, unfortunately, mainly limited to indoor parties) as a folk tale, derived from the traditions of Italian peasantry, the name of Punch derives from the *Commedia dell'arte* character, Pulcinella. It came to us through

Frontispiece of one of the few large-paper copies of *Punch and Judy* – its first appearance in English. This copy has the 24 full-page copperplate engravings coloured by hand.

the French, Polichinelle, and the anglicised Punchinello, but the irascible hero or villain has throughout retained his hooked nose, humped back, and aggressive nature. The first printed text of *Punch and Judy* is, surprisingly, dated as late as 1828. John Payne Collier (1789–1833), remembered unhappily for his falsifications of ancient documents and his forgeries of marginal corrections of the text of Shakespeare in the 'Perkins folio', had to his credit the distinction of being the first to record the text of the famous puppet-show. At the instigation of Samuel Prowett of Pall Mall, the publisher of the work and a collector of puppets, Collier accompanied George Cruikshank to a Punch and Judy show. Here, the artist made his series of drawings to illustrate the book while Collier took notes for the text. By this means, as the editor tells his readers in the preface, the publisher was able 'to fill up a *hiatus* in theatrical history'. A second edition of *Punch and Judy* appeared the same year, with the 24 full-page engravings of scenes from the play again hand-coloured, and within a few years abridged versions of the text with fresh sets of illustrations were being issued by many of the best-known publishers of children's books. The drama of Mr Punch and his wife Judy (originally Joan) was watched by Samuel Pepys in the theatre at Covent Garden as long ago as the 1660s and has never failed to fascinate audiences of every age since then.

Wonderful Stories for Children, 1846, is the first translation into English of the tales of Hans Christian Andersen (1805–75), whose fairy stories had been appearing in his native Denmark since 1835. Further collections of his tales for children were issued at regular intervals, and after 1848 he abandoned his other literary activities and wrote little else but the fairy stories that have brought him immortality throughout the world. *The Ugly Duckling*, *The Tinder Box*, *The Emperor's New Clothes*, *The Snow Queen*, and many others are known and loved by children of all ages. The famous statue of the mermaid on a rock in Copenhagen harbour is a lasting tribute to Andersen and his story, *The Little Mermaid*. During an early visit to Britain he met Charles Dickens and befriended Mary Howitt (1799–1888), the author of a number of natural history books for children and wife of William Howitt (1792–1879), author of *The Boy's Country Book*, 1839, and other works. *Wonderful Stories for Children* was translated by Mary Howitt, who had gone to the trouble of learning Danish specially for this purpose. It was published in a straight-grained, full-cloth binding, blocked in blind and gilt, and with a complement of four full-page hand-coloured plates. She took the fact that she had spelled the author's name incorrectly on the title-page of the first edition as an ill-omen, (it was printed 'Anderson') and in fact the work did not pay for the cost of printing. This was probably due to two other rival editions appearing later in the same year, just in time to capture much of the Christmas trade in books for the young. William Pickering published a translation by Caroline Peachey, and a similar selection of Andersen's works was made by Charles Bower and issued by Joseph Cundall. The following year, 1847, saw the publication of *A Picture-Book without Pictures*, by Hans Christian Andersen, translated by Meta Taylor from the German translation of de la Motte Fouque. *The Ice-Maiden*, 1863, was translated from the Danish by Mrs Bushby, the original story having been published in Copenhagen in 1862. From that time onwards, English editions of collections of Andersen's tales and of individual stories appeared every few years, many lavishly illustrated by the foremost artists and engravers of the day. *Ole Lukoie*, *The Daisy*, *The Naughty Boy*, *Tommelise*, *The Rose-Elf*, *The Garden of Paradise*, *A Night in the Kitchen*, *Little Ida's Flowers*, *The Constant Tin Soldier*, and *The Storks*, all appeared in the first English edition of 1846, and the rest of his stories at short intervals after their original appearance in Danish.

By the 1840s, collections of fairy stories were becoming commonplace. One of the landmarks of the period was the appearance of Sir Henry Cole's *The Home Treasury of Books*, which he published under the pseudonym of 'Felix Summerly'. The first title to appear was *Bible Events*, 1843, but he then turned his attention to such popular and saleable extravagances as *Little Red Riding Hood*, *Reynard the Fox*, *Beauty and the Beast*, *Traditional Nursery Songs*, and *Sir Hornbook*. Henry Cole (1808–82), had been dissatisfied with the quality of books available for young people when he had visited the recognised juvenile bookshops seeking story books for his own children. He became determined to design and produce books for the young himself and advertised a new ven-

An illustration from the first in the series of *Gammer Gurton's Pleasant Stories*, 1845, printed at the Chiswick Press by Charles Whittingham, and edited by 'Ambrose Merton, Gent.' the pseudonym of William John Thoms (1803–85). The publisher, Joseph Cundall, commissioned John Franklin and John Absolon for the illustrations.

Size of page: 16 cm × 12.2 cm.

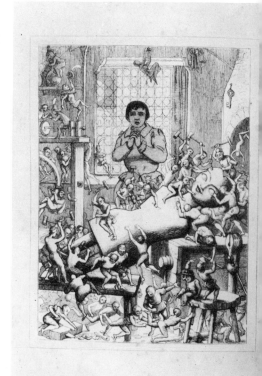

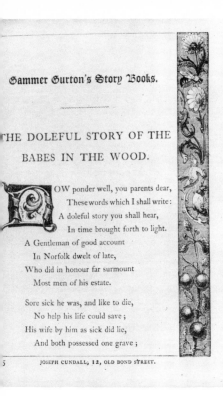

The first book written by Mark Lemon (1809–70), one of the founders, and later the sole editor, of *Punch*. It was published in 1849 by Bradbury & Evans, in a format of glazed pictorial paper-covered boards, with illustrations by Richard Doyle.

Size of title-page:
17.7 cm × 12.5 cm.

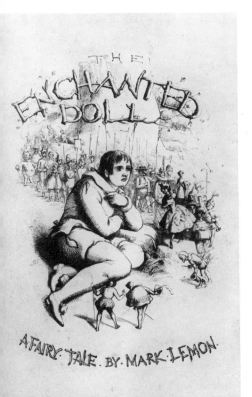

ture, to be called *The Home Treasury of Books, Pictures, Toys, etc., purposed to cultivate the Affections, Fancy, Imagination, and Taste of Children.* In the prospectus, he told his would-be readers that 'Little Red Riding Hood and other fairy tales hallowed to children's use, are now turned into ribaldry as satires for men . . . this is hurtful to children. . . .' The books he published set a new standard of quality in works for young people. The format in which they were issued, although expensive, was influential in moulding the taste of the public that could afford to purchase them for their children. This led eventually to a demand for finely produced, illustrated books in the 1860s and later. With *Reynard the Fox*, 1843, Cole aimed much too high and did not repeat the experiment. It contained 40 coloured plates by Everdingen and was sold in the shops at £1 11s. 6d. ($3.78), an unprecedented price for a children's book in those days. The rest of the bound books in the series retailed at 2s. (24 cents) or 2s. 6d. (30 cents), depending on which of the two alternative bindings you selected, the plates being plain, or at 3s. 6d. (42 cents) or 4s. 6d. (54 cents), with the plates hand-coloured. The bound books were followed by a series selling at 1s. a copy; and then by what was probably a remainder issue, entitled *Gammer Gurton's Story Books*, issued at 9d. (9 cents), with only a single illustration to each. None of 'Felix Summerly's' titles are easy to find. All were finely printed by Charles Whittingham at the Chiswick Press, and are collected as much by those whose interest lies in the history of typography and publishers' binding styles as by the collectors of early children's books.

A number of authors were by this time trying their hand at writing fairy stories for the young, the difficulty of finding new and unused plots presenting obstacles that few were able to overcome successfully. *The Enchanted Doll. A Fairy Tale for Little People*, 1849, by Mark Lemon (1809–70), remembered as one of the founders, and later the sole editor, of the magazine *Punch*, was illustrated in characteristic fashion by Richard Doyle, the famous 'Dicky' Doyle (1824–83), who designed a famous front cover for the periodical mentioned above. *The Enchanted Doll* is a most difficult first edition to find in acceptable condition for it was issued in a rather fragile binding of glazed, pink paper-covered boards, pictorially-printed on the front and back covers. Doyle's most sought after book is the folio, *In Fairyland – A Series of Pictures from the Elf-World*, 1870 (second edition 1875), a masterpiece of book-illustration and an outstanding example of the colour printing of the equally well-known Edmund Evans (1826–1905), a craftsman whose work for Walter Crane, Randolph Caldecott, Kate Greenaway, and other writers and illustrators put him at the top of his profession. *In Fairyland*, the text supplied by a poem by William Allingham (1824–89), is one of the finest books ever produced for children, and from the collector's point of view a most desirable item to add to any library of juvenile works, especially as copies in the original green, morocco-grained, full-cloth bindings, pictorially blocked in gold on the front cover, can still be found for as little as £50 ($120). It is a work that can be expected to rise in price rapidly over the next few years. Allingham was an Irish poet who became a friend of Leigh Hunt and was introduced to the Pre-Raphaelite Brotherhood by Coventry Patmore. His poem, *The Fairies*, first published in *Poems*, 1850 (which he withdrew from circulation), and later in his most famous work *The Music Master*, 1855, has been recited by several generations of children.

> Up the Airy mountain,
> Down the rushy glen,
> We daren't go a-hunting,
> For fear of little men.

The Fairies (1883), with illustrations by E. Gertrude Thomson, was published by Thomas de la Rue & Co., London. The following year, Andrew Lang (1844–1912) wrote a new story to accompany Richard Doyle's original pictures used for *In Fairyland*, and the book was issued, undated, by Longmans, Green & Co., London, as *The Princess Nobody, a Tale of Fairy Land*.

Original stories inspired by folk tales and fairy legends appeared in a succession of titles throughout the latter half of the 19th century. John Ruskin (1819–1900) contributed *The King of the Golden River*, 1851, three editions appearing in the same year. Published anonymously, the story was written some ten years before at the request of twelve-year-old Euphemia ('Effie') Chalmers Gray, a girl whom Ruskin subsequently married in 1848. The marriage was later annulled. William Makepeace Thackeray (1811–63) is remembered by children for *The Rose and the Ring; or, The History of Prince Giglio and Prince Bulbo*, 1855, written under his pseudonym of 'M. A. Titmarsh'. The publication of *The Water Babies: A Fairy Tale for a Land-Baby*, 1863, containing two delightful illustrations by J. Noel Paton, showed a return to a book with a moral to preach. The author, Charles Kingsley (1819–75), had first published the tale serially from August 1862 to March 1863, in *Macmillan's Magazine*. The first issue of the first edition in book form is distinguished by a leaf with the poem *L'Envoi*, which the author suppressed during the printing. Only a few hundred copies escaped before the alteration was made. *The Water Babies* has become a classic in children's literature, and new editions, illustrated by a variety of artists and engravers, have appeared ever since. His other works for children did not attain quite the same success, although two which young people have adopted as their own, *Westward Ho! or, The Voyages and Adventures of Sir Amyas Leigh*, 3 vols. 1856, and *Hereward the Wake, 'Last of the English'*, 2 vols. 1866, have remained firm favourites. His fairy tales include *The Heroes; or, Greek Fairy Tales for my Children*, 1856, with eight full-page illustrations by the author; but his other tales, *Glaucus; or, Wonders of the Shore*, 1855, and *Madam How and Lady Why*, 1870, could more properly be included under the heading Natural History.

Fairy tale and fantasy reached their culminating point of triumph with the publication of *Alice's Adventures in Wonderland*, 1865, and *Through the Looking-Glass, and what Alice found there*, 1872. Both works are written with a fascinating, dream-like blend of strange logic and wild fancy. Both are in many senses 'children's books for grown-ups', and one must admit that although many children thoroughly enjoy reading *Alice in Wonderland* and its companion volume, there are a percentage that remain totally unimpressed. The author, the Revd. C. L. Dodgson (1832–98), is known to young and old by his pseudonym 'Lewis Carroll', a title derived from Dodgson's first two names, Charles Lutwidge: Lutwidge equates with Ludwig, of which Lewis is the Anglicised version, and Carroll is another form of the name Charles. Dodgson delighted in amusing demure little girls of a certain age; he had first met Alice, the daughter of Dean Liddell of Christ Church, Oxford, in 1856, and it was for her that he wrote his masterpiece. By the time the book was published his pretty little girl had just entered her teens, and he complained in a letter that she had 'changed a good deal, and hardly for the better. . . .' The model for the illustrations had to be a new child-friend of the same age as his heroine Alice Liddell in his imagination when he wrote the book.

A review of *Alice's Adventures in Wonderland* appeared in the Christmas annual volume of *Aunt Judy's Magazine*, 1866, from the pen of the editor Mrs Alfred Gatty, a writer of children's stories whose *The Fairy Godmothers and Other Tales*, 1851, had been published by George Bell, London. She was enthusiastic, and began: 'Forty-two illustrations by Tenniel! Why there needs nothing else to sell this book, one would think. But our young friends may rest assured that the exquisite illustrations do but justice to the exquisitely wild, fantastic, impossible, yet most natural history of Alice in Wonderland.' Sir John Tenniel (1820–1914) was knighted in 1893, during a long career as joint cartoonist with John Leech of the magazine *Punch*, in which he gained great fame for the originality and wit of his political satires. It was the harmony of Dodgson's text with Tenniel's inimitable series of illustrations that combined to produce the work the world knows (in almost any language you care to mention) as *Alice in Wonderland*, and immortalised the names of 'Lewis Carroll' and John Tenniel. Never, before or since, has any illustrator caught the mood and atmosphere of a story in so faithful a fashion. The characters imagined in the mind's eye equate exactly with the pictures seen as the leaves of prose are turned. *Alice*, without Tenniel's illustrations, is unthinkable. The story of their first appearance and subsequent disappearance is well known, but can be repeated here. Dodgson commissioned Macmillan & Company to publish the book, paying the expenses of its production out of his own pocket to be set later against the income from the sale of the work. He was an irascible and extremely fussy man, meticulous in his attention to detail and almost hysterically anxious that the work should appear without blemish of any sort, to greet an expectant public from the bookstalls. He admitted later that he had 'inflicted on that most patient and painstaking firm about as much wear and worry as ever publishers have lived through . . .' and Macmillan's staff must have heaved a sigh of relief when the final proofs were pored over and grudgingly

Alice's Abenteuer

im Wunderland

von

Lewis Carroll.

Aeberſetzt von Antonie Zimmermann.

Mit zweiundvierzig Illuſtrationen
von
John Tenniel.

London:
Macmillan und Comp.
1869.

The Wonderland

Postage-Stamp Case

approved by the author and the printers allowed to proceed. The book was printed by the Oxford University Press and they delivered 2,000 sets of sheets to his rooms at the university on 30 June 1865, which Dodgson promptly despatched to Macmillan & Company, asking for fifty copies to be bound up as soon as possible, plus one special copy in white vellum which he presumably wished to present to Alice Liddell. Having seen and handled the book in its binding of red cloth, he began to have qualms regarding the quality of the printing, especially that of the illustrations. After days of worry, he finally persuaded himself that the entire work must be reprinted and the fifty copies already in circulation must be retrieved if possible and replaced when a fresh set of sheets were available for binding. Most of the friends and relations to whom he had presented copies of the first edition, dated 1865, returned them to him and were given in exchange copies of the newly printed edition, dated 1866. This edition, now known as the first published edition, was in the bookshops in December 1865, in time for the Christmas book-buying spree. Dodgson found himself some £350 out of pocket on the whole exercise; but Macmillan managed to dispose of the balance of the first 2,000 sheets of the 1865 dated edition to Appleton & Company, New York, and sent him a cheque for £120 in payment. In the meantime, *Alice's Adventures in Wonderland* was selling in a fashion that far exceeded the author's hopes and a new edition marked 'Fifth Thousand' and dated 1867 was needed to supply the demand. From that time onwards, success was assured, the 1868 edition being marked 'Twelfth Thousand' and by 1874, Macmillan & Co., were printing the words 'Forty-Fifth Thousand' on the title-page. Throughout all these many editions and those which followed in the author's lifetime, the format of the book remained the same. The red cloth was retained, blocked in gold on the front cover with a picture of Alice holding the pig, and on the back with the smiling head of the Cheshire cat, and with the leaf edges gilded. Foreign translations soon appeared, the first French edition *Aventures d'Alice au Pays des Merveilles*, dated 1869, as was the first German edition, shown in the illustration. Both were available at the shop of P. Rolandi, 20 Berners Street, London, a bookseller whose extensive circulating library was devoted to foreign books. By the 1880s *Alice* had been translated into most European languages, the first Italian edition, *L'Avventure d'Alice nel paese delle merviglie*, 1872, being followed by the first Russian edition, *Sonya v tsarstve diva* (a literal translation of the title, reading 'Sonya in the Kingdom of Wonder'), published in Moscow, dated 1879. The success of *Through the Looking Glass* was hardly less marked, and Dodgson wrote several other stories for children in the intervals of producing mathematical treatises of varying degrees of complexity. *The Hunting of the Snark – an Agony in Eight Fits*, 1876, a book of nonsense rhymes, had a delightful series of grotesque illustrations by Henry Holiday.

> 'Just the place for a Snark!' the Bellman cried,
>   As he landed the crew with care:
> Supporting each man on the top of the tide
>   By a finger entwined in his hair.

Sylvie and Bruno, 1889, and *Sylvie and Bruno Concluded*, 1893, the last written five years before his death, are not so successful and have fallen into well-deserved neglect.

It will be obvious from what I have written above that the first (suppressed) edition of *Alice's Adventures in Wonderland*, 1865, is an extremely rare work to find in any sort of condition, and the few copies which come on the market are invariably worn and tattered. Despite this, any complete copy of the 1865 *Alice* now fetches well in excess of £1,000 ($2,400). The second issue of this first edition (i.e. the American edition with the 1866 Appleton imprint) is next in value and is catalogued at about £300 ($720); while the first published edition of 1866 which contains the reprinted sheets, is now priced at over £100 ($240). The first edition of *Through the Looking-Glass*, 1872, is easier to find and is worth in the region of £40 ($96).

Collections of fairy tales continued to appear during the period when the works of 'Lewis Carroll' were selling by the thousand. Joseph Jacobs (1854–1916), an eminent Jewish historian and the editor of the magazine *Folk-lore*, supplied an original collection of five volumes of fairy tales for children. At the end of each volume were several pages of scholarly notes and references, preceded by a leaf which warned his juvenile readers that 'The fairy tales are now closed – little boys and girls must not read any further.' The series was illustrated by John D. Batten, and consisted of *English Fairy Tales*, 1890, *Celtic Fairy Tales*, 1892, *Indian Fairy Tales*, 1892, *More English Fairy Tales*, 1894, and *More Celtic Fairy Tales*, 1894. A particularly attractive, limited edition of large-paper copies of the series was issued, printed on Japanese vellum paper, and signed by the publisher David Nutt. (Each plate appeared twice, in sepia, and in black.) In contrast, the twelve-volume collection of 'coloured' fairy books made by Andrew Lang (1844–1912), looks best in the brightly gilt and coloured cloth-bound issue, rather than the soberly clad, large-paper limited edition which appears drab and uninteresting by the side of its gaily-coloured shelf-mates. First edition dates of Lang's most eagerly sought after collection of coloured fairy books are: *Blue*, 1889, *Red*, 1890, *Green*, 1892, *Yellow*, 1894, *Pink*, 1897, *Grey*, 1900, *Violet*, 1901, *Crimson*, 1903, *Brown*, 1904, *Orange*, 1906, *Olive*, 1907, and *Lilac*, 1910. All were reprinted many times. Among the author's other collections of folk tales and fairy tales for children, published in similar style and format, were *The Arabian Nights Entertainments*, 1898, *The Book of Romance*, 1902, *The Red Romance Book*, 1905, *The Book of Princes and Princesses*, 1908, and *The All Sorts of Stories Book*, 1911, the last two titles compiled by his wife and edited by Andrew Lang. To range with them were a series of six other titles that collectors commonly keep on the same shelves, although most are stories taken from real life with only the occasional folk or fairy tale. H. J. Ford, who supplied most of the illustrations to the fairy books, was again commissioned, with other artists, to create the pictures to illustrate the texts; the titles being: *The Blue Poetry Book*, 1891, *The True Story Book*, 1893, *The Red True Story Book*, 1895, *The Animal Story Book*, 1896, *The Red Book of Animal Stories*, 1899, and (by Mrs Lang), *The Red Book of Heroes*, 1909.

The belief that fairy tales and fantasies present little difficulty and are an easily won literary achievement, even by writers endowed with only modest talents, is nonsense. It appears deceptively simple to create a plot and then to magic away any doubts, difficulties, and unwanted characters and situations you may encounter as the tale unfolds, into thin air 'as from the stroke of the enchanter's wand'. In practice, the original folk stories and traditional fairy tales between them have utilised such an infinite variety of basic plots, that to discover a refreshingly new one is all but impossible without the inventive genius of a Hans Christian Andersen or a Lewis Carroll. The two *Alice* books are fantasy rather than fairy stories, but the distinction between the two *genres* is sufficiently blurred by the similiarity of magical ingredients contained in each for both fairy tales and fantasy to be embraced by a single chapter heading. As the 19th century advanced, more and more writers for children interwove the dream-like logic of fantasy with supernatural powers, exemplified by the granting of the three wishes, or the magical help or hindrance accorded to humans by benevolent or spiteful beings. One of the most gifted of the Victorian writers of fairy stories in this vein was George MacDonald (1824–1905), a poet and novelist, whose *Phantastes: a Faerie Romance for Men and Women*, 1858, was followed later by *Dealings with the Fairies*, 1867. He is remembered today for his children's books, especially *At the Back of the North Wind*, 1871, which first appeared in the magazine *Good Words for the Young*, with illustrations, by Arthur Hughes (1832–1915), a member of the Pre-Raphaelite Brotherhood, which exactly fitted the mood of the book. The story is a religious allegory, telling how little Diamond, the son of a poor coachman, lives out his harsh and straightened existence in working-class London, while dissolving into a dream-world in which he travels with the North Wind in the shape of a beautiful woman with streaming long black hair. In this fantasy, Diamond shelters and finally dies, to find peace at last 'at the back of the North Wind'. *The Princess and the Goblin*, 1872, *Gutta Percha Willie: the Working Genius*, 1873, *The Princess and Curdie*, 1883, and *The Light Princess, and other Fairy Stories*, 1890, are amongst Macdonald's best-known tales, none of which are easy to find in first edition form. This same observation applies to the stories of Jean Ingelow (1820–97), with such titles as *Tales of Orris*, 1860, published at Bath, republished as *Stories told to a Child*, 1865, London (omitting one story); *Mopsa the Fairy*, 1869; and *The Little Wonder-horn*, 1872; all are extremely difficult to find.

In the 20th century, children have delighted in the whimsical fantasies of writers such as J. M. Barrie (1860–1937), whose book, *The Little White Bird*, 1902, contained chapters which first introduced the world to 'Peter Pan'. Barrie's play *Peter Pan, or the Boy who wouldn't grow up*, opened at the Duke of York's Theatre, London, on 27 December 1904, with Nina Boucicault playing the part of Peter, and has been in almost continuous production in theatres throughout the world ever since. In book form, the title first appeared as *Peter Pan in Kensington Gardens*, 1906, accompanied by a series of fifty coloured plates by Arthur Rackham, each guarded by tissues with descriptive letterpress. This is a sought-after book by the many collectors of Rackham's illustrations, especially the limited signed edition with vellum spine which is now catalogued at around £80 ($192). The story of the play was published as *Peter and Wendy* (1911), illustrated by F. D. Bedford; but the play itself was not printed in book form until seventeen years later, being issued by Hodder & Stoughton, London, as *Peter Pan or the Boy who would not grow up*, 1928, in their series, *The Plays of J. M. Barrie*. The author created several vivid and unforgettable characters, including the fearsome Captain Hook, with his steel hook in place of his missing hand; the ticking crocodile; Tinker Bell, the angry little fairy; Peter Pan himself; and of course Wendy, principally for the sake of her name, invented by Barrie, but bestowed on generations of little girls by fond parents ever since.

Three other established classics of children's literature in this field were produced by Rudyard Kipling (1865–1936). *Just So Stories for Little Children*, 1902, was illustrated by the author, and the best of the many later editions is that of 1913, containing a series of coloured plates by J. M. Gleeson. The other two works are *Puck of Pook's Hill*, 1906 and *Rewards and Fairies*, 1910. Neither *The Jungle Book*, 1894, nor *The Second Jungle Book*, 1895, can properly find a place in this chapter, but this most desirable pair of classics in the field of animal stories will always fill a place of honour in any library of children's books. The first of the two is the most difficult to find, and the most expensive, and a pair in fine condition will now cost the collector in the region of £70 ($168).

The fairy tale, though falsely attractive to a seemingly endless stream of hack writers with little fresh to say, still lures poets and scholars of the highest calibre. Walter de la Mare (1873–1956) wrote many poems and stories in which dreams and reality, fairies and animals, are delightfully blended; while in our own day J.R.R. Tolkien (b. 1892), one-time Merton Professor of English language and literature, has published a succession of tales based on a mythology of his own, including *The Hobbit*, 1937, and *The Fellowship of the Ring*, a sequence in three volumes: *The Lord of the Rings*, 1954, *The Two Towers*, 1954, and *The Return of the King*, 1955, all of which appeal equally to grown-ups and older children.

THE·KING·AWAKES·

An illustration from *The Royal Illuminated Book of Legends* (1871), published by William P. Nimmo, Edinburgh, and illuminated in gold and colours by Marcus Ward, who later became a pioneer in the design and colour-printing of children's books.

Size of illustration:
27 cm × 19 cm.

Books of Instruction, Natural History and Travel

The first edition (1818) of a book displaying an early attempt by George Cruikshank at illustration. The work purports to give a boy at boarding-school news of his father's adventures in India.

Size of title-page: 17.2 cm × 10.3 cm.

Up to about the middle of the 18th century, almost every book produced for children had as its primary aim the instruction of youth in religious affairs, the morals and manners of the day, or in the basic rules of grammar, mathematics or classical history. An exception could be made for the chapbooks and

FRONTISPIECE.

Cruikshank del.   *Roberts sculp.*

This is honest Ben Trayford who rode on Jack.
see page 30.

Published Dec. 20, 1818, by J. Bysh, 52 Paternoster Row.

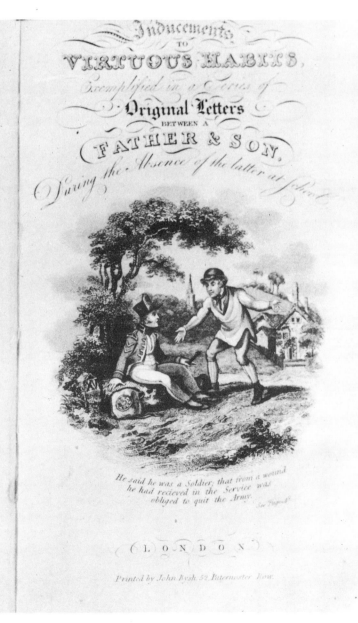

Inducements TO VIRTUOUS HABITS, Exemplified in a Series of Original Letters BETWEEN A FATHER & SON, During the Absence of the latter at School

He said he was a Soldier; that from a wound he had recieved in the Service was obliged to quit the Army.
See Frontisp.

LONDON

Printed by John Bysh, 52 Paternoster Row.

ballad-sheets that children often read and enjoyed; but these were intended for the adult market and were annexed by young people as being the only form of reading matter that afforded a little light relief from the puritanical tracts and devotional manuals their elders thought fit to allow them. There were a few exceptions that children could look at or read with real pleasure, notably Jost Amman's picture book for children published in the final quarter of the 16th century, and Comenius's *Visible World* that appeared in the middle of the 17th, both of which have already been discussed in the chapter dealing with juvenile incunabula. Such works were few and far between, and, despite going through a number of editions, would have found only a very limited audience.

Grammars and schoolbooks were being issued in the latter half of the 16th century, at a time when horn-books were in common use. Alphabets were available in English for the use of children or interested adults soon after the turn of the century, one of the earliest survivors being *The B.A.C. booke in latyn and in Englysshe* [sic], a quarto issued undated in 1538 by T. Petyt, London. *The A.B.C. set forth by the Kynges majestie*, an octavo published by W. Powell about 1545, was followed by *A.B.C. for children* (1561), and then by one of the earliest English grammars, *A Booke at Large for the Amendment of Orthographie for English Speech*, 1580, by William Bullokar. This last work was obviously meant for adults, but he followed it with an abbreviated *Pamphlet for Grammar*, 1586, which may well have been meant for young people, as *The Petie Schole of spelling and writing in English*, 1587, by F. Clement, most certainly was.

By Lady Eleanor Fenn, who sometimes used the pseudonym 'Mrs Teachwell'. This undated first edition was published in 1783, and carries nine full-page copperplate engravings of animals, insects, etc.

Size of title-page: 16.7 cm × 10.3 cm.

"Then most delighted, when we could see
"The whole mixed animal creation round
"Alive, and happy".

THE

RATIONAL DAME;

OR,

HINTS TOWARDS SUPPLYING

PRATTLE

FOR

CHILDREN.

" We cannot fee God, for he is invifible; but we can fee his Works; and worfhip him for his Gifts."

Hymns in Profe for Children.

LONDON:

Printed and Sold by John Marshall and Co. at No. 4, Aldermary Church Yard, in Bow-Lane.

Kk was a King,
And
governed
a Mouse.

Ll was
a Lady,
And had
a white
Hand.

Mm was
a Merchant,
To some
foreign
Land.

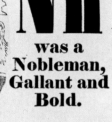 **Nn** was a
Nobleman,
Gallant and
Bold.

 **Oo** was
an Oyster-
girl,—
One that
could
Scold.

 **Pp** was
a Parson,
And wore a
black
Gown.

Trip and goe, heave and hoe,
Up and down, to and fro,
from the town, to the Grove
So merrily trip and goe

Other text books appeared in quantities that soon covered the entire field of learning in all its branches, only a few of which can be quoted here. *A lytel booke of good manners for children*, 1532, by Robert Whytyngton, was a translation of *De civilitate morum puerilium*, 1526, by Erasmus. Some of the early mathematical books had no concern with the education of children, such as *The Mathematical Jewel*, 1585, by John Dansie, although scholars in their 'teens would have made use of them. *Arithmeticke abreviated*, 1634, by W. Barton, was suitable for use in schools, but the far earlier *The Ground of Artes, teaching the woorke and practise of Arithmetike* (*c.* 1542), by Roberte Recorde, has a title-page in the later edition of 1558 displaying a picture of the teacher confronting a class of grown men. Latin text books were common, but other foreign languages were not taught in school and parents must have had a special reason for wishing their children to study *An Introductorie for to lerne Frenche* (*c.* 1534), by Giles Duwes, or *A Worlde of Wordes, Italian and English*, 1598, by John Florio.

The pace quickened in the next few decades, and after the Restoration, a series of popular works made their appearance, some of which remained in print in modified and corrected form for over sixty years. *Cocker's Arithmetic, a plain and familiar method suitable to the meanest capacity*, 1678, by John Hawkins, who used the international reputation of Edward Cocker (1631–76), a writing master and educationalist, as an advertisement for his books on mathematics for the young, was followed by the latter's *Cocker's Morals, or the Muses springgarden . . . for all public and private grammar and writing-schools*, 1685. *The British Youth's Instructor*, 1754, by Daniel Fenning, preceded his very successful *A New Grammar of the English Language*, 1771, which passed through six editions in less than twenty years. John Newbery was an early publisher in this field with his *An Easy Introduction to the English language*, 1745, which was the second volume in his series *The Circle of the Sciences*. It was published the same year as Volume I, which he had entitled *Grammar made familiar and easy to Young Gentlemen, Ladies, and foreigners*. *English Grammar, adapted to the different classes of Learners*, 1795, by Lindley Murray, published at York, had a phenomenal sale and became the standard text book on the subject for the use of schools. Well over one hundred editions of the work appeared, and it was still in print as late as 1871. An abridgement of the text was issued in 1797.

Books of instruction were becoming more sophisticated, both in contents and external appearance. The solid fare of learning was being sweetened for younger minds by the addition of stories and anecdotes, or was given in the form of question and answer while the supposed narrator and his or her pupils were on nature walks or studying the heavens through telescopes, for example. Typical of the didactic works of the period was *The Rational Dame; or, Hints towards supplying Prattle for Children* (1783), by Lady Eleanor Fenn, some of whose works for children have been noticed in a previous chapter. In her preface to this title, she tells the parents of the children who are to benefit from the information contained in the volume:

Children frequently receive their first notions from the most illiterate persons: hence it is the business of some years to make them unlearn what they acquired in the nursery . . . What employment could be more delightful to a mother, than thus, 'Dispensing knowledge from the lips of love?' Curiosity is in children an *appetite* craving perpetually for food; but alas! how often are its cravings disregarded; or, still worse, appeased with trash! . . . In making amusement the vehicle of instruction, consists the grand secret of early education . . . Early impressions are, perhaps, never totally erased – who forgets the nonsense of the nursery? . . . Children listen with avidity to tales – let us give them none but rational information – amuse them with real wonders – entertain them with agreeable surprises – but no deceit; tell them plain, simple truth – there is no need for invention; the world is full of wonders. It is my ambition to have my little volume be the pocket companion of young mothers when they walk abroad with their children; it is my wish to assist them in the delightful task of forming in those children an habit of amusing themselves in a rational manner during their hours of leisure . . .

The engraved frontispiece is followed by six full-page copperplate illustrations, divided into compartments, each containing a species of animal or insect. Although the preface points to the book being intended for parents and guardians as an instructional manual for the children in their care, the text is couched in simple language suitable for younger children, and is full of pertinent observations on the behaviour of animals both domestic and wild. That on the cat is typical of the rest:

Cats have much less sense than dogs, and less attachment; their affection is more to the house, than to the persons who inhabit it.

Her advice to make amusement the vehicle of instruction was by no means a new idea and had been employed from before the time of John Newbery, yet Lady Fenn was an influential figure in her day. The fluency with which children could read her books and absorb the half-hidden truths, due more to her use of simple language than to the extent of her scientific knowledge, had its effect on other writers of the period and on those who followed after. *Rational Sports* (1783), also published by John Marshall, was a companion volume to that quoted above, and was once again 'designed as a hint to mothers how they may inform the minds of their little people respecting the objects with which they are surrounded'.

The chapter on 18th-century children's books has dealt with the work of a number of writers who, in the manner of the age, produced books of instruction and, they fondly hoped, enjoyable interest for the young, with the emphasis almost inevitably on the first intention. This trend continued during the first quarter of the 19th century, but with the bias gradually weighing the other way.

Books on natural history, written especially for children, had appeared during the last quarter of the 18th century. *The Natural History of Birds; intended for the Amusement and Instruction of Children*, 3 vols. 1791, by Samuel Galton, has a fine series of hand-coloured copperplate engravings. His *Natural History of Quadrupeds for the Instruction of Young Persons*, followed in two volumes

This large folio entitled, *Proposal for County Naval Free-Schools, to be Built on Waste Lands*, 1783, by Jonas Hanway, is a book about children rather than for them. But the magnificent copperplate illustrations depict in so vivid a fashion the type of training then considered ideal for boys that the book must have provided considerable entertainment and instruction for young readers.

Size of double-page spread: 45 cm × 38 cm.

in 1801, both works being published anonymously. Natural history books, especially those dealing with birds and animals, have always been best-sellers in the juvenile market, and publishers were not slow to exploit the interest of children in furred and feathered creatures. From several shelves of bird and animal books published for children in the first half of the 19th century, I have space to mention only a representative selection of titles. *A Natural History of Birds, Intended Chiefly for Young Persons*, 2 vols. 1815, by Charlotte Smith (1749–1806), issued in plain, paper-covered boards with leather spines, by John Sharpe, at his Juvenile Library, London Museum, Piccadilly, contains 24 engravings of birds that are hand-coloured in some copies. Despite being

An illustration from *Animal Biography*, by Revd. W. Bingley, first published in 4 vols. 1820.

Size of page: 17.8 cm × 10.5 cm.

Plate III.

Vol. I. P. 132.

J. Shury del. et sculp.

1. Spectre Bat. 2. Elephant. 3. Zebra.

London Published by Longman & Co Oct. 1820.

issued nearly ten years after the author's death, this is a first edition, the work having been found in manuscript amongst her belongings. Mrs Smith, who wrote to help support her eight young children, was the sister of Mrs Dorset, author of *The Peacock "at home"*, whose help she had received when compiling her earlier *Conversations introducing poetry: chiefly on subject of Natural History*, 2 vols. 1804. *Natural History for Children*, 1819, was published in 5 vols. by Baldwin, Cradock, and Joy, London, at 10s. 6d. ($1.26) a set. Each was devoted to a different aspect of natural history, quadrupeds, birds, insects, fishes and reptiles, and trees and plants, forming separate volumes. There was a full-page engraved frontispiece and numerous woodcuts in the text. *The Natural History of the Bible*, 1825, by T. M. Harris, describes itself as 'A new edition, with plates'. This thick 12mo of some 400 pages and 12 full-page plates of animals, birds and plants, is unusual in not having the pages numbered, which, in a book of this size, must have led to considerable confusion. It was issued in drab paper-covered boards with a paper-labelled spine, and was obviously aimed as much at the adult market as at the juvenile.

Three of the 84 copperplate engravings in *Scenes of British Wealth*, 1823, which were designed by Revd. I. Taylor, a Nonconformist minister at Ongar, Essex. This was the first of Isaac Taylor's instructional works for 'little tarry-at-home travellers', as described on the title-page, *right*. Size of page: 17.6 cm × 10.5 cm.

Books of instruction and learning put out by the specialist children's book-sellers were invariably of a far higher quality, both in their contents and general format, than their rivals, the general booksellers, could achieve. In 1828 John Harris conceived the idea of issuing *The Little Library*, which he described as being 'a familiar introduction to the various branches of useful knowledge' for older children. It was an ambitious venture in which he employed many of the leading writers, scientists and artists of the day, the series finally extending to eighteen volumes. Each was published in a distinctive square octavo, lavishly illustrated with full-page engravings and woodcuts, the binding being a choice between full smooth cloth, with paper-labelled spine and front cover, or the more familiar full morocco-grained cloth, with red leather spine, titled in gold. The series extended over seven years, and the first title to appear was *The Mine*, 1829 (fifth edition, 1834), by Revd Isaac Taylor. It seems possible that Harris intended Taylor to be general editor of the entire series, but he died in 1829 soon after finishing the second of the *Little Library* volumes, *The Ship*, 1830. The rest of the series, in order of publication, are: *The Forest*, 1831,

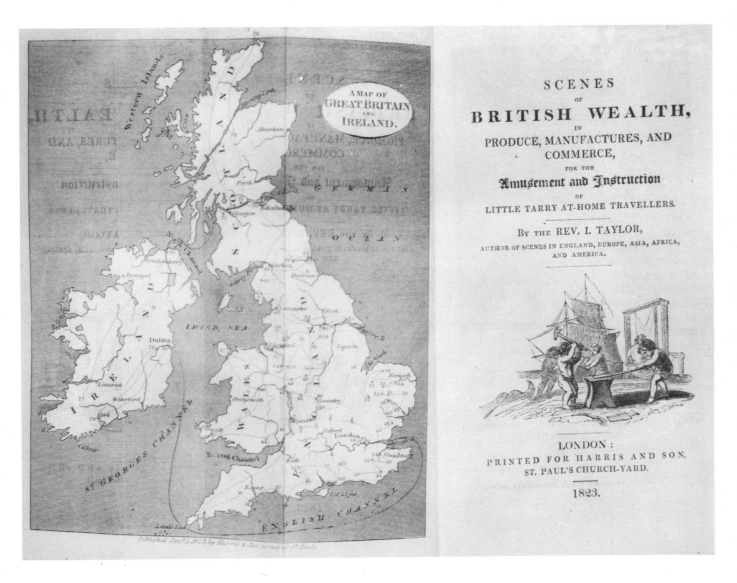

by Jefferys Taylor; *The Public Buildings of Westminster*, 1831, by Christian Isobel Johnstone (1781–1857), published anonymously; *The Public Buildings of the City of London*, 1831, by the same author; *The Garden*, 1831; *Bible Illustrations*, 1831, by Revd Bourne Hall Draper; *The Farm*, 1832, by Jefferys Taylor; *Ancient Customs, Sports and Pastimes, of the English*, 1832, by Jehoshaphat Aspin (a work originally issued by Harris in 1825 under the title *A Picture of the Manners, Customs, Sports, and Pastimes of the Inhabitants of England*); *The British Story Briefly Told*, 1832; *The French History Briefly Told*, 1833; *The Ocean*, 1833; *Natural History of Quadrupeds*, 2 vols. 1834, by Frederic Shoberl, with illustrations by Thomas Landseer; *Francis Lever, the Young Mechanic*, 1835; *The Little Botanist*, 2 vols. 1835, by Caroline A. Halstead; and *The Natural History of*

Birds, 1836, by Frederic Shoberl, with the illustrations again by Thomas Landseer. The sixteen various titles (in a total of eighteen volumes), dated as shown above, make up a complete set of first editions, and I searched for many years before I was successful in making a complete collection. There is usually difficulty with a series extending in time over many years; readers bought part of the set, or individual volumes, but few completed a collection as they were issued new by the booksellers. Sets have therefore to be made up by present-day collectors from various sources, and often one or two titles elude the search for many years. *The Little Library* deservedly passed through many editions, and during the course of issue, the text of some volumes was altered or extended, new plates were added or appeared hand-coloured, and the bindings underwent various changes of a minor nature. Coloured frontispieces were standard with certain titles such as *The Little Botanist. The Ship*, at the publication of the fourth edition in 1835, had its series of sixteen full-page illustrations extended to twenty by the addition of four plates of hand-coloured national flags and pendants.

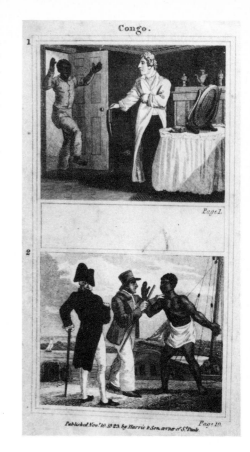

One of the most comprehensive early works on travel and exploration written for children was *Historical Account of the most celebrated Voyages, Travels, and Discoveries, from the Time of Columbus to the Present Period*, 10 vols. 1796 (last three volumes dated 1797), by William Mavor (1758–1837). Each volume had three full-page copperplate engravings, volume seven having a folding plate of the death of Capt Cook which is sometimes missing. The series was issued by Elizabeth Newbery, and proved so successful that a further ten volumes, all dated 1797, were published at the end of that year. Once again the final volume of the ten finished with a general index; but in 1801 a further five volumes were published, bringing the series up to date with the latest voyages and discoveries. A full set of the twenty-five volumes in first edition form is now worth in the region of £100 ($240). The same year saw the appearance of *The Juvenile Travellers*, 1801, by Priscilla Wakefield (1751–1832), complete with a large folding hand-coloured map of the world, a companion

Inhabitants of California.

FRONTISPIECE.

Mercury introducing a Youth to the Island of Locuta.

volume to her *Excursions in North America*, 1806, similarly embellished. A particularly attractive publication by John Harris was *Cosmorama; A View of the
Costumes and Peculiarities of All Nations* (1827), by Jehoshaphat Aspin, issued in
the firm's standard binding of pictorially-printed paper-covered boards with
red leather spine. There are eighteen hand-coloured copperplate engravings,
each divided into four compartments, showing the manners, dress, and
customs of the inhabitants of the lands described. Aspin was gifted with an
unconscious humour which was accentuated by his forthright opinions on the
unfortunate members of the human race not lucky enough to have been born
British. The Dutch he describes as:

. . . generally below the middle stature, inclined to corpulency, and remarkable for a heavy awkward mien . . . The love of money is their ruling passion,
and the spring of all their actions. They never lose a moment in the gratifica-
tion of malice, the indulgence of envy, or the assumption of those petty
triumphs, which, in other countries, fill life with much unnecessary misery.

The American nation fares just as badly:

In the towns, no very striking difference exists among the inhabitants: the
same tall, stout, well-dressed men every where appear, much at their ease,
shrewd, and intelligent; but indolent; and, though boasting of freedom,
generally slaves to idleness . . . The use of tobacco pervades the whole frame
of society, from the President of the United States to the meanest pauper;
neither the chair of state, the senate, the pulpit, the bar, nor the drawing-
room, is exempt from this annoyance and its loathsome consequences, the
marks of which are witnessed upon the floors and walls even of the best apart-
ments. Another prevailing vice is excessive drinking, and the pernicious
practice of swallowing ardent spirits in large quantities, is indulged in by all
classes.

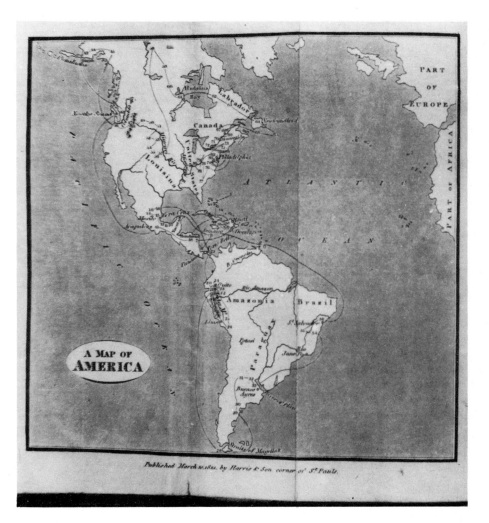

A MAP OF
AMERICA

Published March 10.1821. by Harris & Son corner of St Pauls.

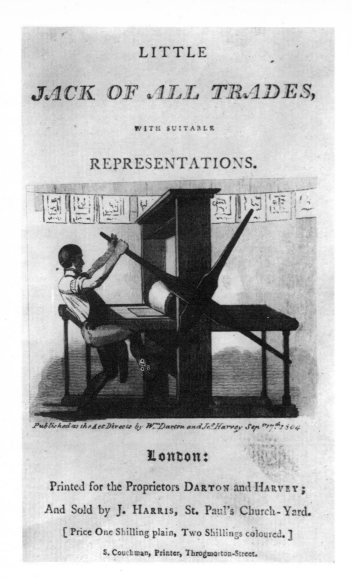

More and more books written solely for the amusement and entertainment of children were published in London and the provinces, until, by mid-century, stimulated by the increase in literacy amongst the young, the trickle of books to be read just for amusement became a flood. Authors who leavened their stories and tales too heavily with moral platitudes and pious sermons directed at saving their young readers from an eternity of hell-fire and damnation did not sell as well as those who produced the straightforward romance in which the young heroes of the tale acted in a credible but still strictly Christian way. Commercial considerations saw to it that they were gradually shouldered aside by their more forthright rivals, who nevertheless were every bit as God-fearing, at least on the printed page. Despite the increasing emphasis of this trend, there was also an expanding market for educational and instructional works for the young. Two distinct types of books emerged, the one instructive, the other amusing, but each no longer apologised for not doing both. This division did not happen overnight, but by the 1850s a story book was usually a story book and not a religious catechism disguised, or a thinly-veiled didactic work on deportment and manners. By the time that Charles Dickens (1812–70), came to write *A Child's History of England*, 3 vols. 1852–3–4, another minor literary revolution had been accomplished and had passed unnoticed. Books of instruction for children now had to evolve attractions of their own, both in their binding styles and in the general format of their texts and illustrations. *The Playbook of Metals*, 1861, is an example of a serious work of instruction that has been specifically designed to be attractive and interesting to young readers. Issued, like its companion volume, *The Playbook of Science*, in a bead-grain full-cloth binding, pictorially blocked on the front cover and spine in gold and blind, and with leaf edges cut and gilded, it contained on its 504 pages a total of nearly 300 woodcut illustrations by Edmund Evans and others. The *Playbook* was an encyclopaedia of knowledge that any boy would have been proud to own. It contained some of the very

56

A profusely-illustrated work of 504 pages written as a companion volume to the author's *Boy's Playbook of Science*. An interesting and surprisingly accurate book for boys in their 'teens.

Size of title-page:
18 cm × 12 cm.

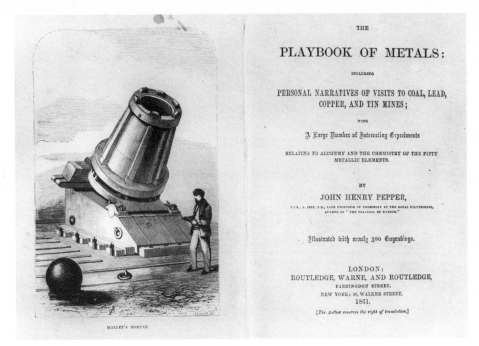

THE

PLAYBOOK OF METALS:

INCLUDING

PERSONAL NARRATIVES OF VISITS TO COAL, LEAD, COPPER, AND TIN MINES;

WITH

A Large Number of Interesting Experiments

RELATING TO ALCHEMY AND THE CHEMISTRY OF THE FIFTY METALLIC ELEMENTS.

BY

JOHN HENRY PEPPER,

F.C.S., L. INST. C.E., LATE PROFESSOR OF CHEMISTRY AT THE ROYAL POLYTECHNIC, AUTHOR OF "THE PLAYBOOK OF SCIENCE."

Illustrated with nearly 300 Engravings.

LONDON:
ROUTLEDGE, WARNE, AND ROUTLEDGE,
FARRINGDON STREET,
NEW YORK: 56, WALKER STREET.
1861.
[*The Author reserves the right of translation.*]

MALLET'S MORTAR.

latest scientific information and theories, including those expounded by Charles Darwin in *On the Origin of Species*, 1859, published only two years before, and, more surprisingly, the first illustrated and detailed explanation of the now popularly accepted theory of Continental Drift, supplied by M. A. Snider, from his work entitled *La Création et ses Mystères dévoilés*.

In the USA, one of the most active writers in the field of children's literature in general, and school text books and primers in particular, was Samuel Griswold Goodrich (1793–1860), universally known by his pseudonym 'Peter Parley', a name soon appropriated by publishers in Britain for works by other authors. His first book using this name was *Peter Parley's Tales of America*, 1827, published in Boston. It was here that the legendary figure first introduced himself to children:

Here I am! My name is Peter Parley: I am an old man.
I am very gray and lame. But I have seen a great many things, and had a great many adventures, and I love to talk about them.
I love to tell stories to children, and very often they come to my house, and they get around me and I tell them stories of what I have seen and of what I have heard.
I live in Boston.

Goodrich probably coined the name from a character created by Hannah More (1745–1833), whom she had named 'Old Parley the Porter'. It is known that he had read and admired her works, and the fact that Miss More had described Parley as 'always talking about his experiences and adventures', may well have prompted Goodrich to borrow the name when he was seeking a pseudonym behind which to write his children's books. The contents of his *Tales of America*, as with his other books of history and travel, were 'designed to give to the child the first ideas of Geography and History', for which reason he was careful to research thoroughly, and to present what was then considered to be a factual background, although today his bias is obvious. The secret of his success was once again the use of simple language coupled with an interesting text, full of action, and a real-life atmosphere, in which the heroes occasionally ended up dead and the wicked escaped from justice. At the foot of many pages were series of simple questions relevant to the text immediately above, which children could ask themselves or each other as they read the book. Typical of Goodrich's prose style is this extract from his first book for children, taken from near the end of his *Tales of America*:

In the year 1607, some English people, about one hundred in number, came to Virginia, and made a settlement on James River.
The first town they built they called Jamestown. I need not tell you, that no

people but Indians lived in this part of North America at that time. The great towns, such as Boston, New York, Philadelphia, and others, did not exist then. Vast forests extended over the whole country, and in those forests lived numerous tribes of Indians. These Indians were generally unfriendly to the white people, and would often kill them if they could.

One day, Captain Smith, who was one of the people of Jamestown, had been up a river in a boat. He was discovered by the Indians, seized by them, and carried before Powhattan, who was their king. Powhattan and his counsellors decided that he should be put to death. Accordingly, he was brought forward, and his head laid upon a stone. Powhattan then took a club, and raised it in the air to strike the fatal blow. What was his astonishment to see his daughter, a beautiful Indian girl, run shrieking between him and Smith, and place herself in a situation to shelter him from the club of her father!

The solid fare of fact sugared with the instant drama and excitement of a real-life (or backwoods-fiction) hair's-breadth escape from death at the hands of the Redskins. Youthful attention had seldom time to flag.

By the mid-1830s the name of Peter Parley was a household word with the juvenile reading public of the United States of America, but it was 1835 before the first of his collection of tales appeared in Britain. *Tales about Europe, Asia, Africa, and America*, 1835, was published by Thomas Tegg & Son, London, and printed by C. Whittingham at the Chiswick Press. This unauthorised version was issued in the same format as Peter Parley's American editions, a square octavo, in this case containing 500 pages, with a total of 137 woodcut illustrations in the text. The four tales were originally published separately in Boston, but were here collected into a single volume. *Tales of Animals, Comprising Quadrupeds, Birds, Fishes, Reptiles and Insects*, 1835, followed almost immediately, once again published by Thomas Tegg, who had obviously acquired a set of texts of the American editions.

Once Goodrich realised he had discovered a magic formula, he started churning out titles at a speed that led William Howe, writing later in *The Cambridge History of American Literature*, to describe him as 'the most prodigious literary hack of his day'. His first Peter Parley tale was followed by over a hundred others, and that number can be at least doubled by the titles that appeared over the same signature, but were in fact written by other authors in Britain and America. Tegg in London dutifully republished all the titles he could lay his hands on, and *Tales About the Sun, Moon and Stars*, 1837, was followed by numerous others. But well before he issued *Tales about Rome and Modern Italy*, 1839, other London publishers were on the scent. *Peter Parley's Visit to London during the Coronation of Queen Victoria*, 1838, was issued by Charles Tilt and almost certainly written by him. Another bookseller, Edward Lacy, had earned the title of 'remainder man' due to his habit of making a substantial business out of buying up the printed sheets left unsold with other publishers, casing them up in flashy cloth bindings, and then issuing them with newly tipped-in title-pages, always undated, containing his own imprint. Often he changed the title of a work, especially on some of the annuals. With the children's books he issued under Peter Parley titles, he simply bought up sheets containing stories by other authors, tore out the original and correct titles and then inserted new and false ones, such as *Grandfather's Tales*, by Peter Parley. Goodrich eventually found out about this and was extremely displeased, as he tells his readers in his autobiographical *Recollections of a Lifetime*, 2 vols. New York, 1857. The demand for Peter Parley tales was now so great that Tegg was obliged to commission a hack writer, George Mogridge (1787–1854), whose many pseudonyms included 'Old Humphrey' and 'Ephraim Holding', besides his later assumed title of 'Peter Parley'. His task was to compose a series of tales in the style of those originally written by Goodrich. *Peter Parley's Tales about Christmas*, 1839, and *Peter Parley's Shipwrecks and Disasters at Sea*, 1840, were two of the many titles from his pen. Tegg eventually made a furious Samuel Goodrich an *ex gratia* payment of £400 ($960) in reluctant acknowledgement of his debt to the author, but books of instruction disguised in the Peter Parley manner were by this time available in quantity from several London publishing houses, notably Darton and Clark. John Maw Darton, and his business associates Samuel Clark and William Martin, systematically pirated every Peter Parley title they could lay their hands on.

Within a few months of the first titles being issued, Samuel Clark, who was Darton's brother-in-law, began turning out fictitious Peter Parley books under the pseudonym of the 'Revd. T. Wilson', a name he used with much success on a long series of *Popular School Catechisms* (1845–8), which embraced subjects as diverse as geography, music, natural philosophy, astronomy, bible history, and botany, among others. A number of the Peter Parley books contained a letter, apparently from Goodrich (although his initials are incorrect), stating:

Gentlemen – I think it is now understood between us that I am to prepare a series of books, of which you are to be Publishers. I undertake this task with pleasure, because it is my wish to be judged in England by what I do write, and not by what has been written for me. I have been much vexed, since my arrival in this country, to see the name of Peter Parley attached to a number of books published in London, which I never saw or heard of, and which contain much of which I wholly disapprove, and consider to be contrary to good morals. I have also seen my books mutilated and altered so that I could scarcely recognize anything in them as my own, except the title and some disfigured fragments.
It is therefore a real satisfaction to me, that my future works are to make their appearance in England in a genuine form . . .
S. E. Goodrich.
London; Aug. 1842.

Whether this letter was genuine or not, the activities of Darton & Clark finally led to Goodrich issuing writs for damages against the firm in the Supreme Court of New York State, where he obtained judgement in his favour in the sums of $7,816.40 damages, plus $138.76 costs. It is unlikely that the London firm ever paid him anything in settlement of this action. Acts of literary piracy were not, however, confined to England, and publishers in the USA were equally guilty. Goodrich himself was as blameworthy as those he sued, for in 1819 he had published an eight-volume edition of the works of Walter Scott without obtaining the author's consent or paying him a penny in royalties.

Before leaving the subject of Goodrich's almost painless method of imparting facts, figures, and a wealth of miscellaneous information to the young, mention must be made of the long series of annuals that appeared in England using his well-known pseudonym. Issued as a magazine in monthly parts during 1839, the first *Peter Parley's Annual: A Christmas and New Year's Present for Young People*, was published at the end of that year, dated forward to 1840. It was issued in a binding of straight-grained green cloth, blocked on the front cover and spine in gold and blind, with yellow end-papers and the leaf edges trimmed. The publishers were Simkin, Marshall & Co., London, and the unknown editor of the first volume told his young readers: 'I have had only one end in view; that is, your improvement. I do not think that you will complain of these pages ever being dry or tedious; but your *instruction* has been my *first* aim.' From the first issue a high standard was set; each volume had a series of full-page steel-engravings finely executed by leading artists and engravers, and the numerous woodcuts in the text were above the average quality found in children's books of that period. The issue for 1843 had the frontispiece and engraved title-page printed by a two-colour patent chromographic process invented by Griffith. In the meantime, Darton & Clark had purchased an interest in the enterprise and their advertisements were tipped in the back of the volumes from 1842 onwards. In 1845, they took over the series completely from Simkin, Marshall & Company, and substituted a bright-red cloth binding, blocked in gold and blind, in place of the drab green, brown, or plum-coloured cloths used previously. The issue dated 1846 contained some startling innovations and was a milestone in the annals of book production for children. Darton had never been afraid to experiment with new processes and his books were printed on the newly installed steam presses of D. A. Doudney, Long Lane, London, from the mid-1840s onwards. He was also the first publisher to have colour-printed illustrations inserted in children's books, a more expensive process at that time than hand-colouring, especially for comparatively short runs. When the 1846 *Peter Parley's Annual* appeared in the bookshops, there was a brightly coloured frontispiece and title-page, both taken from designs by the young and as yet unknown artist Harrison Weir (1824–1906), who had been apprenticed to the famous George Baxter. These illustrations had been printed in about ten colours from wood-blocks by Gregory, Collins & Reynolds of Charterhouse Square, and from that time onwards each new annual contained plates colour-printed by various processes. The enterprise well deserved the success that attended it, and for a total of 55 years, until 1894, it was on sale in the bookshops in time for Christmas.

In later years, as Daniel Roselle tells us in his biography of the author, published by the State University of New York Press, 1968, Samuel Goodrich even came to resemble the fictitious character he had created – gouty foot, silver hair, stout wooden cane, and all. He deserves a niche in the annals of American literary history as the author of some of the most popular and widely read books produced for the instruction, amusement and education of 19th-century children, books they read with a great deal of pleasure and by which they were introduced to a world of interests they would not otherwise have known. He also deserves the thanks of collectors of early children's books: our shelves are brightened with the pictorial spines of lines of Peter Parley books blocked in gold on a rainbow of coloured cloths, not only from his own pen, but from imitators who recognised the value of his approach.

Issued in time for the opening of the World's Industrial Fair, 1884, in New Orleans, USA, *A Peep at the World's Fair*, by Raphael Tuck & Sons, London, was illustrated by Adrien Marie, Walker Hodgson, and W. & F. Brundage. It was No. 413 in their list of Juvenile Gift and Toy Books.

Size of front cover:
24.5 cm × 18.5 cm.

Poetry
and
Nursery Rhymes

Of the poetry and verse of the 18th century written for children, the only rhymes composed especially for reciting and singing in the nursery, the true nursery rhymes as opposed to spoken poetry and verse, were the rhyming alphabets, the lullabies, and perhaps the little songs that sometimes accompany children's ritual games. Poetry and verse written for the entertainment, much less the amusement, of young people was almost unknown until well into the 1740s. The 17th century had provided them with a few emblem books in which the morals were set out in verse, but these were intended for adults and were only commandeered by children because of the attraction of the pictures and the fact that the verses themselves were sometimes printed in the shapes of altars, crosses, and even such oddities as bottles and swords. John Bunyan had contributed *A Book for Boys and Girls; or, Country Rhimes for Children*, 1686 (see page 16), a work of religious instruction that children were most unlikely to turn to in their leisure moments. Earlier than this was *Artificial Versifying or; The School-Boy's Recreation*, 1677, at first glance a light-hearted treatise on schoolboy doggerel rhyme, until the rest of its title-page is read. It turns out to be severely instructional in character and as didactic as any 17th-century schoolmaster could wish, although the anonymous author, John Pater, has a quaint wryness of style, as the composition of the sub-title seems to show: *A New Way to make Latin Verses. Whereby Any one of ordinary Capacity, that only knows the A.B.C. and can Count 9 (though he understands not one word of Latin, or what a Verse means) may be plainly taught, (and in as little time as this is Reading over,) how to make Hundreds of Hexameter Verses, which shall be True Latin, True Verse, and good Sense.*

Verses printed in chapbook form were sometimes aimed at the juvenile market, and Nathaniel Crouch (1632?–1725?), the author of many books attributed on the title-pages to 'R.B.' or 'Robert (or Richard) Burton', published *Youth's Divine Pastime*, 1691. It consisted of thirty-six Bible stories in verse each illustrated with a crude woodcut, and each calculated to instil a fear of the wrath of God into the hearts of youth.

> When Men by Sin and Violence
> Did stain the Earth with Blood,
> God did resolve to wash them thence
> By Waters of a Flood.
>
> Yet did he warn before he struck,
> *Noah* was sent to tell
> They by their Sins would God provoke
> To cast them down to Hell.

Some of the first printed verse to be recited with at least a modicum of amusement by children, for many of the rhymes jingle in the memory long after the book is read, were contained in *Divine Songs, Attempted in Easy Language; for the Use of Children*, 1715, by the Nonconformist schoolmaster and hymnologist Isaac Watts (1674–1748). The work was an immediate and lasting success, and at least twenty editions in book and chapbook form were called for in less than seven years. Watts had realised that children commit to memory most easily items of prose and verse that they have enjoyed reading, and that the power of understanding complex religious argument is not given to the very young. His moral propaganda was sugared with catch-phrases in tramping rhymes, as well as glimpses of the comedy and tragedy of everyday life, and the thunderous religious drama of his day. He could move from the gentleness of *A Cradle Hymn*, with its lullaby of words:

> Hush! my Dear, lie still and slumber,
>   Holy Angels guard they Bed!
> Heavenly Blessings without Number
>   Gently falling on thy Head.
>
> Sleep, my Babe; thy Food and Rainment,
>   House and Home thy Friends provide;
> All without thy Care or Payment,
>   All thy Wants are well supply'd.

to the grim Janeway warnings and the dark threats of his verses *Against Lying*:

> The Lord delights in them that speak
>   The Words of Truth; but ev'ry Lyar
> Must have his Portion in the Lake,
>   That burns with Brimstone, and with Fire.
>
> Then let me always watch my Lips,
>   Lest I be struck to Death and Hell,
> Since God a Book of Reck'ning keeps
>   For ev'ry Lie that Children tell.

Many of his verses are remembered today in the form in which Lewis Carroll parodied them, but children in the early 18th century read the words as he wrote them. They were a task set at school and repeated in front of the class of other young hopefuls awaiting their turn; most of whom no doubt had their revenge when they had children of their own:

> Let Children that would fear the Lord
>   Hear what their Teachers say:
> With Rev'rence meet their Parents Word,
>   And with Delight obey.
>
> Have you not heard what dreadful Plagues
>   Are threaten'd by the Lord,
> To him that breaks his Father's Law,
>   Or mocks his Mother's Word?

Any 18th-century copy of Watts' *Divine Songs*, whether in the authorised versions or in one of the many piracies that appeared throughout the succeeding decades, is a prize that deserves a prominent place in any collection of early children's books. Despite the number of editions that appeared before the turn of the century, they are difficult to find, a tribute to the number of times the little books were handled and read. Reprints, extending to the present day, are legion, one of the most attractive of the earlier ones being *Songs, Divine and Moral*, 1826, published by W. Simkin, R. Marshall, and J. Johnson, London, in a binding of pictorially printed paper-covered boards, with the leaf edges left uncut. There are sixty fine-quality woodcut illustrations, the text is enclosed in ruled borders; the work is designed, edited, and printed by J. Johnson, whose *Typographia; or, Printer's Instructor*, 1824, was well known in its day.

62

Little Master's Miscellany, 1743, is discussed in a previous chapter, and an illustration of the 1750 edition reproduced. Most of the verse by the unknown author appears to be original and most is directed at improving the morals of the young. Children are advised to model themselves on the paragons of virtue the versifier holds up to the light:

> Their Parent's hopes they'll not defeat,
>   By passion for a tinsel Dress,
> Appearing modest, plain, and neat,
>   Nor Laws of decency trangress.
>
> Such are the little Trifflers gay,
>   Sweet objects of our Hopes and Fear,
> That sooth our Thoughts, by Night and Day,
>   – Our Joy, or Sorrow centers here.

But children lucky enough to obtain a copy of this first juvenile miscellany of prose and verse, had a wide choice of reading, with a selection of poems on the tulip, the woodlark, fishing, hunting and fowling, or, if they chose, on death, deformity, lying and detraction, as well as stories, dialogues and a succession of fables in verse. Of particular interest to literary historians and the students or collectors of the works of Samuel Johnson (1709–84) is a conversation that takes place between a brother and his young sister in a bookshop:

> Here's a Poem just now from the Printer come in;
> 'Twas Puff'd I presume in the last *Magazine*!
> My Master Sir! never descended so low,
> Mr. Cave I believe, knows the Author, – or so!
> Here's *London* Sir! wrote in an elegant Style,
> That would make the old Satyrist Juvenal smile . . .

This reference to Johnson's *London: A Poem, In Imitation of the Third Satire of Juvenal*, 1738, and to Edward Cave (1691–1754), a printer and publisher who founded *The Gentleman's Magazine* and employed Johnson in a journalistic capacity for many years, is surprising in a children's book and points to the possibility of this portion of the work having first appeared as long ago as 1738.

First published in 1823, this second edition runs to 480 pages. William Mavor (1758–1837), was at one time headmaster of Woodstock Grammar School, near Oxford.

Size of title-page: 17.5 cm × 10 cm.

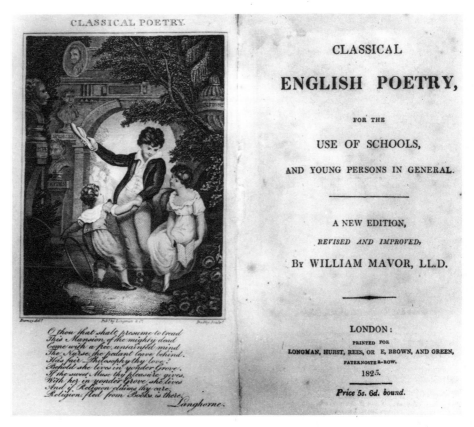

CLASSICAL POETRY.

O thou that shalt presume to tread
This Mansion of the mighty dead
Come with a free, untainted mind
The Nurse, the pedant leave behind.
It's fair Philosophy thy love;
Behold she lives in yonder Grove.
If the sweet Muse thy pleasure gives,
With her in yonder Grove she lives.
And if Religion claims thy care,
Religion fled from Books is there.
        —Langhorne.

CLASSICAL

ENGLISH POETRY,

FOR THE

USE OF SCHOOLS,

AND YOUNG PERSONS IN GENERAL.

A NEW EDITION,

REVISED AND IMPROVED,

By WILLIAM MAVOR, LL.D.

LONDON:

PRINTED FOR
LONGMAN, HURST, REES, OR E, BROWN, AND GREEN,
PATERNOSTER-ROW.
1825.

Price 5s. 6d. bound.

The first nursery rhyme book that we know of was printed about 1744. *Tommy Thumb's Pretty Song Book*, was published in two miniature volumes, but the date is conjectural, and so for that matter is the existence of Volume One, for only a single copy of the work is known to have survived. This is in the British Museum, but comprises Volume Two only, and we are lucky to have even this small fragment. It is there, for the first time in print, we read of 'Bah, Bah, a black sheep'; 'There was a little Man, And he had a little Gun'; 'Who did kill Cock Robin?'; and over thirty other songs, most of them illustrated with woodcuts which the Georgian artist thought appropriate to the rhyme. How these rhymes came to be collected by the original editor of the work we shall never know, but there is at least a slim chance that we shall one day discover the contents of the missing Volume One and see the songs and rhymes it contained. The missing first edition of *Little Goody Two-Shoes*, 1765, came to light only a year or two ago, and the first volume of *Tommy Thumb's Pretty Song Book*, or the two volumes bound up together, may still be lying hidden in a hat-box in an attic, or in the proverbial old oak chest in a well-aired cellar. A copy of *The Famous Tommy Thumb's Little Story-Book*, published about 1760, is in the collection of Iona and Peter Opie, joint editors of *The Oxford Dictionary of Nursery Rhymes*, 1951, and of *The Oxford Nursery Rhyme Book*, 1955, invaluable reference works for collectors in this field. The concluding part of *Tommy Thumb* gives the text of 'pretty stories that may be sung or told', in which we read for the first time of 'This pig went to market' and 'Little Boy Blue'. The work soon appeared in America, and was advertised by John Mein in *The Boston Chronicle* of 29 August 1768, as available: 'price two coppers'. Another edition, published under the imprint of John Boyle, Boston (1771), is now in the Boston Public Library.

The Top Book of All, for Little Masters and Misses (c. 1760), contains eight well-known nursery rhymes, including 'Jack Nory', and 'The Three Jovial Welshmen'. *A Little Pretty Pocket Book*, 1744, has already been mentioned as the first book for children published by John Newbery on his arrival in London to set up business. In its verses, it describes a number of children's games, including the well-known refrain 'Boys and Girls come out to Play', as well as a rhyming alphabet, giving the version commencing 'Great A, B, and C'. The earliest known example of this device for teaching children the alphabet is that contained in *A Little Book for Little Children* (c. 1710), by 'T. W.' and sold at the Ring in Little Britain, a district in central London where many booksellers had their stalls. The version given here commences:

> A was an Archer, and shot at a Frog;
> B was a Blind-man, and led by a Dog:
> C was a Cutpurse, and liv'd in disgrace;
> D was a Drunkard, and had a red Face:
> E was an Eater, a Glutton was he;
> F was a fighter, and fought with a Flea:
> G was a Gyant, and pul'd down a House;
> H was a Hunter, and hunted a Mouse:

and so on, to the end of the alphabet. The rhyme was printed at Boston, USA, as early as 1761. Many of the later versions have a second line couplet for each letter:

> A was an Archer and shot at a frog,
> But missing his mark shot into a bog;
> B was a Butcher and had a great dog,
> Who always went round the streets with a clog . . .

Visions in Verse, for the Entertainment and Instruction of Younger Minds, 1751, published anonymously by Nathaniel Cotton (1705–88), can claim a place in a library of early children's books chiefly by virtue of its title. Cotton was a physician who had studied at Leyden, before settling at St Albans, where he established a general practice and a private madhouse which later housed the poet William Cowper. *Visions in Verse* was popular in its day (the tenth edition appeared in 1782) and consists of nine allegories, including slander, pleasure and health, marriage, life, and death, aimed, one would have

Right, above
An illustration engraved and printed at the Racquet Court Press by Edmund Evans, for *Four and Twenty Toilers* (1901), published by Grant Richards. The pictures are by F. D. Bedford and the verses by E. V. Lucas.

Right, below
'Solomon Lovechild' was one of the many pseudonyms of Lady Eleanor Fenn (1743–1813) and the above title, first issued in two separate parts, is a new edition of c. 1855. The original editions appeared in 1783–5.

SKETCHES
OF
LITTLE BOYS
AND
GIRLS.

SOLOMON LOVECHILD

THOMAS DEAN & SON THREADNEEDLE STREET.

CHRISTMAS EVE — A DREAM.

thought, at parents and guardians rather than the children in their care. Political and social satire is used freely, and in so obtuse and oblique a form that no youth under the age of eighteen could possibly have understood the author's allusions. Despite this, he tells his readers that:

> Childhood and Youth engage my Pen,
> 'Tis Labour lost to talk to Men.
> Youth may, perhaps, reform, when wrong,
> Age will not listen to my Song.
> He who at Fifty is a Fool,
> Is far too stubborn grown for School.

On quite another level, and one that could be comprehended by all children over the age of twelve who took pleasure in reading, was John Newbery's

An illustration by Joseph Wolf for *Reynard the Fox*, 1887, by Thomas James Arnold, taken from the German of Goethe. This expensively produced quarto was issued with a set of twelve proof engravings by Wolf, printed on India paper, as well as 60 further pictorial designs by Wilhelm von Kaulbach on the text paper.

Size of page: 20 cm × 13 cm.

Left
The frontispiece to *A Christmas Tree Fairy*, (1886), by Lizzie Mack and R. E. Mack, was lithographed by Ernest Nister, Nuremberg, Germany, for Griffith, Farran, Okeden & Welsh, of London. The high quality and relative cheapness of German colour-printing caused many British publishing houses to have their plates processed and printed abroad.

J. Wolf. del.   R.H. Roe. sc.

REYNARD THE FOX.

And he would tell his beads and seem to pray.
And smite his breast, and so pass on his way.

65

Circle of the Sciences, the first three volumes of the series advertised in *The Penny London Post*, 18 January 1745. It is the fourth volume that concerns us here, entitled *Poetry made familiar and easy to Young Gentlemen and Ladies*. I have been able to find only the third edition, published by Newbery and Carnan, 1769, but luckily this little book is still in its original binding of blue paper-covered boards with green vellum spine on which is Carnan's printed label giving the title and the volume number. Complete sets of any edition of *Circle of the Sciences* dated before 1780 are rarely encountered, and it is doubtful if a complete set of the first edition has survived. The successor in the business, Elizabeth Newbery, published several books of verse, including a number by John Huddlestone Wynne (1743–88), an eccentric whose promise to his mother on her deathbed that he would 'shun horses, and never go into a boat or a belfry' led him, when drunk, to step backwards under a hackney carriage when avoiding an approaching horse. He survived with a crippled leg for another ten years. *Choice Emblems . . . for the Improvement and Pastime of Youth*, 1772, was the first of several similar poetical works from his pen. *Tales for Youth; in thirty poems*, 1794, contains a delightful series of woodcuts by John Bewick that rank with the very best of his work. The most sought after of Wynne's books for children are issues of the first edition of *Fables of Flowers, for the Female Sex*, 1781, containing six engraved plates, each divided into five scenes. This series of illustrations is not always present in all copies.

Books of poetry and nursery rhymes were also being produced in Europe, one of the earliest being *Kleine Lieder für Kinder*, 1777, published at Leipzig. *Little Songs for Children*, to give the work its English title, is of the utmost rarity. It was issued as an oblong octavo with an engraved title-page and twelve engraved plates of music and words. Only a handful of copies appear to have survived.

As the 18th century drew to a close, poetry books for children were issued in increasing numbers by provincial as well as London booksellers (the term being synonymous with publisher at that time). *Pretty Little Poems for Pretty Little Children* (c. 1790) appeared with a Gainsborough imprint, while *The Twelfth Cake. A Juvenile Amusement consisting of Little Ballads to be Sung*, was published undated at about the same time. The only copy I have been able to find of *The Bee, a Selection of Poetry from the best Authors*, 1793, proclaims itself to be a 'New Edition' on its engraved title-page. This collection of poetry for children, published by Darton & Harvey, London, must have sold extremely well, for new editions were still appearing well into the first quarter of the 19th century.

The first appearance of *Poetry for Children*, by Lucy Aikin (1781–1864), was in 1801; the book was composed in part of original work by the young author, but with the majority of the poems selected from the works of past and present writers as far apart in time and the quality of their verse as John Dryden and Mrs Barbauld. Five editions were published in the space of the ensuing seven years and the work was still in print in the 1850s. This may have been the collection used by Lewis Carroll when he selected the poems he parodied so successfully in the *Alice* books. The Isaac Watts verses he used are here, and also 'The Old Man's Comforts and how he Gained them', by Robert Southey (1774–1843), starting with the well-known line ' "You are old, father William," the young man cried'. Lucy Aikin was the daughter of John Aikin, man of letters and physician, who was himself joint-author with his sister, Mrs Anna Laetitia Barbauld (1743–1825), of *Evenings at Home; or, The Juvenile Budget Opened*, 6 vols. 1792–96, mentioned in a previous chapter, a collection of stories, poems, and dialogues that was warmly praised by Maria Edgeworth.

It was in June, 1803, that the publishers William Darton and Joseph Harvey planned a poetical miscellany for children. They wrote to several correspondents who had previously submitted poems asking for 'something in the way of moral songs (though not songs) or short tales turned into verse'. The result was the publication of one of the most popular books of verse for children. Many bibliographical experts consider it to have been an important influence in the development of the genre, for subsequently, 'moral songs' became widely successful, with their characteristic combination of pedestrian rhymes and sweet sentiment. *Original Poems, for Infant Minds, by Several young persons*, 2 vols. 1804–5, was principally the work of Jane Taylor (1783–1824),

The most important of Lucy Aikin's several books for children, and a work which remained in print throughout the 19th century. It was revised and enlarged several times.

Size of title-page: 14 cm × 8.5 cm.

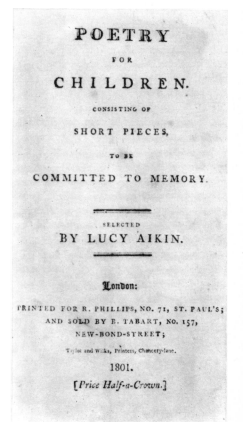

POETRY

FOR

CHILDREN.

CONSISTING OF

SHORT PIECES,

TO BE

COMMITTED TO MEMORY.

SELECTED

BY LUCY AIKIN.

London:

PRINTED FOR R. PHILLIPS, NO. 71, ST. PAUL'S; AND SOLD BY B. TABART, NO. 157, NEW-BOND-STREET;

Taylor and Wilks, Printers, Chancery-lane.

1801.

[*Price Half-a-Crown.*]

and Ann Gilbert, née Taylor (1782–1866), although Isaac Taylor, their brother, and possibly their father Isaac Taylor of Ongar, also contributed verses, as well as Bernard Barton, and Adelaide O'Keeffe, the last named having thirty-four poems accepted, although completely unknown to the Taylor family. In her autobiography, published in 1874, Ann complained that having 'written to order we had no control over the getting out of the volumes and should have been better pleased if contributions from other hands had been omitted'. Jane wrote, for the most part, about nature and the countryside. while Ann's poems are centred more on town life and the domestic scene. The first poem in the book is from her hand and is almost certainly drawn from a scene she remembered from early childhood.

> Little Ann and her mother were walking one day,
> Through London's wide city so fair;
> And bus'ness oblig'd them to go by the way
> That led them through Cavendish Square.
>
> And as they pass'd by the great house of a lord,
> A beautiful chariot there came,
> To take some most elegant ladies abroad,
> Who straightway got into the same.
>
> The ladies in feathers and jewels were seen,
> The chariot was painted all o'er,
> The footmen behind were in silver and green,
> The horses were prancing before.
>
> Little Ann, by her mother walk'd silent and sad,
> A tear trickled down from her eye;
> Till her mother said, 'Ann, I should be very glad
> To know what it is makes you cry.'
>
> 'Mamma,' said the child, 'see that carriage so fair,
> All cover'd with varnish and gold,
> Those ladies are riding so charmingly there,
> While we have to walk in the cold:
>
> You say God is kind to the folks that are good,
> But surely it cannot be true;
> Or else I am certain, almost, that he wou'd
> Give such a fine carriage to you.'

By the end of the poem her mother had drawn the inevitable moral; but the work also contained the first appearance of several established favourites, of which the best known and most widely repeated is, perhaps, *Twinkle, Twinkle, Little Star*. Adelaide O'Keeffe (daughter of the dramatist) drew her young readers' attention to a large number of pertinent observations on domestic dramas and tragedies by poems headed 'Never Play with Fire', 'False Alarms', 'The Truant Boys', etc., with 'George and the Chimney-Sweeper' starting:

> His petticoats now George cast off,
> For he was four years old;
> His trowsers were nankeen so fine,
> His buttons bright as gold.
> 'May I,' said little George, 'go out
> My pretty clothes to show?
> May I, papa? may I, mamma?'
> The answer was – 'No no.'

Five editions of *Original Poems for Infant Minds* were called for in a space of less than twelve months and the work was never out of print for the rest of the 19th century. In 1875, a complete edition, finally revised by Mrs Gilbert was published. Many selections of the poems, under a succession of differing

Drawn by Isaac Taylor Jun.ᵗ   Engraved by Ann Taylor

Oh! if she would but come again

I think I'd vex her no no more.

HYMNS

FOR

INFANT MINDS.

BY

THE AUTHORS

OF

" *ORIGINAL POEMS*," " *RHYMES FOR THE*

NURSERY," &c.

————" We use great plainness of speech."————

LONDON:

PRINTED FOR T. CONDER, BUCKLERSBURY:

SOLD ALSO BY

DARTON, HARVEY, & CO., GRACECHURCH STREET; AND

CONDER & JONES, ST. PAUL'S CHURCHYARD.

1810.

titles, were issued, illustrated by the leading artists and engravers of the day, of which *Little Ann and Other Poems* (1883), by Kate Greenaway, is possibly the best known. Ann and Jane Taylor produced several other books of verse. *Rhymes for the Nursery*, 1806, reached its 27th edition in 1835, while *Hymns for Infant Minds*, 1810, went through no less than 60 editions before 1890.

The appearance of *The Butterfly's Ball and the Grasshopper's Feast*, in 1807, ushered in an era where children could sometimes be permitted to be amused without having to pay the penalty of being moralised and sermonised and told to say their prayers, wash their faces, take care of their clothes, and be loving and kind to the brat next door. The verses had first appeared in the November 1806 number of *The Gentleman's Magazine*, and were ready for publication in book form, with a set of plain or coloured engravings above the engraved text after pictures by William Mulready, in January 1807. The author, William Roscoe (1753–1831), was a historian, a banker, a botanist, a biblio-phile with a library of magnificent proportions, a Member of Parliament, and is acknowledged as the first author to write sheer nonsense for the enjoy-ment of boys and girls. The little book, with its fourteen copperplate engrav-ings, was issued in a binding of yellow pictorially-printed wrappers; a second issue, with different illustrations and variations in the text, was published the same year. The work proved immensely popular with several generations of children and soon led to a host of imitators. The best known of these is *The Peacock "at Home"*, 1807, by Mrs Catherine Dorset (1750?–1817?), once again published by John Harris, who had taken over the bookselling business from Elizabeth Newbery on her retirement in 1801. The book was issued in September 1807, in a format that matched with Roscoe's original work, with a blue binding and pictorially-printed covers containing an advertise-ent of *The Butterfly's Ball* on the back. The six copperplate engravings after

This was the first book to be written entirely by Jane and Ann Taylor, daughters of the Revd. Isaac Taylor of Ongar, Essex.

Size of title-page:
14 cm × 8.6 cm.

William Mulready were issued in either plain or coloured form. A total of over 40,000 copies of the two titles were sold before the end of the following year. There were at least twenty unauthorised sequels under various titles, such as *The Elephant's Ball*, by an unidentified 'W.B.', 1807; *The Lion's Parliament*, 1808; *The Horse's Levee*, 1808; *Flora's Gala*, 1808; and *The Lobster's Voyage*, 1808; most of which were published anonymously. Fifty years after the first appearance of *The Butterfly's Ball*, a version with similar verses was compiled by R. M. Ballantyne. In 1856, this same author published *The Three Little Kittens*, which had first appeared in *New Nursery Songs for all Good Children*, 1843, by Eliza Fallen (1787–1860), printed in the USA.

The earlier of these nonsense books paved the way for the appearance of the illustrated limerick books, the first printing of this jingling metrical form being that of *The History of Sixteen Wonderful Old Women*, 1820, which was Number 15 in *Harris's Cabinet of Amusement and Instruction*. Engravings depicting the scenes, hand-coloured in some copies, were printed above the limericks, the first of which reads:

> There was an Old Woman named Towl,
> Who went out to Sea with her Owl,
>   But the Owl was Sea-sick,
>   And screamed for Physic;
> Which sadly annoy'd Mistress Towl.

Anecdotes and Adventures of Fifteen Gentlemen (*c.* 1822), published by John Marshall, with verses attributed to R. S. Sharpe, was described as embellished with 'fifteen laughable engravings', and takes its place as the second limerick book, originally produced for the amusement of children. Edward Lear (1812–88), is a writer whose name is always associated with the limerick form of verse, but he certainly did not invent it and acknowledged that he modelled his verses on those found in the book quoted immediately above. His *Book of Nonsense*, 2 vols. 1846, was published by Thomas McLean, London, in pictorial paper-covered boards, lettered in white, with the spines of a distinctive bright-red linen. Each volume had an illustrated title-page, but complete copies in the original board bindings are seldom found. These lines:

> There was an old Derry down Derry
> Who loved to see little folks merry:
>   So he made them a book,
>   And with laughter they shook,
> At the fun of that Derry down Derry!

was the first of the little verses that were to make his name famous, and which he continued to produce in works such as *A Book of Nonsense and more Nonsense*, 1862, *More Nonsense, pictures, rhymes, botany, etc*, 1872, and *Laughable lyrics: a fresh book of nonsense poems*, 1877.

Amongst other children's poetry books of the period under review, which stand on my shelves is *The Sunflower; or, Poetical Truths*, (1822), by Mary Elliott, née Belson, announced by the authoress as a continuation of her earlier *Simple Truths, in Verse*, 1812. Standing next in line is *Classical English Poetry, for the Use of Schools, and Young persons in General*, 1823, edited by William Mavor (1758–1837), the second edition of which, dated 1825, is described in the inserted advertisements as 'closely printed in Duodecimo'. With 480 pages it appears to be good value for money at 5*s.* 6*d.* (66 cents) a copy. This poetical miscellany covers a range of authors as far apart in time as Shakespeare and Scott, and it is one of the best selections of poetry for children that had appeared up to that time. *Selections from the Poems of William Wordsworth, Esq. Chiefly for the use of Schools and Young Persons*, 1831, published by Edward Moxon, London, is now a scarce and expensive book, especially if it is still in the original binding of drab paper-covered boards, with paper-labelled spine and uncut leaf edges. Copies in this condition would be priced at about £30 ($72). *Pleasant Rhymes for Little Readers or Jottings for Juveniles*, 1864, by 'Josephine' is a work by an unknown author which is sought more for the pleasure of its gold-blocked cloth binding and fine coloured frontispiece by Kronheim, than for the quality of its verse. The work first appeared in 1862, under the title

Edward's Decision.

Deep sunk in thought see Edward stand,
Revolving in his mind,
Which of the articles in hand
He shall most useful find.

Musical box. A Watch.

see Sunflower; Page 70.

London, William Darton, 58, Holborn Hill. 1822.

THE

SUNFLOWER;

OR,

POETICAL TRUTHS,

FOR YOUNG MINDS,

RELIGIOUS, MORAL, MISCELLANEOUS,

AND

HISTORICAL;

FORMING

A COLLECTION OF ORIGINAL POEMS,

And intended as a Continuation of

"SIMPLE TRUTHS IN VERSE."

*Like as the Sunflower spreads its leaves,
To meet the sun's bright rays,
The youthful mind with warmth receives
The Moral—Truth conveys.*

BY MARY ELLIOTT, *(late Belson,)*
Author of "SIMPLE TRUTHS."

LONDON:

WILLIAM DARTON, 58, HOLBORN HILL.

Jottings for Juveniles in Simple Verse, but in an entirely different format.

In the second half of the 19th century, the writing of poetry for children frequently occupied the talents of writers of the highest quality. Others wrote poems that are remembered, while the names of the authors have sunk into the mists never to be recalled. Christina Georgina Rossetti (1830–94), the sister of D. G. Rossetti (1828–82), contributed her earliest writings to *The Germ*, a periodical that made its first appearance on 1 January 1850, as the journal of the Pre-Raphaelite Brotherhood. Her first published work was *Goblin Market and other Poems*, 1862; although *Verses*, 1847, a small book of poems dedicated to her mother, had been privately printed by G. Polidori, and issued as a single sheet in 1842 when Christina was only twelve years of age. *Goblin Market*, published in a binding of straight-ribbed blue cloth, blocked in gilt on the front cover with an *avant garde* motif of lines and roundels designed by her brother, is a comparatively rare book that is currently underpriced at less than £30 ($72). The frontispiece and pictorial title-page were both designed by D. G. Rossetti, who himself was a poet of high repute, as well as an artist of the first rank. As a pioneering book design in complete contrast to the general style of the period, the format is some thirty years ahead of its time. Despite the book's title, the verses could only have appealed to young people in their late teens, whereas *Sing-Song. A Nursery Rhyme Book*, 1872, with a series of 120 delightful woodcut illustrations by Arthur Hughes, engraved by the brothers Dalziel, would have brought pleasure to children of all ages. The first issue of the first edition is blocked pictorially in gold on the front cover and spine, while later issues have the same design blocked in gold and black. Macmillan & Co., issued a 'new and enlarged edition', dated 1893, in a moiré, fine-ribbed cloth binding lettered only on the spine. *Speaking Likenesses*, 1874,

Mary Elliott, a Quaker by birth and persuasion, published her first book of children's verse, *Simple Truths*, in 1816, followed by this continuation of her moral theme in 1822. She also wrote many stories and tales in prose.

Size of title-page:
14.3 cm × 8.8 cm.

An illustration from *Childhood's Golden Days* (1880), a folio published by Dean & Son, London. The photo-lithographic plates were prepared and printed in Dresden, Germany. Size of page: 33 cm × 26 cm.

O
h nurse, what tales you told me!
To school I hardly would go,
And yet we have been so merry
How could you frighten me so?"

"The master was kind, like my father,
We laughed and sang and could play,
And instead of hating it, nursie,
I wish it had lasted all day."

"And bags full of goodies he gave us:
The largest of all was for me,
I'll run home so quick to dear mother
And give her the biggest I see!"

M. SCHERER & H. ENGLER
Registered.
Printed by Römmler & Jonas, Dresden.

again with illustrations by Arthur Hughes, is a fairy story in prose, a fantasy that exhibits many points of similarity with Lewis Carroll's earlier *Alice in Wonderland*. The work deserves an honoured place in any collection of children's books, if only on account of the series of dream-like images which Arthur Hughes, under the influence of Tenniel, drew in a style that exactly captures the atmosphere of the story.

A Child's Garden of Verses, 1885, by Robert Louis Stevenson (1850–94), was an instant success and has seldom been out of print since its original appearance. (Thirty-nine of the sixty-four poems had been privately printed in 1883 under the title *Penny Whistles*.) Issued in a binding of blue cloth over bevelled boards, the top edges of the leaves gilded and the others left uncut, the text printed on stiff paper surrounded by meadows of margin, it is an altogether delightful first edition to own, although becoming an expensive acquisition at about £80 ($192). The second edition, almost identical in format, appeared dated the same year, and the fourth in 1890. The first poem, 'Bed in Summer', displays the delightfully simple style Stevenson employed throughout the work,

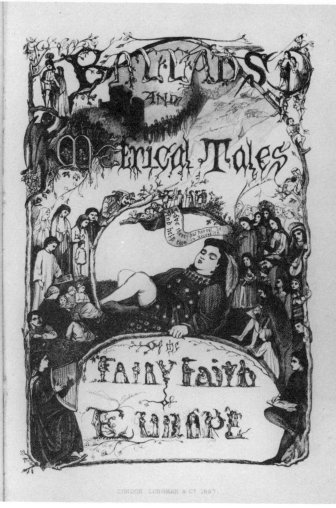

and the ease with which children were able to read and recite the little stanzas:

In winter I get up at night
And dress by yellow candle-light.
In summer, quite the other way,
I have to go to bed by day.

I have to go to bed and see
The birds still hopping on the tree,
Or hear the grown-up people's feet
Still going past me in the street.

And does it not seem hard to you,
When all the sky is clear and blue,
And I should like so much to play,
To have to go to bed by day?

Nonsense verse was still being written during the closing years of the century. *A Bad Child's Book of Beasts* (1896), *More Beasts for Worse Children* (1897), and *The Moral Alphabet* (1899), all by Hilaire Belloc (1870–1953), a versatile writer of essays, novels, history, biography, and verse. His *Cautionary Tales for Children* (1908), was illustrated by a series of line drawings by Lord Ian B. G. T. Blackwood.

The tradition of poetry for children continued through the works of Walter de la Mare, (1873–1956), with his poetical animal fairy tale *The Three Mulla-Mulgars*, 1910, later re-named *The Three Royal Monkeys*, a book which met with small success when it was first issued, but which has since established itself as a children's classic. A. A. Milne (1882–1956), contributed four unforgettable books of stories and verse for children which later generations of adults seem never to tire of reading to their own small offspring. *When we*

Above
'Stiff, archaic, immature, romantic . . .' Forrest Reid called this frontispiece and title-page by Edward Burne-Jones, who was then only twenty-four years of age. Except for the later Kelmscott books he illustrated little else. These early examples of his work are in *The Fairy Family*, 1857.

Size of title-page:
18.8 cm × 12.8 cm.

72

Randolph Caldecott (1846–86), is remembered today more for the series of sixteen picture books he designed and executed for children than for most of his other illustrative works. These were published separately from 1878 to 1885. The one shown is from *A Farmer went Trotting upon his Grey Mare*, which formed the second of the stories in verse in the *Ride A-Cock Horse to Banbury Cross* issue.

Size across one page: 23.5 cm × 20 cm.

were very young, 1924; *Winnie-the-Pooh*, 1926; *Now we are Six*, 1927; and *The House at Pooh Corner*, 1928; the first of which is much the rarest of the quartet, contain verse which is only incidental to the stories of the 'Christopher Robin books', a series illustrated in memorable fashion by E. H. Shepard. But the little verses and songs Milne wrote for Christopher Robin and his animal friends are not easily forgotten and have long since found a niche in *The Oxford Dictionary of Quotations*. A set of the four first editions, all of which were also issued in a strictly limited large-paper edition printed on Japon vellum, is a prize to be cherished by any collector. In 1929 the publishers of the series, Methuen & Company, London, issued *Fourteen Songs*, *The King's Breakfast*, *Teddy Bear and Other Songs*, *Songs from 'Now we are Six'*, *More Very Young Songs*,

The mischievous Raven flew laughing away;
Bumpety, bumpety, bump!
And vowed he would serve them the same the next day;
Lumpety, lumpety, lump!

Below
One of the minutiae which constitute a point of issue, in this case the distinguishing mark between the first and subsequent early editions of *A Child's Garden of Verses*, 1885, by Robert Louis Stevenson. The apostrophe in the word 'Child's' is rounded in the first edition (top in picture) and square in later editions, some of which appeared the same year.

and *The Hums of Pooh*, a set of folio-sized books in pictorially-printed paper-covered boards, in which the words of Milne's songs had been set to music by H. Fraser-Simson, and with the illustrations of E. H. Shepard. These song books are now almost as hard to find in acceptable condition as the original 'Christopher Robin' books themselves.

The last space on my shelf of poetry books for children is occupied by a first edition of *Old Possum's Book of Practical Cats*, 1939, a slim quarto published by Faber and Faber, London, in a binding of bright yellow cloth, blocked pictorially in red. The work was issued, priced at 3s. 6d. (42 cents), in a yellow dust-wrapper: copies in this desirable state are now catalogued at over £40 ($96). The author, T. S. Eliot, (1888–1965), has been a major figure in literary history since the 1920s, and his work is too well known to need quoting here. Yet *Old Possum's Book of Practical Cats* would well deserve a place in any collection of children's books if the author's name was unknown, for with it Eliot produced a minor masterpiece and a classic amongst books of poetry for children. The tale of 'Bustopher Jones: The Cat about Town', like the other titles in the book, caricatures a human counterpart while introducing us to the cat:

Bustopher Jones is *not* skin and bones –
In fact, he's remarkably fat.
He doesn't haunt pubs – he has eight or nine clubs,
For he's the St. James's Street Cat!
He's the Cat we all greet as he walks down the street
In his coat of fastidious black:
No commonplace mousers have such well-cut trousers
Or such an impeccable back.
In the whole of St. James's the smartest of names is
The name of this Brummell of Cats;
And we're all of us proud to be nodded or bowed to
By Bustopher Jones in white spats!

Stories-before 1850

In May 1802 appeared the first monthly issue of *The Guardian of Education*, the first publication of any kind in the world to review books published for children and young people. It was edited by that eminently 'good' woman Mrs Sarah Trimmer, forthright exponent of the strictly moral tale, whose cautionary figure cast a shadow over the publishers of every class of children's literature of her day. Her *Fabulous Histories*, 1786 (or *The History of the Robins*, as it came to be called), has already been discussed, and in addition she had produced a wealth of educational books and pamphlets, including *A Series of Prints of Scripture History* (1786), a set of 32 numbered copperplate illustrations, which had been made to accompany *A Description of a set of Prints of Scripture History: contained in a set of Easy Lessons* (1786), both published by John Marshall, London. These 32 Old Testament stories, and the set of separately issued illustrations, had a wide circulation and passed through numerous editions, as did her similar works *A Series of Prints of Ancient History* (text 1786; illustrations, 2 parts, 1786–8), *A Series of Prints of Roman History* (1789), and *A Series of Prints of English History* (1792). She continued to alter and revise these titles well into the 19th century. *A New Series of Prints, accompanied by Easy Lessons; containing a general outline of Antient History*, 1803, was followed by other revised editions, and the series was still in print in the 1840s.

Mrs Trimmer dominated the scene for over twenty years. Long after she was dead we continue to find her books recommended, and young Victorians were reading them in their classrooms and nurseries, and gazing at the pasted prints of the *Sacred History* which had been sold by Marshall in their thousands, glued to boards 'for hanging – price 10/6 – in sheets 8*d*'. In her *Guardian of Education* she acted as a self-appointed censor, the champion of virtue, and the exposer of the monster Vice, which 'to be hated needs but to be seen'. The

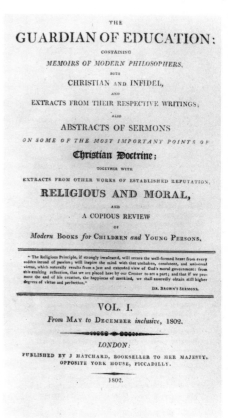

work started as a monthly periodical, but Mrs Trimmer's name did not appear on the title-page until issue No. 9 in January 1803. A total of 28 numbers of the magazine appeared at gradually lengthening intervals, and it finished as a quarterly publication at the end of its fifth volume, in September 1806. The first children's book published by the firm of Newbery which she reviewed was

THE

ADVENTURES

OF

A DONKEY.

••••••••••••••••••

BY

ARABELLA ARGUS,

Author of "THE JUVENILE SPECTATOR."

••••••••••••••••••

LONDON:
PRINTED BY AND FOR WILLIAM DARTON, JUN.
58, HOLBORN HILL.
1815.

Poor little foal of an oppressed race!
I love the languid patience of thy face;
And oft with gentle hand I give thee bread,
And clap thy ragged coat and pat thy head.

Above
The first edition of the most famous of the works of 'Arabella Argus'.

Size of title-page:
13.5 cm × 8.5 cm.

Right
The first edition of another well known work by 'Arabella Argus'; the real name of the author remains a mystery. The writer admits in her preface that she has used a pseudonym, but beyond the fact that she was an elderly lady living in London nothing else is known.

Size of title-page:
17 cm × 10.5 cm.

THE

JUVENILE SPECTATOR;

BEING

OBSERVATIONS

ON THE

TEMPERS, MANNERS, AND FOIBLES

OF

VARIOUS YOUNG PERSONS,

INTERSPERSED

With such lively Matter, as it is presumed will amuse
as well as instruct.

BY ARABELLA ARGUS.

"Teach me to feel another's woe,
To hide the fault I see;
That mercy I to others show,
That mercy show to me."

LONDON:
PRINTED BY AND FOR W. AND T. DARTON,
58, HOLBORN-HILL.
1810.

I cannot kiss you just now Grandmama
said Lucy, for I am writing to such a funny
old Woman about my wax Doll.

E.Burney Del.   J.Springsguth Sculp.

The frontispiece by Edward Burney for *The Affectionate Brothers* (*c.* 1833), by Mrs B. W. H. Hofland, a work that first appeared in two volumes in 1816.

Size of plate: 8.5 cm × 6.5 cm.

Youthful Recreations; containing the Amusements of a Day, 1799. Her advice to parents on how to make it more suitable reading for their young lacks the thunder of some of her later denunciations, but strikes a chill into the heart of a bibliophile:

This little volume has no tincture of the *new School* in its composition, but is well calculated to amuse and instruct young readers. In one particular only we find ourselves at a loss to form a decided judgment – we mean in respect to the account which is introduced of a supposed *haunted house* . . . if a child never had heard of *haunted-houses*, &c. such a story would certainly do harm, by putting him upon inquiries, which would probably lead to his taking up a painful idea he might not easily get rid of; but a pair of scissors will easily rectify this error . . .

Drastic, but simple! Thomas Bowdler (1754–1825), who soon started his task of expurgating the works of William Shakespeare in order to make them fit for 'family reading', and later castrated Gibbon's *History of the Roman Empire* in similar fashion, must have nodded approvingly. The next book to fall into Mrs Trimmer's hands was *The History of Susan Gray, as related by a Clergyman, for the Benefit of Young Women going to Service,* 1802 (published anonymously) the second work of a lady who achieved the astonishing total of over 350 books, tracts, and pamphlets to her credit. (*The Traditions,* 1795, was her first.) Martha Mary Sherwood (1775–1851) later joined in the thick of the fight

From *The Christmas Fire-side*, by Sarah Wheatley. The factory owner is addressing the barefooted children he employs, the sons and daughters of crofters dispossessed by the Enclosure Act. Little is known about Sarah Wheatley; this book, and *The Friendly Adviser*, appear to be her only works.

At a village in Essex, not far from Rumford, some children were playing near a windmill: to see the sails go round was very amusing, but one little boy going to examine them too closely, was struck by one of the sails, which caught him up, and threw him a considerable distance, and when found he was lifeless.

Printed by Darton, Harvey, and Co.
Gracechurch-Street, London.

Above
One of the anecdotes from *A Present for a Little Boy*, 1816, issued in printed paper-wrappers by Darton, Harvey, & Darton.
Size of page: 15.7 cm × 9.5 cm.

Right
One of the rarest of early 19th-century children's stories, the author of which has so far escaped identification.
Size of title-page: 18.3 cm × 10.7 cm.

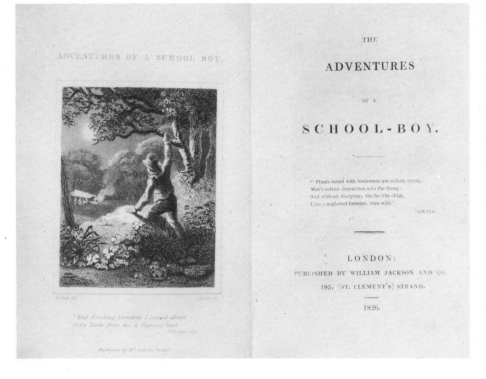

that raged until the 1830s between the strait-laced moral and didactic juvenile tract, and the fairy story and she was very firmly on the side of Mrs Trimmer in opposing the superstitious nonsense that children would persist in reading and enjoying. Although the two women had not at that time had the pleasure of meeting each other, and Mrs Trimmer apparently had been unable to identify the author of the book she was reviewing, she instantly perceived that here was a kindred spirit who could be relied upon to root out vice and lustful indulgence in what ever form it arrayed itself. *The History of Susan Gray* had her warmest approval:

This exemplary tale furnishes a most seasonable and edifying lesson to girls of the lower order; and, with a little accommodation to circumstances, it might be applied with great propriety to the higher classes, for *the love of dress*, and *the desire of admiration*, to which it relates, are equally prevalent, in all the different ranks of which the female part of society is composed. This fatal propensity may, indeed, be justly considered as a pestilential disease of the mind, the baneful contagion of which is daily spreading till it is become almost universal. If any means can check its progress they must, we think, be such as this little book affords . . . It should also, we think, be put into the hands of mothers, with the view of checking in them that thoughtless vanity which frequently contributes to the ruin of their daughters.

Despite the narrow-minded strictures of its editor *The Guardian of Education* is of inestimable value to the literary historian and bibliographer, for many of the books she reviews have been lost to sight and are now known only through the titles she gives and the advertisements contained in other works of the period. This rule applies especially to those ephemeral little publications for children that were issued at prices ranging from one penny to threepence, for their only protection against dirt and damage was flimsy paper-wrappers and their expectation of life was very short indeed.

In the meantime, Mrs Sherwood had sailed for India where her husband Captain Henry Sherwood was on military service. It was here that she came under the evangelising influence of the missionary Henry Martyn, and from that time onwards her intensely righteous books demanded a standard of conduct from children that would have resulted in a juvenile population of cherubs. On her return to England, she completed *The History of little Henry and his bearer*, 1814, published by F. Houlston & Son, Wellington, Shropshire, telling the story of dear little Henry's dogged perseverance that led to the ultimate conversion of his Indian servant to Christianity. The tale enjoyed immense popularity, the title later being changed to *The Story of little Henry*

Come, little preacher, said Emma, come, and teach us
how we are to die, and how we must rise again

See Pages 43 & 44

Published by Thomas Melrose, High Street, Berwick
January 1st 1829

THE

BUTTERFLY.

BY

MRS. SHERWOOD,

AUTHOR OF " LITTLE HENRY AND HIS BEARER," &c.

BERWICK:

PUBLISHED BY THOMAS MELROSE.

MDCCCXXIX.

and his bearer Boosy. So many editions appeared in the space of some thirty years that its success has been compared with that accorded to *Uncle Tom's Cabin.* It remained in print until after 1900, and the provincial firm of Houlston & Son, who published the vast majority of her library of titles, owed much of their prosperity to her unfailing output of tales for youth. *The History of Lucy Clare,* 1815, *The Lady and her ayah,* 1816, *Memoirs of Sergeant Dale, his daughter and the orphan Mary,* 1816, *The Indian Pilgrim: or the progress of the pilgrim Nazarene,* 1818, were followed by the book that she is remembered by today, *The History of the Fairchild family; or, The Child's Manual; being a collection of stories calculated to show the importance and effects of a Religious Education,* 3 parts, 1818-42-7. Mrs Sherwood received the help of her daughter, Mrs Sophia Kelly in writing the final part, and this lady was also responsible for a lively and readable biography of her mother, entitled *The Life of Mrs Sherwood, chiefly autobiographical,* 1854, most of which was extracted from the author's voluminous diary which she kept throughout her life. *The History of the Fairchild family* enjoyed a vogue unsurpassed by any children's book for fifty years or more. The majority of English middle-class children up to the mid-1850s may be said to have been subjected to its rigorous piety to an extent that finally led to a revulsion of feeling when they had married and had children of their own. Someone, somewhere, must have started to giggle, and no work intended for the interest and instruction of the young has ever been so completely ridiculed and as forthrightly condemned by those with the true interests of children and young people at heart. Whatever may have been Mrs Sherwood's aims and intentions, the result of her Calvinistic moralising must surely have been to terrify and subdue, rather than to edify and cheer her young readers. The very sight of Mr Fairchild mincing towards them in

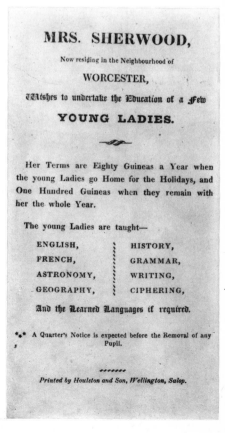

MRS. SHERWOOD,

Now residing in the Neighbourhood of

WORCESTER,

Wishes to undertake the Education of a Few

YOUNG LADIES.

Her Terms are Eighty Guineas a Year when the young Ladies go Home for the Holidays, and One Hundred Guineas when they remain with her the whole Year.

The young Ladies are taught—

ENGLISH,	HISTORY,
FRENCH,	GRAMMAR,
ASTRONOMY,	WRITING,
GEOGRAPHY,	CIPHERING,

And the Learned Languages if required.

• A Quarter's Notice is expected before the Removal of any Pupil.

Printed by Houlston and Son, Wellington, Salop.

their dreams would have chilled them with fear: the smell of death and damnation pervaded every scene he entered:

'Come with me to the gibbet,' said Mr Fairchild, taking the hands of his infants to where the corpse swung slowly in its casket of chains. It had not yet fallen to pieces although it had hung there for some years. However the face of the corpse was so shocking that the children could not bear to look at it.

'Oh! papa, papa! what is it? Let us go, papa!' cried the children, pulling Mr Fairchild's coat. 'Not yet,' said Mr Fairchild sternly, 'I must tell you the story of this wretched man before I allow you to leave this place.'

Another macabre scene relished with gloating piety by the authoress concerns a visit to a cottage in which Mr Fairchild's faithful old gardener, Roberts, has recently died. 'You never saw a corpse, I think?' says Mr Fairchild. 'No, papa,' answers Lucy, 'but we have a great curiosity to see one.' 'And so you shall, dear child.' Off they go through the garden hand in hand, until they arrive at the cottage:

When they came to the door they perceived a kind of disagreeable smell, such as they had never smelt before; this was the smell of the corpse, which having been dead now nearly two days had begun to corrupt . . . the whole appearance of the body was more ghastly and horrible than the children expected . . . At last Mr Fairchild said, 'My dear children, you now see what death is; this poor body is going fast to corruption. The soul, I trust, is in God; but such is the taint and corruption of the flesh, by reason of sin, that it must pass through the grave and crumble to dust . . . Remember these things, my children, and pray to God to save you from sin.'

'Oh, Sir!' said Mrs Roberts, 'it comforts me to hear you talk!'

The works of Mrs Sherwood, and to a lesser degree, those of her sister Mrs Lucy Cameron (1781–1858), became interwoven into the literary fabric of Victorian family life, and were the accepted Sunday afternoon reading of generations of 19th-century children. The extreme rigidity of Mrs Sherwood's theological stance made her works unacceptable to large sections of the reading public as the century drew to a close, but titles written in the early 1820s were still being presented as Church of England Sunday School prizes up to the start of World War I. Despite her manifest faults she possessed a great deal more literary talent than most of her female companions in the field of children's literature, and her often vivid descriptions of domestic life in the Fairchild family live on in the imagination long after her prayers and exhortations have mercifully faded and been forgotten.

One of the first books to show a markedly lenient attitude to the bubbling high spirits and good plain naughtiness in children, was *Holiday House: a Series of Tales*, 1839, by Catherine Sinclair (1800–64), published in Edinburgh by William Whyte & Company, and containing a hand-coloured frontispiece after a design by the authoress. Miss Sinclair was the daughter of a Scottish politician, and came of so tall a family that the path leading to their home was nicknamed 'The Giant's Causeway'. Her first children's book was *Charlie Seymour; or the Good Lady and the Bad Lady*, 1838 (second edition, enlarged, the same year), again with a hand-coloured frontispiece by the authoress, and published by the same firm. In her preface to this work she expressed surprise that a large proportion of the children's books she had examined 'had frontispieces to represent a death-bed surrounded by the clergyman, the physician, and the afflicted relatives of a dying Christian; the memoirs of children *especially*, which I examined, were almost invariably terminated by an early death.' She was determined to portray real-life children, wilful, mischievous, exasperating, stubborn, destructive, often dirty and untidy, often disobedient, and sometimes downright bad. She preferred her children to be like 'wild horses on the prairies, rather than like well-broken hacks on the road'. In *Charlie Seymour* she based the boy's choice between right and wrong, and between living with his indulgent Aunt Jane or his upright and moral Aunt Mary, on actual conversations she had with 'a child of great intelligence'. We may assume this was her nephew, the Hon. G. F. Boyle, son of the Earl of

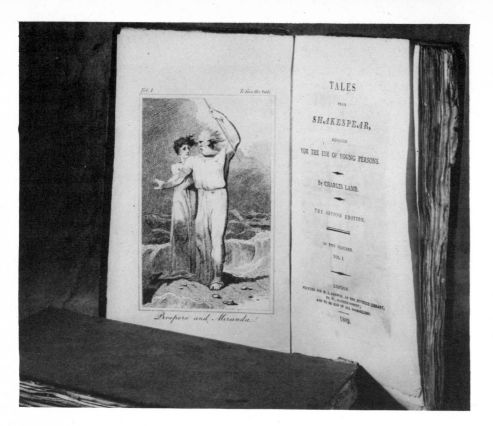

First published in 1807, this second edition in 1809 of Lamb's *Tales from Shakespeare* is unusual: it is in the original publisher's binding of boards with uncut leaf edges. The engravings are by William Blake after designs by William Mulready.

Size of title-page:
19 cm × 11 cm.

Right
Part of a rare set of children's books printed and published in Tokyo, Japan, in English, in 1888. Printed on soft-textured paper from wood-blocks, the fore-edges were uncut and sealed giving a concertina effect when the books were opened. The texts of the Japanese fairy-tales were by B. H. Chamberlain and Mrs T. H. James. The set of twenty little volumes was originally sold in a drop-fronted box by Griffith Farran & Co., London, and may have been intended for the Australian market.

Glasgow, for whom she admitted writing her children's books. Naughtiness and disobedience are shown by the do-as-you-would-be-done-by Aunt Mary to be foolhardy, and she expounds the inevitable moral when little Charlie is ill after having stuffed himself with raspberry cream, or nearly plunges over a cliff in a donkey-cart after missing church on Sunday. But in *Holiday House*, written only a year later, Miss Sinclair positively extols youthful high spirits

First published in 1809, this story by Charles and Mary Lamb did not achieve the popularity of their *Tales from Shakespeare*, 1807. The frontispiece is engraved by James Hopwood the Younger, after a drawing by his brother, William Hopwood.

Size of title-page:
17.5 cm × 10 cm.

and near riotous behaviour in a way not generally countenanced in children's literature for another fifty years. Harry and Laura Graham, the hero and heroine of the tale, start by playfully setting their grandmother's house on fire before indulging in an orgy of destruction in which windows, clothes, toys and furniture all suffer in greater or lesser degree. Their guardian, Uncle David, discovers Laura cutting off all her hair, just for the fun of it, and calls the children together for a mild rebuke:

'I am not so seriously angry at the sort of scrape Laura and you get into, because you would not willingly and deliberately do wrong. If any children commit a mean action, or get into a passion or quarrel with each other, or omit saying their prayers and reading their Bibles, or tell a lie, or take what does not belong to them, then it might be seen how extremely angry I could be; but while you continue merely thoughtless and forgetful, I mean to have patience a little longer.'

Miss Sinclair was certain that the children of her age were far too severely disciplined, but she had no doubt that a strict religious upbringing was their only ultimate hope of salvation. She did believe that each and every child was gifted with a personality that was individual, and that young people could not be drilled and dragooned into unquestioning obedience without extinguishing the joy for life and natural high spirits possessed by the youth of the world, and her attitude marked her as being far in advance of her time both as a writer and as an educationalist.

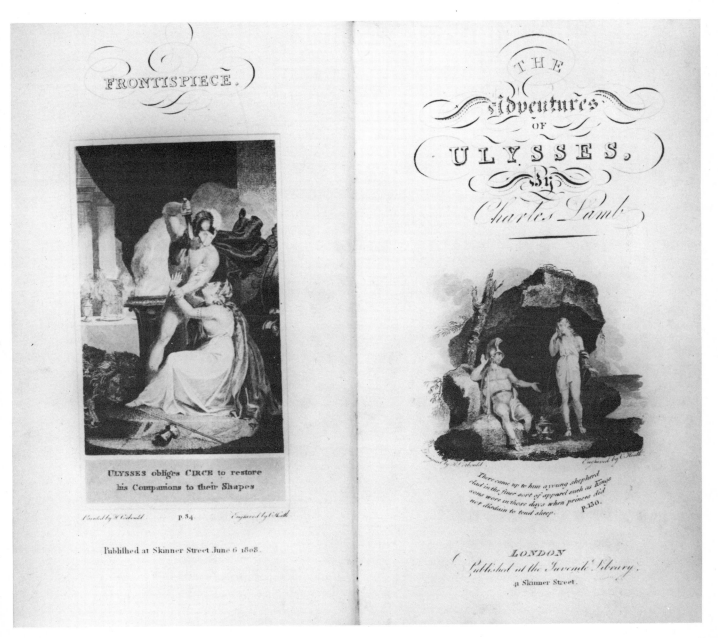

FRONTISPIECE.

ULYSSES obliges CIRCE to restore his Companions to their Shapes

Painted by H Corbould   p. 54   *Engraved by C Heath*

Published at Skinner Street June 6 1808.

THE
Adventures
OF
ULYSSES.
By
Charles Lamb

There came up to him a young shepherd clad in the finer sort of apparel such as Kings' sons wore in those days when princes did not disdain to tend sheep.   p.130.

LONDON
Published at the Juvenile Library,
41 Skinner Street.

For the first time in a children's book, misbehaviour had been set in an amusing and understandable light, but it was many years before other writers in the field dared to let the reins loose and give what she described as 'noisy, frolicsome, mischievous children' their heads. A glance along my shelves soon confirms that her contemporaries were content to be guided by the rules laid down by Mrs Trimmer and her able lieutenant Mrs Sherwood. For the most part they played safe and had their heroes on their knees at least once in every fifty pages, either to ask forgiveness for a series of youthful indulgencies, or to thank God for granting them a station in life, however lowly, and for the ability to resist temptations into which their feckless playfellows had fallen. The prig still received the plaudits of the crowd, but the cheers were becoming gradually fainter, and occasionally, as the titles neared the middle of the century, he might inadvertently fall flat on his face in the nettles, or end up having to make his way unaided out of the village duck-pond. Good was still good, but badness was being defined as shades of grey darkening to the pitch black of 'unwholesome thoughts'. The real-life story for children was taking a good deal longer to escape from didacticism than had the fairy tales and fantasies; but *Holiday House* was a milestone pointing the way ahead, allowing real children to become involved in the genuine troubles and scrapes of childhood, and to act as the sort of unpredictable individuals that child readers could recognise as themselves.

Women writers still dominated the world of children's literature. Mary Hughes, née Robson, contributed *Aunt Mary's Tales; for the enlightenment and improvement of little Girls*, 1813; *The Ornaments Discovered*, 1815; *The Alchemist* 1818; and, amongst many others, *The orphan girl: a moral tale*, 1819, in all of which the influence of her friend Maria Edgeworth is clearly discernible.

A story by Mary Hughes that first appeared in 1815. It relates the adventures of the orphan Fanny, who is happily bequeathed a legacy before the end of the tale. Mrs Hughes and her husband emigrated to the USA in 1817, where she ran a school for young ladies in Philadelphia.

Size of title-page:
14.3 cm × 8.4 cm.

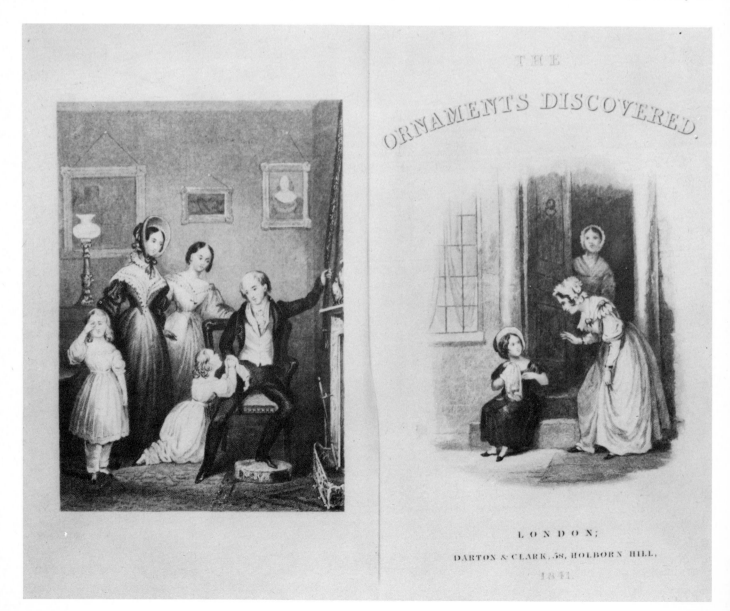

Agnes Strickland (1796–1874), is remembered for *The moss-house*, 1822, and for *The rival Crusoes, or The shipwreck* (1826), in which she collaborated with her sister Elizabeth. Her *Lives of the Queens of England*, 12 vols. 1840–8, achieved considerable success and was followed by a number of similar works, some of which, in abbreviated form, became established as school text-books. Her other sister, Jane Margaret Strickland (1800–88), who was later the editor of *Fisher's Juvenile Scrap-Book*, wrote *National Prejudice; or, The French prisoner of war*, 1828, and a number of other children's historical works.

A mixed bag of titles of early 19th-century children's books taken at random from a shelf largely filled by the publications of John Harris; Taylor & Hessey; Longman, Hurst, Rees, Orme, Brown, & Green; Harvey & Darton; A. K. Newman & Co.; and Whittaker & Company who between them dominated the market in juvenile literature up to the 1840s, reveals a complexity of formats and binding styles and a considerable variation in the quality of the illustrations. Three volumes standing next to each other all have connections with Sheffield. *The History of an Officer's Widow*, 1814, by Mrs Barbara Hofland (1770–1844), who was herself the widow of a wealthy Sheffield merchant, T. B. Hoole, was written two years before her second marriage, this time to T. C. Hofland, the artist. An earlier work in much the same style had been extremely successful, *The Clergyman's Widow, and her Young Family*, 1812. It sold well over 20,000 copies in the space of ten years, and apparently intent on backing a winning horse she added yet another title to the same stable with *The History of a Merchant's Widow and her Young Family*, 1823. Mrs Hofland's best-known children's book today is probably *The Son of a Genius*, 1812, dedicated to her son Frederick Hofland. *The Blind Man and His Son*, 1816, was published anonymously by Samuel Roberts (1763–1848), the Sheffield social

A group of children's books published by John Harris, London, in the 1820s. The printed paper-covered boards and leather spine blocked with horizontal gold lines was a format that was quickly copied by rivals in the trade.

Height of standing books: 17 cm approximately.

reformer who became known as the 'Pauper's Advocate'. The profits from all his numerous books, pamphlets, and broadsheets, were always contributed to the various charities in which he had an interest, especially anti-slavery societies and those concerned with the abolition of child labour. *Tales of the Poor, or Infant Sufferings*, 1813, was his first children's book. The poet James Montgomery (1771–1854), was a close friend of Samuel Roberts and had contributed the second part of *The Four Friends*, a poetical fable, to *The Blind Man and His Son*. For that reason I have allowed *The Chimney-Sweeper's Friend, and Climbing-Boy's Album*, 1824, which Montgomery wrote while in Sheffield,

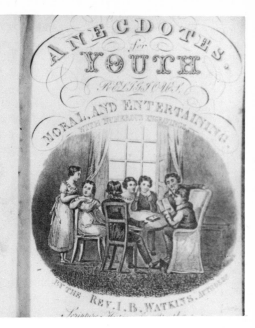

to stand next to it on the shelf, although it has no real place in a chapter devoted to story books for children. It epitomises the sufferings of a class of unfortunate young boys of the period, and the impressive list of contributors, under the editorship of Montgomery, included Charles Lamb, Sir John Samuel Roberts, 'The Pauper's Advocate', as he came to be known, vowed never to publish for profit. This is his second book, published in 1816.

Size of title-page: 16.5 cm × 9.5 cm.

THE BLIND MAN AND HIS SON.
Page 3.

THE

BLIND MAN AND HIS SON:

A TALE FOR YOUNG PEOPLE.

THE FOUR FRIENDS:

A FABLE.

AND

A WORD FOR THE GIPSIES.

Any profits arising from the sale of this publication will be applied in aid of the Society for the relief of Aged Females in Sheffield.

LONDON:
PRINTED BY T MILLER;
FOR TAYLOR AND HESSEY, 93, FLEET-STREET.
1816.

Bowring, Allan Cunningham, Mrs Hofland, Samuel Roberts, and several other well-known names. The work is also of importance for containing the first separate printing of William Blake's poem *The Chimney Sweeper* from his *Songs of Innocence* (first published in book form by William Pickering in 1839).

Two anonymous tales that have fictional adventure stories woven into a factual background of travel in foreign parts are *Fire-Side Stories; or, Recollections of my School-Fellows*, 1825, a tall 12mo issued by Harvey & Darton in a binding of printed paper-covered boards with leather spine, and described as by the author of *The Picture Gallery*; and *The Wanderings of Tom Starboard; or the Life of a Sailor*, 1830. The advertisements at the end of the volume add the information, by 'I.J.T.' who also claimed credit for *The Children's Fire-Side*, and *The Young Wanderer's Cave*. These fictional tales of travel were amongst the precursors of the boys' adventure stories of the 1850s and later. Another was *Minor Morals for Young People*, 3 vols. 1834-5-9, by Sir John Bowring (1792-1872), his only children's book. This is a most difficult first edition to acquire as a complete set in the original full glazed-cloth binding with paper-labelled spines. The first two volumes were issued by Whittaker & Company, London, and the third volume some five years later (in a matching binding) by William Tait, Edinburgh. All the full-page plates in the last two volumes are by George Cruikshank, but in the first volume he contributed only the frontispiece, and the rest of the illustrations were by William Heath. As well as tales of travel, *Minor Morals* contains several interesting fairy tales translated into English for the first time.

By the 1840s James Fenimore Cooper had already published his series of *Leather Stocking Tales*, and Captain Marryat was at work on his adventure

To face the Title.

THE

CHIMNEY-SWEEPER'S

FRIEND,

AND

CLIMBING-BOY'S ALBUM.

DEDICATED,

BY THE MOST GRACIOUS PERMISSION, TO

𝕳𝖎𝖘 𝕸𝖆𝖏𝖊𝖘𝖙𝖞.

The child of misery baptized with tears.   LANGHORNE.

ARRANGED BY

JAMES MONTGOMERY.

WITH ILLUSTRATIVE DESIGNS BY CRUICKSHANK.

LONDON:

PRINTED FOR

LONGMAN, HURST, REES, ORME, BROWN, AND GREEN,

PATERNOSTER-ROW.

1824.

stories for boys, both of which are discussed in the chapter dealing with that subject. Children began to have a diversity of stories and tales to choose from, allowing them a wide choice of interest and ideas. In the USA, Jacob Abbott (1803–79), a congregational clergyman and educator, brought pleasure to children with his list of 28 titles detailing the adventures of Rollo, Lucy and Jonas, of which *Rollo's Vacation*, 1839, published in Boston, is typical. The 'Rollo' books achieved an immense popularity, and were originally modelled on Jacob Abbott's son, later known as Revd Lyman Abbott, a distinguished minister and editor. In Germany *Das Blumenkörbschen*, by Johann Christoph von Schmid (1768–1854), enjoyed an immense sale, but it was not translated into English direct from the German edition until 1867, when Frederick Warne & Company issued the story as *The Basket of Flowers; or, Piety and Truth Triumphant*. Published in a full-cloth binding over bevelled boards, blocked in gold and black, this undated edition deserves a place in any collection of children's books. The numerous coloured plates were printed direct on to the text paper by Edmund Evans, and represent a new departure in colour-printing, each chapter having a half-page coloured plate at its head. Earlier English editions of *The Basket of Flowers* had used a translation taken from the French by G. T. Bedell, or had used a modified translation taken from an American edition. The story was a favourite with children for many years, and lent itself admirably to the talents of illustrators and book designers. Thomas Nelson & Sons, Edinburgh, published an edition in 1871 with a series of illustrations by steel engravings from designs by William Harvey; while Milner & Company issued a particularly attractive edition with colour-printed floral margins in the text, and with the coloured plates of flowers tipped on to an ornamental gilt background. The tale is centred around a stolen diamond ring, taken when a village girl, Mary, the daughter of a poor gardener, calls at the castle with a basket of flowers to present to the Countess on her birthday. Arrested on the false evidence of a jealous maid, she steadfastly refuses to confess even when whipped and tortured, and she and her aged father are banished in disgrace from the Count's domain. But there is a happy ending when a tree in the castle garden is cut down and the missing ring is discovered in a magpie's nest. Margaret, the covetous maid is struck down by a mysterious illness in retribution for her false evidence, and dies 'at the age of twenty-three, a melancholy example of the misery that sin never fails to bring along with it. We cannot add that there was any hope in her death'. Mary marries the son of the judge who had previously condemned her, and the diamond ring is given to her by the Countess for her wedding ring. A happy, well-rounded, ending, and one which many a young reader must have sighed over. English editions of other of Johann Schmid's tales were *Eustace, the Christian Warrior*; *Genevieve, and other tales*; *Itha, Countess of Toggenbourg*; *The orphan child, or, The Story of little Sophia*; *The pet Lamb, and other tales*; and *The Two Brothers, and other tales*; most of which appeared originally in Germany in the 1840s, and were issued in England in the 1850s. According to publisher's advertisements, well over a million copies of *The Basket of Flowers* were issued in Britain before 1855, and it was undoubtedly the most popular tale to appear in England during that decade. The story remained in print well into the 1920s.

Viewed as a whole half-century of endeavour in the field of children's literature, one has to admit that the progress achieved during the period 1800–50 was fitful and unspectacular. Yet conventions were breached, inviolate rules were broken, and by the middle of the century the didactic age was all but finished. Entirely new kinds of books were being written for children, and adult fiction was also in an exciting state of transition. In books for young people, the day of the real-life romance and adventure story, unmoralised and unashamed, was close at hand. The energetic, questing, business-like spirit of the Victorians was gradually loosening the puritanical straight-jacket that had stifled almost all attempts at an honest portrayal of everyday life in juvenile books. The few exceptions that had thumbed their noses at the hell-fire and damnation school can be counted on the fingers of one hand. But they had pointed the way to a new era, in which writers of the highest talent gave their best for young people, and in which a number of works specially written for children were ultimately to take their well-earned places as classics of English literature.

Stories - 1850 and after

By the mid-1850s, the changes that had been gradually taking place during the previous twenty years in the style and character of literature produced for young people had reached a critical stage. Children's books had altered to a degree that makes 1855 a dividing line between the old and the new, between soul-saving didacticism and the modern children's book. The overlap either way was considerable; nevertheless, it can be stated that after that date the majority of children's books contained characters who resembled real children in their attitudes to the family and the world. They were no longer paragons of virtue with all the saint-like attributes; neither were they black-hearted little sinners plunging rapidly to hell.

There was a considerable change of attitude on the part of responsive adults towards the obvious desire of intelligent young people for books that would amuse and entertain them, without at the same time seeking to impose a nagging load of moral responsibility on their unwilling young shoulders. This liberal-minded shift in the public view of children's literature was soon re-

"I HAVN'T TIME TO LOOK AT DOLLS NOW."

flected in the attitude of the more progressive and commercially-minded publishing houses. Stories in which the action was not too heavily clogged by the gum of piety sold better, and tales by these authors were requested more often than those in which sermonising occupied a third of every chapter. A new generation of talented writers was rapidly replacing the black-browed divines and camphorated females who had haunted story books for so long. *Moralise less and sell more* became the unspoken watchword of the leading London publishers, and those in the provinces were not slow to follow their lead.

The literate population of Britain was growing at a pace that must have gladdened the hearts of all those concerned with the book-publishing trade, and the increasing use of the steam-driven printing-press was gradually bringing down the price of books to a level that made them readily accessible. Publishers began to more clearly understand the contrasting and varying needs of boys and girls in different age groups. Children's books began to grow up in size as well as contents. Bindings were re-styled, with spines and covers pictorially blocked in gold on vividly coloured cloths, in order to catch the eyes of teenagers who could now be expected to make their own choice of titles. Books for younger children were designed in formats which the publishers hoped would appeal equally to the mothers, fathers, aunts and uncles who had to foot the bill. Led by Darton & Clark, London, and Thomas Nelson, Edinburgh, who were pioneers in the craft, extensive use began to be made of colour-printed illustrations in children's books. Many of the leading artists and engravers of the day were employed to supply the wood-blocks and plates. The calibre of writing of many children's authors improved to a degree that gave the world a host of titles that are now household names and classics of English literature.

Two great landmarks in the annals of children's books are more fully discussed elsewhere in this work: but it can be said that the appearance of *Alice in Wonderland*, 1865, marked a decisive victory over the now scattered exponents of moral earnestness and that the battle was finally won with the publication of Stevenson's *Treasure Island* in 1883. Children could identify themselves with the Jim Hawkins of the apple-barrel perhaps more easily than Alice in her dream-world of fantasy and make-believe, but both were rational human beings who became as easily excited, bored, irritated and bad-tempered as the boy or girl who turned the pages of their books.

Works specially written for older girls were something of an innovation, and the lead was set by Charlotte Yonge (1823–1901), who in the midst of her 150 or so novels and tales wrote *The Daisy Chain*, 2 vols. 1856, the second edition being issued (also in 2 vols) by Bernhard Tauchnitz, Leipzig, the same year. Miss Yonge's first book, *Le Chateau de Melville*, 1838, was published when she was only fifteen years of age. From 1850 onwards she averaged at least three books a year, as well as acting as a critic, reviewer and as editor of the magazine *The Monthly Packet*, from 1851 to 1894. *The Trial*, 1864, was a continuation of *The Daisy Chain*, her most popular children's book. Amongst her other works for young people were *Henrietta's Wish; or, Domineering*, 1850; *The Little Duke; or, Richard the Fearless*, 1854; *The Railroad Children*, 1855; *Little Lucy's Wonderful Glove*, 1871; and *P's and Q's; the Question of Putting upon*, 1872. She is remembered today for the novel *The Heir of Redclyffe*, 2 vols. 1853, three editions of which appeared that same year. Charlotte Yonge was one of the last of the old guard of children's writers, and to the modern child most of the characters she portrayed would seem the ghosts of another age, like old-fashioned wax-faced dolls bowing and scraping at the pull of a string. Filial obedience was her constantly reiterated theme:

> The things my parents bid me do,
> Let me attentively pursue.

The Stokesley Secret, 1861, and *Countess Kate*, 1862, are the two best books she wrote for children, the latter giving what is probably a pen-portrait of herself as an excitable, wilful, and headstrong little child. The glimpses she gives us of mid-Victorian children released from the drudgery of the schoolroom and scampering home to tea are amongst the many vignettes of family life she recorded so vividly. The Merrifield children in *The Stokesley Secret*, while

The first appearance in book form of one of Mrs Henry Wood's stories for children. Published about 1875 in a particularly vivid cloth binding, the volume contains two other short stories by other authors. The tale was first printed in *The Golden Casket*, 1861, edited by Mary Howitt.

Size across both covers: 22 cm × 17 cm high.

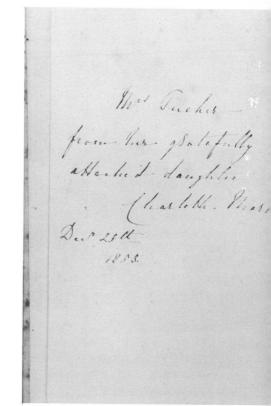

enduring the boredom of the classroom are still recognisable as the ghosts of our own youth breaking up for the holidays:

What an entirely different set of beings were those Stokesley children in lesson-time and out of it! Talk of the change of an old thorn in winter to a May-bush in spring! that was nothing to it!

Poor, listless, stolid, deplorable logs, with bowed backs and crossed ankles, pipy voices and heavy eyes! Who would believe that these were the merry capering creatures, full of fun and riot, clattering and screeching, and dancing about with ecstasy at Sam's information that there was a bonfire by the potatoe-house!

A story which became a best-seller in the juvenile market was *Ministering Children: A Tale dedicated to Childhood*, 1854, by Maria Louisa Charlesworth (1819–80), a vicar's daughter whose children of the title of her book devote their every leisure moment to ministering to the needs of the poor. The book became enormously popular and by the time the continuation of the work appeared some thirteen years later, nearly 100,000 copies had been sold. *Ministering Children, A Sequel*, 1867, is an easier first edition to acquire than the earlier title, but neither work is common. The latter was issued in a binding of full bead-grain cloth over bevelled boards, with the title ornamentally blocked in gold on the front cover and spine. The frontispiece and engraved pictorial title are particularly attractive, and were engraved by C. H. Jeens after the well-known artist J. D. Watson who was famous for his book illustrations. Of Miss Charlesworth's other works for children, her series of 'Reward Books', selected from *Sunday Afternoons in the Nursery*, comprised six little paper-wrappered Bible stories, sold in a packet by Seeley, Jackson & Halliday, London, priced at one shilling. They remained as favourite Sunday school prizes for several decades.

The name of Charlotte Maria Tucker (1825–93) did not appear on any of her 160 works. From the time of publication of her first book, *Claremont Tales; or, Illustrations of the Beatitudes* (1852), she insisted on using the pseudonym 'A.L.O.E.' the initials of the title 'A Lady of England'. *Sketches of the Life of Luther* (1853), was followed by *The White Shroud, and other Poems* (1853), all published by Gall & Inglis, Edinburgh, a house that persisted in not dating the title-pages of the books it issued. One of her earliest children's books was *Wings and Stings*, 1855, followed by *Upwards and Downwards; or, The Sluggard and the Diligent; A Story for Boys*, 1856. But it was not until the appearance of *The Rambles of a Rat*, 1857, published by Thomas Nelson & Sons, Edinburgh, that she found her place in the hearts of children as a storyteller. The adventures of 'Oddity' the piebald rat and his seven brothers who lived in 'a large warehouse, somewhere in the neighbourhood of Poplar, and close to the River Thames', contained little moralising and was a story read with enjoyment by many Victorian children. Like all her early books, this is a difficult first edition to find in the original cloth binding, blocked in blind on the covers and pictorially in gilt on the spine with a picture of a sheaf of corn around which three of the mischievous rats in the story are disporting themselves. *The Giant-Killer*, 1856, and its sequel *The Roby Family*, 1857, were followed by *The Story of a Needle*, 1858; *The Mine; or, Darkness and Light*, 1858; *The Silver Casket; or, The World and its Wiles*, 1864; and *Fairy Know a-bit*, 1866, all published by Thomas Nelson & Sons. Collectors must exercise considerable care when acquiring what they believe to be first editions of works issued by this particular publishing house. Nelson & Sons had a rule that all editions should be dated on the title-pages, not just the first edition as was the practice with many other publishers. But the fact that they dated their titles and gave no indication whatsoever that editions of the same work had been issued previously has made for considerable confusion in the ranks of bibliographers, not least for the late Michael Sadleir. In his *XIX Century Fiction*, 2 vols. 1951, he more than once fell into error with books published by Nelson & Sons, notably with *Martin Rattler*, 1858, by R. M. Ballantyne, which he dated 1859 and then took other bibliographies to task for marking it differently. Nelsons were one of the most prominent and successful publishers of children's books in the 19th century, but it is wise to be cautious when examining the many thousands of juvenile works they issued.

Charlotte Maria Tucker (1825–93) used the pseudonym 'A.L.O.E.' (i.e., A Lady of England) and produced over 160 titles, mostly for children. This presentation copy to her mother, published in 1853, is the rarest of her many works.

Size of title-page:
16.3 cm × 9.6 cm.

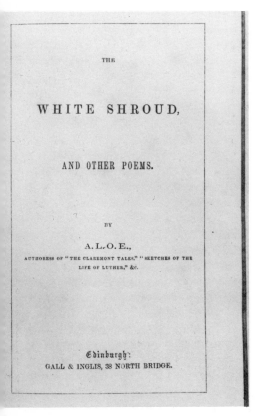

FERN'S HOLLOW.

MARTHA REPULSES THE INVADERS.

[Page 72.

LONDON:
THE RELIGIOUS TRACT SOCIETY;
Instituted 1799.
DEPOSITORIES, 56, PATERNOSTER ROW, 65, ST. PAUL'S CHURCHYARD,
AND 164, PICCADILLY; AND SOLD BY THE BOOKSELLERS.

The first book written by 'Hesba Stretton', shown here as the first issue of the first edition, published undated in 1865.

Size of title-page:
16.4 cm × 9.8 cm.

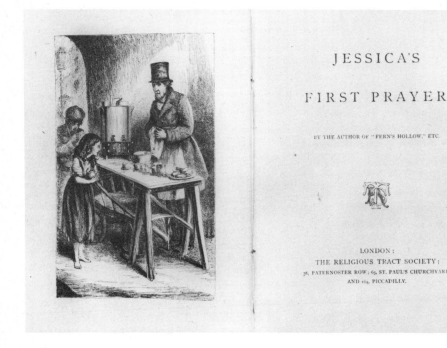

JESSICA'S
FIRST PRAYER

BY THE AUTHOR OF "FERN'S HOLLOW," ETC.

LONDON:
THE RELIGIOUS TRACT SOCIETY;
56, PATERNOSTER ROW; 65, ST. PAUL'S CHURCHYARD;
AND 164, PICCADILLY.

The first issue (with only one previous title mentioned) of a book that sold nearly two million copies and was translated into at least twenty different languages. Written by Sarah Smith (1832–1911), who used the pseudonym 'Hesba Stretton', this first edition was published undated in December 1867, and brought her lasting fame.

Size of title-page:
15.5 cm × 12 cm.

I have said that with Gall & Inglis, who were 'A.L.O.E's' other main publisher, we had the equal difficulty of undated title-pages, and this observation applies to the hundreds of titles issued by The Religious Tract Society. The R.T.S., as it came to be known, published a number of best-sellers in the field of children's books, including the phenomenally successful *Jessica's First Prayer* (1867), by 'Hesba Stretton', the pseudonym of Sarah Smith (1832–1911). She was the daughter of the bookseller, Benjamin Smith, of Wellington, Shropshire, and the word 'Hesba' represented the initial letters of the names of her brothers and sisters. 'Stretton' was a village near her home. Her first appearance in print was a story in *Household Words*, 1859, a magazine edited by Charles Dickens, who gave her every encouragement to continue her career as a writer. Her most famous book, *Jessica's First Prayer*, was first published in the periodical *Sunday at Home*, in 1866, before passing through countless editions in book form. The first issue of the first edition can be identified by the illustration shown above. The distinguishing mark is that only one previous title, *Fern's Hollow*, appears on the title-page. Later issues carry the names of several of her other works, and editions other than the first have an ornamental device of leaves and berries across the top of the title-page. In still later issues, the publisher's monogram is contained in a circle on the centre of the page. Well over a million-and-a-half copies of one of the most popular stories of the Victorian age were sold during the author's lifetime, and the work was translated into every European language and the majority of Asiatic and African tongues. She was undoubtedly the most gifted writer of what has come to be called the 'street-arab school': authors who excited pity on the part of their comfortable and prosperous readers with edifying stories of the horrors of the gin-sodden slums. Hesba Stretton's first book *Fern's Hollow* (1865), is extremely rare (see head of facing page), and few of her first editions are easy to find. *Little Meg's Children* (1868), *Alone in London* (1869), *Under the Old Roof* (1880), and *No Place Like Home* (1881), to name only a few of her many children's books, all follow much the same formula of *Jessica's First Prayer*, in which the little girl in the title, daughter of a brutal and vindictive mother, is brought to an understanding of God's mysterious ways. Barefoot and dressed in rags, she shivers with the cold in the doorway of a fashionable chapel, having been beaten and turned out of doors by her mother. The minister's children discover her, and are faced with a dilemma when they ask her in to hear their father preach:

The little outcast was plainly too dirty and neglected for them to invite her to sit side by side with them in their crimson-lined pew, and no poor people attended the chapel with whom she could have a seat.

These sentiments seemed quite rational to Hesba Stretton's young readers, who rejoiced in Jessica's ultimate good fortune in being looked after by the caretaker and his wife, and being given a job by the minister. 'And many a happy day was spent in helping to sweep and dust the chapel, into which she had crept so secretly at first, her great delight being to attend to the pulpit and the vestry, and the pew where the minister's children sat . . .' Stories of the little street-arabs of London remained firm favourites with the reading public during the whole of the latter half of the 19th century, and R. M. Ballantyne's *Dusty Diamonds Cut and Polished – A Tale of City-Arab Life and Adventure*, 1884, was still in print in 1914. Another particular favourite that sold several hundred thousand copies was *Christie's Old Organ; or, "Home Sweet Home."* (1874), by Mrs O. F. Walton, about a little boy who inherits a barrel-organ from his dying friend and master, old Treffy, and ends his days as a Scripture-reader in the homes of the poor. *A Peep behind the Scenes* (1877), telling the story of the privations suffered by a little girl in a travelling fair, also went through several editions, but none of Mrs Walton's other books achieved quite the popularity of Christie and his little organ. One other evangelistic lady must be mentioned; all the space that can be afforded to the school of pity-the-poor-in-their-proper-place writers for young (and prosperous) readers, whose works crowded the bookshops. Mrs George Cupples (1839–98), was as prolific as her rivals in trade, and her slim little books with such catching titles as *Alice Leighton; or, A Good Name is rather to be chosen than Riches*, 1869, were 'bright cheerful stories, each having for its object the inculcation of the principle implied in the second title of the books', to quote the publisher's advertisements. *Hugh Wellwood's Success; or, Where there's a will there's a way*, 1869, *Bluff Crag; or, A Good Word costs Nothing*, 1882, and *Young Bright-Eye; or, Charlie Harvey's First Voyage* (1878), are typical of her works.

School stories for boys made their appearance in the 1840s, notably with the tale of *The Crofton Boys*, by Harriet Martineau (1802–76). This was first published in 1841 as the last of the four volumes of a series of tales called *The Playfellow*, and was issued as a separate work in 1856. But it was the publication of two books that caused school stories to take the prominent place in children's literature that they held for close on a hundred years. Both works were internationally popular. *Tom Brown's School Days. By an Old Boy*, 1857, was published anonymously by Thomas Hughes, and issued by Macmillan & Co., over a Cambridge imprint. This was the first school story to give a genuine picture of life in an English public school, and was dedicated to Mrs Arnold, the wife of the redoubtable Thomas Arnold. Thomas Hughes (1822–96), was himself educated at Rugby School, where Arnold was headmaster, and his first-hand knowledge of the schoolboy cruelties and firm-chinned loyalties exercised there enabled him to depict school life in a way that swept the book

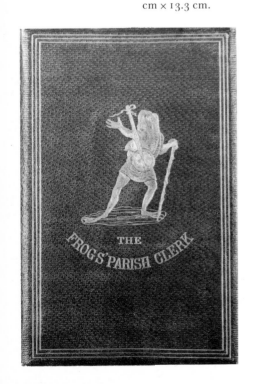

A fairy story by Thomas Archer, published in 1866.

Size of cover: 20.2 cm × 13.3 cm.

into the best-selling bracket within a few months of its first appearance. The work had a considerable influence on the attitude of parents to public schools, but its sequel, *Tom Brown at Oxford*, 3 vols. 1861, was much less successful. Both titles are anything but easy to acquire in the original cloth bindings. The only other work by Hughes that concerns us here is *The Scouring of the White Horse; or, The Long Vacation Ramble of a London Clerk*, 1859, illustrated in characteristic fashion by Richard Doyle who also designed the gold-blocked pictorial covers. It is a book that must have been read by older teenage children with amusement, and a work that is collected today by those interested in the evolution of publishers' binding styles and the history of 19th-century book production, as well as by those seeking a copy of the text.

Within twelve months of the publication of *Tom Brown's School Days* the second notable title depicting boarding-school life appeared. *Eric or Little by Little – A Tale of Roslyn School*, 1858, by Frederic W. Farrar (1831–1903), was published by Adam & Charles Black, Edinburgh. It was the future Dean of Canterbury's first book and one that brought him immediate and lasting fame. Written when he was still a master at Harrow School, the work had little to do with the muscular Christianity of Hughes's earlier tale. The phrase 'little by little' sums up the gradual decline into sinful ways of the hero, Eric Williams, while a boarder at public school. Before the story has progressed very far Eric starts to swear, and then, to secretly smoke. Soon, he downs pints of porter in a low pothouse, punches a master on the nose, steals pigeons from a loft, and almost, but not quite, purloins some cash. Wrongly suspected of theft he runs away to sea, to conditions of the utmost cruelty. In these scenes the author's powers of description seem perceptibly heightened. After the lad has almost broken his leg he is ordered by the brutal captain of the ship to help the rest of the crew hoist sail, but collapses under the effort. He is immediately tied up, his shirt ripped from his back, and then the captain and the crew stand in a semi-circle around the unresisting young boy while the author allows his imagination full play:

Again the rope whistled in the air, again it grided across the boy's naked back, and once more the crimson furrow bore witness to the violent laceration. A sharp shriek of inexpressible agony rang from his lips, so shrill, so heart-rending, that it sounded long in the memory of all who heard it. But the brute who administered the torture was untouched. Once more, and again, the rope rose and fell, and under its marks the blood first dribbled, and then streamed from the white and tender skin.

This passage was suppressed in later editions; but it gives us something of the flavour of the rest of this remarkable work, and indeed it is a vivid example of the style of writing which caused the French to invent a phrase for the '*maladie d'anglais*', sadism. The young hero only just survives his whipping and returns home to learn that he is forgiven. Later, he dies repentant, with a smile on his lips. Farrar's other novels for youth include *Julian Home; A Tale of College Life*, 1859; *St Winifred's; or, The World of School*, 1862; and *The three Homes; A tale of Fathers and Sons*, 1873, issued under the pseudonym 'F.T.L.'.

School stories remained firm favourites for generations, and some of the earlier examples are extremely difficult to find in anything approaching original condition in first edition form. *Tom Brown's School Days* now commands well over £100 ($240) at auction, for copies that could be described as well short of fine condition. *Eric or Little by Little*, although a difficult 'first' to find, fetches less than half this amount.

Another exponent of the saga of school life was Talbot Baines Reed (1852–93), an author who reacted strongly against the sentiments of both Hughes and Farrar by producing his *The Fifth Form at St Dominics*, 1887; *The Cockhouse at Fellsgarth* (1893), and *The Master of the Shell* (1894). The last two titles appeared undated under an R.T.S. imprint, as did his most famous book, *The Adventures of a Three-Guinea Watch* (1883). It was left to Rudyard Kipling to upset all the accepted traditions of school stories with his memorable *Stalky & Co.*, 1899, a deliberately unsentimental and largely autobiographical tale of life in the United Services College in North Devon, a school which the author had attended. H. G. Wells described the three boy heroes of the story as 'mucky little sadists', and one feels the remark well justified after reading of the shoot-

CLIMBING THE FIR-TREE AFTER THE KESTREL'S NEST. P. 263.

An illustration by Arthur Hughes for the 1878 edition of *Tom Brown's School Days*, by Thomas Hughes.

Size of page: 18.8 cm × 12.5 cm.

ing of the school cat (later buried beneath the floorboards of a rival dormitory in order that the subsequent stench would make life unbearable to its inmates), and of the detailed, eight-page description of the slow torture of two tied-up bullies captured in a school ambush. The vigour and stark realism of *Stalky & Co.* had far-reaching effects, not least in seeming to expose the naïvete of all past and contemporary school stories for boys.

The wide diversity of stories and romances for children and young people during the last few decades of the 19th century makes it impossible to give more than a thin cross-section of titles available during this extremely active literary period. The passing of the Elementary Education Act of 1870, and the consequent hunger for books by the increasing number of children who could now read and write, led to expansion and prosperity for publishing houses in general and to those specialising in children's books in particular. The demand for school text-books, school prizes in book form, library books for schools, and a host of other literary needs created a thriving seller's market.

Women writers were still pre-eminent in the story-book world of children, but, with the exception of Anne Bowman (q.v.), they left the field of boys' adventure stories clear for their masculine colleagues. In the USA Louisa M. Alcott (1832–88), wrote *Little Women*, 1868, one of the most popular juvenile books ever published. Drawing on her memories of home, the authoress portrayed the daily lives and doings of four girls – Jo, Meg, Beth, and Amy March – in a New England family of the 19th century, although the influence of Charlotte Yonge's *The Daisy Chain*, 1856, is discernible in the character of Jo, who owes something to the Ethel May of the earlier book. In fact, in the third chapter of *Little Women* Jo is discovered in the attic, 'eating apples and crying over *The Heir of Redclyffe*'. *Little Women* and its sequels passed through countless editions and were translated into almost every foreign language. *An Old Fashioned Girl*, 1870, and *Little Men*, 1871 were the best of her later works, and Louisa Alcott is also remembered as the editor of the successful children's magazine *Merry's Museum*, started in 1867.

Juliana Horatia Ewing (1841–85), was the daughter of Mrs Margaret Gatty (1809–73), whose first book *The Fairy Godmother and Other Tales*, 1851, was followed by her frequently reprinted *Parables from Nature*, issued in five separate series during 1855–71, and later translated into nearly every European language. Mrs Gatty was assisted by her daughter in preparing *Aunt Judy's Tales*, 1859, and the sequel *Aunt Judy's Letters*, 1862, illustrated by Clara Lane and published by Bell & Daldy, London. In May 1866, she founded *Aunt Judy's Magazine*, and her daughter Juliana became the Aunt Judy to whom children addressed their letters. At the same time Juliana was writing books on her own account. The first of her many children's books was *Melchior's Dream, and Other Tales*, 1862, and there was then a gap of nearly seven years before the appearance of *Mrs Overtheway's Remembrances*, 1869, although this story, like a great many others that followed, had been published as a serial in *Aunt Judy's Magazine*, running from May 1866 to October 1868. She took considerable pains over all her many books for the young, polishing the text with infinite care, and revealing a compassionate heart so far as juvenile misbehaviour was concerned, as well as a sense of humour. She married Major Alexander Ewing in 1867, and for many years was forced to live the unsettled existence of an army officer's life. A number of her later books reflected this aspect of her career and had an army setting. These were special favourites of Rudyard Kipling, who said of her *Six to Sixteen*, 1875 (actually a story for girls that first made its appearance in *Aunt Judy's Magazine* in 1872), that he owed more 'in circuitous ways to that tale than I can tell you. I knew it, as I know it still, almost by heart.' All her stories found a wide readership, and all passed through several editions in the course of a few years, after making their first appearances as serials. The most popular were *The Brownies and Other Tales*, 1870; *A Flat Iron for a Farthing*, 1873; *Lob-lie-by-the-Fire; or, The Luck of Lingborough*, 1874: *Jan of the Windmill*, 1876; *Jackanapes* (1884); *Daddy Darwin's Dovecot* (1884); and *Dandelion Clocks* (1887), the earlier titles being published by Bell & Daldy, and the last three by the S.P.C.K. As far as I am aware they did not date any of the many thousands of works issued under their imprint. Mrs Ewing's works attracted the talents of the foremost book illustrators of her day, George Cruikshank, Randolph Caldecott, Gordon Browne, Helen Paterson (afterwards Mrs William

Frontispiece of *The Adventures of a Three-Guinea Watch*, by Talbot Baines Reed. This first edition of the author's first book was published undated in 1883, in an elaborate binding of diagonal fine-ribbed cloth, blocked in gold, silver and black. It was marked as No. 1 in a series called 'The Boy's Own Bookshelf' and later passed through numerous editions.

A Walter Crane frontispiece to the first edition of *The Adventures of Herr Baby*, one of Mary Molesworth's most famous works. She wrote well over a hundred books for children.

"Oh look, look, Baby's made Peepy-Snoozle into 'the parson in the pulpit that couldn't say his prayers,'" cried Denny.—P. 5.

Allingham), J. A. Pasquier, and R. André, among the most prominent names.

From the modern viewpoint, Juliana Ewing's reputation as a writer for juveniles seems to have worn less well than either of her two foremost rivals in the same field, although as mid-Victorian picture story-books they radiate a charm that has endeared them to several generations of collectors of early children's books. Most of them can still be purchased for a few pounds apiece; but to try to acquire her entire output of first editions in book form would be a long and time-consuming task. One tends to bracket her as a writer with Mrs Molesworth and Mrs Hodgson Burnett, the more so since the appearance of Marghanita Laski's excellent review of their work and social backgrounds in her book *Mrs Ewing, Mrs Molesworth and Mrs Hodgson Burnett*, 1950. Their books stand together on my own shelves, those of the last two ladies impressive in full-cloth bindings heavily blocked pictorially in gold, while Mrs Ewing's slim little volumes stand rather primly in a corner in their paper-covered boards. Mary Louisa Molesworth (1839–1921), was a formidable dreadnought of a woman, stately of carriage, precise and dignified in her demands on life and on those around her. As her cousin Mrs Dyson-Laurie later confessed, 'her manner was distant and one worshipped from afar'. Her earliest books were written under the pen name of 'Ennis Graham' and her first children's book *Tell me a Story*, 1875, published by Macmillan & Co., London, and illustrated by Walter Crane, was the forerunner of over a hundred 'child novels'. "*Carrots:*" *Just a Little Boy*, 1876, brought her work to the notice of a wider public, and from that time onwards hardly a year passed without at least one or two books from her pen appearing on the booksellers' counters in time for the Christmas trade. She used a fairy-tale fantasy in many of her

A heavily-gilt pictorial binding on diagonal fine-ribbed cloth. The book was published in 1895.

Size of front cover: 20.6 cm × 14.5 cm.

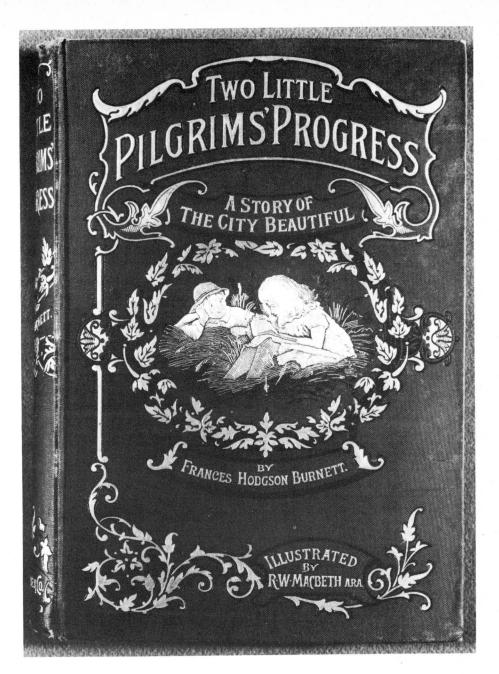

stories, including *The Cuckoo Clock*, 1877; *Four Winds Farm*, 1887; and *An Enchanted Garden*, 1892. Her real-life tales of romance and adventure captured a wide audience of children into their early 'teens. The best of these were *The Tapestry Room, a Child's Romance*, 1879; *A Christmas Child*, 1880; *The Adventures of Herr Baby*, 1881; *Two Little Waifs*, 1883; *"Us", an Old-fashioned Story*, 1885; *The Old Pincushion* (1889); *Nurse Heatherdale's Story*, 1891; '*Farthings*', 1892, and *The Carved Lions*, 1895. The most difficult of her books to find in first edition form is *An Enchanted Garden*, published by T. Fisher Unwin, London, in a binding of 'pinafore' blue and white design cloth, and issued as the eighth volume in their series *The Children's Library*.

The last of our trio was Mrs Frances Hodgson Burnett (1849–1924), an Anglo-American novelist, born in Manchester, England, of poor parents, who emigrated to the USA with her family in 1865, settling near Knoxville, Tennessee. Her first work to be published in book form was *That Lass O' Lowries*, 1877, New York, which appeared as a serial in *Scribner's Magazine* the same year. *Haworth's*, her next novel, was published in 1879; but she is forever remembered by the title that has long since become a household name and a derogatory term: *Little Lord Fauntleroy*, 1886, again issued under a New York imprint. This saccharine picture of a beautifully bred child first appeared as a serial in *St. Nicholas Magazine*, New York, from November 1885 to October 1886. The first English edition, dated 1886, was issued by Frederick Warne & Co., London, and promptly 'ran through England like a sickly fever', to quote the words of F. J. H. Darton in his *Children's Books in*

England, 1932. The story was dramatised in 1888, and a film version appeared in the late 1930s. In less than four years twenty editions of the story were issued in England alone, and it was subsequently translated into nearly every European language. She wrote many other successful children's books, including *Sara Crewe; or, What happened at Miss Minchin's*, 1888; *The Captain's Youngest; Piccino; and Other Stories*, 1894; *Two Little Pilgrim's Progress*, 1895; *In the Closed Room*, 1904; and *Racketty Packetty House*, 1907, all of which appeared first in the USA followed by London editions dated the same year. *The Secret Garden*, 1911, displayed her insight into child psychology and is probably the book that will be accorded pride of place among her works. *The One I Knew the best of All*, 1893, is an autobiographical account of her own childhood, and the first English edition of the same year, published by Frederick Warne & Company, deserves an honoured place in any collection of books devoted to publishers' binding styles of the 19th century. In a diagonally-striped full-cloth binding over bevelled boards, blocked in gold and colours on the front cover and spine, with pictures and emblematic designs by the American artist Reginald Birch, it is a delightful volume to own and admire. A first (American) edition of *Little Lord Fauntleroy* in the original pictorial-cloth binding would now be worth about £50 ($120), but most of the rest of her many titles can be purchased for less than £5 ($12).

Susan Bogart Warner (1819–85) was an American novelist who wrote under the name of 'Elizabeth Wetherell'. She sprang to immediate and lasting fame with her *The Wide, Wide World*, 2 vols. 1850, New York, a pious and sentimental story in which the principal characters are in tears on every other page. Despite the almost complete lack of incident and a paper-thin plot, her description of the emotions of her characters apparently compensated for the absence of action in this and her other stories. *The Wide, Wide World* became a best-seller within a few months of its first appearance and it was as popular in Britain as it was in the USA. *Queechy*, 2 vols. 1852, New York, her next book, was also a success, the first English edition being published by James Nisbet, London, also dated 1852. (It was reissued, dated 1853, the following year.) This two-volume edition appeared in a binding of wavy-grain cloth, with the title blocked in gilt on the front covers and spines. In order to be first in the field, Nisbet rushed copies into the booksellers without having had time to supply any illustrations for the work. The first English illustrated edition was published by George Routledge & Co. London, as a single volume dated 1853, and contained a pictorial title-page and frontispiece. The same firm also issued a single-volume of *The Wide, Wide World*, dated the same year and containing illustrations by William Harvey. Susan Warner's other works for young people include *The Old Helmet*, 1863; *Melbourne House*, 1864; and *Mr Rutherford's Children*, 2 vols. 1853–55, of which she was co-authoress with her sister Anna Warner (1827–1915), who used the pseudonym 'Amy Lothrop'. Anna wrote several novels and children's books in a style similar to that of her more famous sister.

Queechy appeared the same year as *Uncle Tom's Cabin*, 1852, 2 vols., published by John P. Jewett & Company, Boston. Written by Harriet Beecher Stowe (1811–96), it was a book that children the world over annexed as one of their own. It had made its first appearance as a serial in the American magazine *National Era* in 1851–52. The first English edition of Mrs Stowe's famous anti-slavery novel was issued by Clarke & Co., London, dated 1852, but there was not time to incorporate any illustrations. Most other British publishing houses used the text of Clarke & Company's version, and over twenty different editions, all dated 1852, appeared that same year. Children's illustrated editions were legion within a space of a few years, the text often abbreviated and amended. The story was subsequently translated into twenty-three languages.

The tradition of 'man the friend of animals' was a favourite theme in children's books. *Black Beauty: the Autobiography of a Horse* (1877), by Anna Sewell (1820–78), was published by Jerrold & Son, London, and has been in print ever since that date. The story was told in the equine first person singular and its success brought forth a crop of similar works employing every type of animal, reptile, insect, and even plants. The authoress, a Quaker, had been crippled by a leg-injury since she was fourteen years of age, and by the time she came to write *Black Beauty*, her one and only book, she was bedridden. She died a few months after its publication, too early to realise the

The mortality rate among miniature books for children was extremely high; but a few have survived to become sought-after collector's pieces. As an example of size, the red morocco copy in the centre of the picture measures 3.2 cm × 2.5 cm, and dates from *c*. 1845. A sheet of the original embossed-and-gilt Dutch flowered paper extensively used for binding children's books can also be seen.

CHILDREN'S
BREAD;
OR,
DAILY TEXTS FOR THE
YOUNG.

FOURTH EDITION.

RELIGIOUS TRACT SOCIETY
56, PATERNOSTER ROW,
AND 65, ST. PAUL'S CHURCHYARD.

SMALL RAIN
UPON THE
TENDER HERB

LONDON
Religious Tract Society
56 Paternoster Row

Adam & Eve

Cain & Abel

Cinderella was so happy, she entirely
forgot her Godmother's warning; and
the time had passed so quickly, she
did not think it was more than
eleven, when the first stroke of
midnight sounded. She jumped up
from her seat by the side of the
Prince, rushed
across the room,
and flew downstairs.

The Prince ran after
her; but he was
too late.

Left
A design by Edouard de Beaumont for
Cinderella and the Two Gifts, 1887, a portfolio
of thirty-three printed and hand-coloured
single-sided leaves issued in a drop-sided
box.

Size: 40 cm × 30 cm.

extent of its phenomenal success. A first edition, in the original orange-brown cloth, is now worth in the region of £150 ($360). Another famous title in the same field is *Tarzan of the Apes*, 1914, by Edgar Rice Burroughs (1875–1950), which must have the imprint of A.C. McClurg & Co., Chicago, to be a first edition. The book remained in the best-sellers list for years, and over 25 million copies of it and its sequels have been purchased. Amongst his later books were *The Return of Tarzan*, 1915, *The Beasts of Tarzan*, 1917, *Tarzan the Terrible*, 1921, *Tarzan the Invincible*, 1931, and *Tarzan the Magnificent*, 1939, all first issued under American imprints. He was also early in the field of science fiction and contributed *A Princess of Mars*, 1917, *The Warlord of Mars*, 1919, and *Lost on Venus*, 1935. None of the Tarzan books are easy to find as first editions, and *Tarzan of the Apes*, 1914, is now catalogued at well over £100 ($240).

Kate Greenaway (1846–1901) is represented in the collection by half a shelf of slim volumes in assorted sizes, starting with the first book she illustrated, *Diamond and Toads*, 1871, and then her second, *School Days in Paris* (1874), by Margaret S. Jeune. Neither of these works display in her drawings any of the quaintly dressed little children that were later to capture the public taste, or the fluency of style that has made her work sought after by collectors on both sides of the Atlantic. It was not until *Under the Window* (1878), made its appearance in its glazed pictorially-printed paper-covered boards, engraved in colour by Edmund Evans, that her name became widely known to the general public. Despite the fact that a first edition of 20,000 copies was printed, the volume is always extremely difficult to find in clean original condition, and now fetches anything up to £35 ($84). *A Day in a Child's Life* (1881); *Mother*

Published in 1902 by Macmillan & Co., the first edition was illustrated by the author, who also designed the pictorial cover.

Size of cover: 24 cm × 18 cm.

Goose (1881); *Language of Flowers* (1884); and *The Pied Piper of Hamelin* (1888) by Robert Browning were all illustrated in the inimitable style that made her an equal favourite with children and adults. *The Queen of the Pirate Isle* (1886), by Bret Harte, was one of the most successful examples of her talents as a book illustrator and was described by her friend John Ruskin as 'the best thing you have ever done – it is so real and natural'. Also collected by children of her day, but now in a price bracket that puts them beyond the reach of collectors of moderate means, are her series of little almanacks, although they have no real place in this chapter. A complete set, from its beginning in 1883 to the conclusion of the series in 1897 (missing the year 1896 for which there was no issue) comprises a total of fourteen volumes. Most of them were originally published in envelope dust-wrappers, marked ready for the post. The issue for 1897, bound in leather, is much the rarest, and that for 1889 is also difficult to find. A full set in good condition in their original pictorially-printed boards could now be priced in antiquarian booksellers' catalogues at anything up to £500 ($1200). Her *Queen Victoria's Jubilee Garland*, published in illustrated wrappers in 1887, was also engraved and printed by Edmund Evans, whose press was responsible for all her important work. It now fetches in the region of £60 ($144). *Kate Greenaway's Carols*, printed in colours by Edmund Evans on a stiff board, for hanging in the nursery, is a rare item and very few copies appear to have survived. George Routledge & Sons, London, published the majority of her first editions; those bearing the imprint of Frederick Warne & Co., London, are late editions of little value. Finally, I must mention the definitive work that has long been a collector's item in its own right, *Kate Greenaway*, 1905, by M. H. Spielmann and G. S. Layard, published by Adam & Charles Black, London. The edition-deluxe of this magnificent volume was limited to 500 copies, each of which contains an original pencil drawing by Kate Greenaway inserted at the front of the book. This is the standard reference book on the artist, and the limited edition is now catalogued at over £200 ($480).

An American author who found his most popular works pirated by British publishers was John Habberton (1842–1921), who is today remembered almost exclusively for his best-selling novel *Helen's Babies*, 1876, which he published anonymously as 'by their latest victim, Uncle Harry'. He was one of the first writers to amuse his readers with his own vocabulary of baby language and the lisps and inversions of early youth. *Helen's Babies* can be read today with almost the same amusement one finds in reading *The Diary of a Nobody* (1892), by George and Weedon Grossmith, a work quickly discovered by teenage children as a hilarious piece of domestic strife, although never meant for their eyes. The first English edition of *Helen's Babies*, 1877, was published in December 1876, by David Bryce & Son, Glasgow, complete with a pictorial title-page, and issued as a square octavo in a smooth-cloth binding with gilt leaf-edges. Another edition, also dated 1877, appeared later in that year and was published in a pictorial binding (but without illustrations) by William Mullan & Son, London. To find any early edition in good condition is difficult, the book having apparently been nearly 'read to death'.

Much the same fate awaited the first edition of *The Story of the Treasure Seekers*, 1899, by Edith Nesbit (1858–1924), afterwards Mrs Hubert Bland. She had previously tried her hand at several styles of writing with little success, but the enthusiastic reviews of Andrew Lang brought her to the notice of a wide public. She and her first husband were founder members of the Fabian Society. Although she aspired to be recognised as a poet, her children's books brought her fame. From the time that *The Story of the Treasure Seekers* appeared, she was established as a leading writer of what came to be known as 'modern' children's stories of family life. The book was episodic, and various chapters previously appeared in the *Pall Mall Magazine*, the *Windsor Magazine*, *The Illustrated London News*, and *Nister's Holiday Annual*, during 1898. The adventures of the Bastable children in search of a fortune (to quote the sub-title of the work) continued in *The Would-be-Goods*, 1901, dedicated to the authoress's son, Fabian, who died suddenly in his sixteenth year, and ended in the last of the trilogy, *New Treasure Seekers*, 1904. All three volumes were published by T. Fisher Unwin, London, and illustrated by Gordon Browne and Lewis Baumer. Her stories had a direct appeal to the imaginations of children and

The first edition of a popular children's book by 'F. Anstey' (T. A. Guthrie), published in 1903.

Size of front cover:
21.3 cm × 15.5 cm.

E. V. Lucas (1868–1938), journalist, essayist, and critic, also wrote several stories for children. *The Slowcoach*, 1910, was published by Wells, Gardner, Darton & Co., with 16 full-page coloured plates and a map.

Size of front cover:
20 cm × 13.5 cm.

have been popular ever since their first appearance, with several still in print today. Of the thirty or so that followed the best are probably *The Story of the Amulet*, 1906, *The Railway Children*, 1906, *The Enchanted Castle*, 1907, *The Magic City*, 1910, *Wet Magic* (1913), and *Five of Us – and Madeline*, 1925.

Vice Versa: or A Lesson to Fathers, 1882, published by Smith, Elder, & Co., London, has always been a difficult 'first' to acquire, and the author, Thomas Anstey Guthrie (1856–1934), better known by his pseudonym of 'F. Anstey', is far from easy to collect complete. *Paleface and Redskin*, 1898, and *Only Toys!*, 1903, are the best known of his later children's books, although he achieved a considerable reputation as a novelist with such titles as *Voces Populi*, 1890; *The Man from Blankley's*, 1893; and *The Brass Bottle*, 1900; all of which had a considerable appeal for older children. So did the novels of John Meade Falkner (1858–1932) although he wrote only four. The last, just completed and still in manuscript form, he left in a railway carriage and never saw again. *The Lost Stradivarius*, 1895, *Moonfleet*, 1898, and *The Nebuly Coat*, 1903, have been read by generations of older teenagers and adults, and the second has established itself as a near-classic adventure story in the tradition of Stevenson's *Treasure Island*. Entirely different in concept were the stories and tales of G. E. Farrow (1866–1920), who achieved considerable success with *The Wallypug of Why* (1895), and its six sequels of which *The Wallypug in London*, 1898, and *In Search of the Wallypug*, 1903, are typical examples. *The Missing Prince*, 1896, *The Little Panjandrum's Dodo*, 1899, *Baker Minor and the Dragon*, 1902, and *Professor Philanderpan*, 1904, are amongst his many other stories, most of which were published by C. Arthur Pearson, London.

Two other minor authors whose books were widely read by children in the older age groups were E. H. Knatchbull-Hugessen (Baron Brabourne) (1829–93) a great-nephew of Jane Austen; and Sir Edward Abbott Parry (1863–1943), most of whose works were inscribed by 'His Honour Judge Parry'. Knatchbull-Hugessen contributed stories derived from folk tales and legends, including *Stories for my Children*, 1869, *Tales at Tea-Time*, 1872, *Queer Folk*, 1874, *Whispers from Fairyland*, 1875, and *River Legends*, 1875, this last work with illustrations by Gustave Doré. Judge Parry's tales covered a wider spectrum: *Katawampus: its treatment and cure*, 1895, was followed by a sequel entitled *Butterscotia; or, A Cheap Trip to Fairy Land*, 1896. *The First Book of Krab*, 1897, was illustrated by Archie MacGregor and published by David Nutt, London, as were the author's first two books. *The Scarlet Herring*, 1899, and *Gamble Gold*, 1907, are both fine examples of publishers' binding styles of the period, while *Don Quixote of the Mancha, retold by Judge Parry*, 1900, is one of the most difficult Walter Crane illustrated books to find in acceptable condition. A book standing alone on the same shelf that well deserves a mention is *Toyland*, 1875, by Arthur and Eleanor O'Shaughnessy. This was the Irish poet's only children's book, and one in which his wife was co-author.

The name of Kenneth Grahame (1859–1932), is now as famous as the book which has brought him lasting fame, *The Wind in the Willows*, 1908, published by Methuen & Co., London, with a frontispiece by Graham Robertson. This is a difficult and expensive first edition to acquire, and as it is almost indistinguishable from the second edition (also published in October 1908) a word of warning is necessary. In the past, copies have been sold to collectors as 'firsts' when in fact they are later editions, with the tell-tale words carefully erased from their title-pages. There is one sure method to distinguish the true first edition from subsequent fakes. The first edition of 1908 is blocked on the front cover pictorially in gold, while later early editions are blocked in blind only. Otherwise the spine, and the rest of the book is much the same, although in unsophisticated copies the words 'second edition' (or later) are printed on the title-page and the number of impressions on the verso of the same leaf. *Toad of Toad Hall*, 1929, by A. A. Milne, was the first printing of the play made from Grahame's book. *The Golden Age*, 1895, was partly derived from the author's first book, *Pagan Papers*, 1894, which has a title-page designed by Aubrey Beardsley. *Fun O' the Fair*, 1929, was Grahame's last children's book and was adapted from his essay *Sanger and his Times*. Issued in a binding of orange-coloured paper-wrappers as one of J. M. Dent & Sons *Elian Greeting-Booklets*, its fragile binding has ensured that not many copies will survive the ravages of time.

Several ladies no bibliographer of children's books would wish to ignore

HOOPS.

PRISONER'S BASE.

IN THE PLAY-GROUND.

IN THE GARDEN.

RACKETS.

PEG IN THE RING.

HARE AND HOUNDS.

WIDDY WIDDY WAY.

Left and right
Two pages from *Warne's Picture Book* (1878), a folio-sized volume with 'upwards of 500 illustrations by every artist of eminence during the last twenty years'. The book was issued in a binding of coloured pictorially-printed paper-covered boards, with 96 pages of pictures.

Size of pages: 32.5 cm × 25 cm.

Angela Brazil (1868–1947), was herself once head-girl at a boarding school, and is distinguished as founder of a genre of girls' school stories, of which she wrote over 60.

Size of title-page: 18.5 cm × 12 cm.

must be mentioned before I bring this all too short a chapter to a close. Mrs Gene Stratton-Porter (1863–1924) was one of the most popular American novelists during the early part of the 20th century, and many of her books have become firm favourites with children on both sides of the Atlantic Ocean. *Freckles*, 1904, *A Girl of the Limberlost*, 1909, *Laddie*, 1913, and *The Keeper of the Bees*, 1925, are typical of her titles in which idealism, sentimentality, and the joys of the outdoor life receive equal prominence. *A Girl of the Limberlost* has never been out of print since its first appearance. Bertha Upton (1849–1912) supplied the text for a memorable series of oblong story books in verse, while her daughter, Florence K. Upton (1873–1922), brought them to life with her pictures of wooden dolls and the universally loved nursery favourite the 'Golliwogg'. Florence invented both the name and the little shock-haired figure who first appeared in this unique series of picture books, all published by Longmans, Green & Co., London. *The Adventures of Two Dutch Dolls* (1895) was the first of the many titles in which Mrs Upton and her talented daughter co-operated, all issued in oblong-quarto format, in a binding of glazed pictorially-printed paper-covered boards with cloth spines, and each having 64 pages of text and illustrations. *The Golliwogg's Bicycle Club* (1896), the first issue of which has the copyright declaration printed on the front cover but has no mention of other titles in the series; *The Golliwog at the Sea-Side* (1898); *The Golliwogg in War* (1899); *The Golliwogg's Polar Adventures* (1900); and continuing in similar style until the appearance of *The Golliwogg in the African*

THE APPLE STALL. DRESSING UP.

THE SNOW MAN. THE SQUIRREL.

Jungle (1908). Two books issued in identical format, but not featuring the Dutch dolls Sarah Jane, Peg, Meg, Weg, and the Midget, this last being a tiny version of her bigger sisters, or the longed-for Golliwogg, lacked the magic that endeared the rest of the titles to several generations of children: *The Vege-Men's Revenge* (1897), and *The Adventures of Barbee and the Wisp* (1905), were experiments not repeated. Due to their unusual size and shape, and the fact that their covers easily soil, Golliwogg books are difficult to find in good condition and dealers ask high prices for those that have managed to survive intact. During World War I, Florence Upton gave her entire collection of manuscripts, drawings, and the original Golliwogg and Dutch dolls, to the Red Cross. They were auctioned in London and fetched nearly £500 ($1200), the money being used to buy an ambulance. The purchaser, Miss Faith Moore, donated the collection to Chequers, the British Prime Minister's official country residence in the Chilterns, and there Golliwogg and his friends have found a permanent resting place in an illuminated glass-case in the Long Gallery.

Helen Bannerman (1863–1946), married an army doctor and spent much of her life in India. In 1899, when she was returning there after leaving her two small daughters to be educated in her native Scotland, she wrote and illustrated a miniature book which she called *The Story of Little Black Sambo*. She sent it to her children who loved it so much that friends sent it to a London publishing house. It was published, dated 1899, as No. 4 in the series *The*

Dumpy Books for Children, which Grant Richards were issuing at eighteen pence each. It passed through five editions in the course of twelve months, and before another year was out *Little Black Sambo* was a household name in both Britain and the USA. The last copy of the first edition to be catalogued was priced at exactly £100 ($240). Although Helen Bannerman never achieved quite such a startling success with her many later stories and tales, most of which were issued in a similar miniature format by James Nisbet & Co., London, all of her titles were popular with smaller children and all passed through several large editions. *The Story of Little Black Mingo*, 1901; *The Story of Little Black Quibba*, 1902; and *The Story of Little Black Bobtail*, 1909; are typical titles.

Beatrix Potter (1866–1943), also wrote and illustrated little books. She insisted they should remain tiny to suit the little hands into which they were meant to find their way. She lived in the Lake District, near Ambleside, Westmorland, and there, at 'Hill Top' Farm, she produced the diminutive volumes that young people the world over have loved and enjoyed ever since. *The Tale of Peter Rabbit* (1901), was the first to appear, privately-printed by Strangeways & Sons in an edition of 250 copies; to be followed by a second privately-printed edition of 200 copies in February 1902, with the text revised and corrected. It was when the first published edition of 1902 appeared, under the imprint of Frederick Warne & Co., that success was quickly apparent. In the meantime Beatrix Potter wrote and privately published *The Tailor of*

From *The Motor Car Dumpy Book*, the earliest children's book to have a 'motor car' title-page. The series of *Dumpy Books for Children*, 1900–5, extended over thirty titles at 2s. each.

Left
A selection of the first published editions of tales by Beatrix Potter (1866–1943) which became known as the 'Peter Rabbit' series.
Size of *Squirrel Nutkin*: 14.5 cm × 10.5 cm.

From *Number One Joy Street*. The first of the series of 'Joy Street' books was published in 1923 by Basil Blackwell, Oxford. They contained a medley of prose and verse by leading writers of the day, with coloured plates tipped-in on tinted paper.

Size of page: 24.3 cm × 18 cm.

Below and below left
Two small first editions exceedingly difficult to find in their original cloth bindings. *The Oogley OO* (1903), by Gerald Sichel, with text by S. C. Woodhouse, caught the imagination of children and was a popular favourite before World War I. *The Story of Little Black Mingo* (1901), by Helen Bannerman, followed her successful *The Story of Little Black Sambo*, 1899.
Height: 13.5 cm.

THE STORY OF

LITTLE BLACK MINGO

Gloucester, 1902, a story she described as her 'favourite among the little books'. It, too, was published by Warne, dated 1903, continuing a run of her works that became famous as the 'Peter Rabbit' books. First editions carry the Warne imprint and are dated on their title-pages as well as having a copyright inscription on the verso. The first privately-printed issues fetch anything up to £120 ($288); while the rest of her titles vary from £5 ($12) to £25 ($60). These include *The Tale of Squirrel Nutkin*, 1903; *The Tale of Benjamin Bunny*, 1904; *The Tale of Two Bad Mice*, 1904; *The Pie and the Patty-Pan*, 1905; *The Tale of Mr. Jeremy Fisher*, 1906; *The Tale of Jemima Puddle-Duck*, 1908; *The Tale of the Flopsy Bunnies*, 1909; *The Tale of Timmy Tiptoes*, 1911; and *The Tale of Mr. Tod*, 1912. Two titles issued in a larger format were *The Roly-Poly Pudding*, 1908; and *Ginger and Pickles*, 1909; while *The Tale of Little Pig Robinson*, 1930, was a late addition to her list of works for children. Her last book to appear was published posthumously in 1956 by Frederick Warne & Co., under their New York imprint, and was titled *The Tale of the Faithful Dove*.

Few children's story books of the 1920s are still genuinely alive in the sense of being reprinted for modern reading, or achieved sufficient success in their own decade to be sought after by literary historians and bibliographers. The long series of 'William' books from the pen of Miss Richmal Crompton Lamburn (1890–1969), who wrote under the name of Richmal Crompton, is an exception. Originally a school-teacher, she started her career as a writer by submitting schoolboy stories to the *Home Magazine* in 1920, and later to the more popular *Happy Magazine*. The publishers, Newnes, decided to issue a collection of her stories in book form. *Just William*, 1922, was the first title in a series that continued for over 45 years (36 different stories were published by the end of 1966), and brought their authoress both fame and fortune. *More William*, 1922; *William Again*, 1923; and *William the Fourth*, 1924; are typical of a series of hilarious tales about a mischievous schoolboy that have now sold over ten million copies.

The early 1930s witnessed the beginning of a new and exciting trend in English children's literature by the appearance of *Swallows and Amazons*, 1930, by Arthur Ransome (1884–1967), written when he was forty-six years of age with over a quarter of a century's writing for adults behind him. The first edition had no illustrations and caused little stir; but the publication of the second edition, with illustrations by Clifford Webb and end-paper maps by Steven Spurrier, was praised by reviewers and did much to ensure the work's continuing success. *Swallowdale*, 1931, was followed by *Peter Duck*, 1932, a book received enthusiastically by critics. The trio now really began to sell, and sell extremely well. By the time that *Winter Holiday*, 1933, had made its appearance Arthur Ransome was established as one of the foremost writers for children. *Coot Club*, 1934; *Pigeon Post*, 1936; *We Didn't Mean to Go to Sea*, 1937; *Secret Water*, 1939; *The Big Six*, 1940; *Missee Lee*, 1941; *The Picts and the Martyrs*, 1943, and *Great Northern*, 1947; include all his famous children's holiday stories, now known as the 'Swallows and Amazons' books, each deserving a place in any collection devoted to the history of children's books.

The revival of interest in children's literature both here in Britain and in the USA during the first half of the 20th century is shown by the institution of medals and awards for writers and others concerned in the production of children's books. The USA has The Newbery Medal, awarded annually to the author of the most distinguished contribution to literature for children in the country. The first two winners were Hendrik Willem van Loon for his *The Story of Mankind*, 1921; and Hugh Lofting for his *The Voyages of Dr Dolittle*, 1922. The Caldecott Medal has been awarded annually since 1938 to the best American picture book for children. Britain has two principal awards in the field of children's books, both presented annually by the Library Association, whose magazine *The Junior Bookshelf* has been a most successful and useful publication since its first number in 1936. The Carnegie Medal has been awarded annually since 1936 (when it was won by Arthur Ransome with *Pigeon Post*) for an outstanding book for children published during the preceding year and written by a British subject living in the country. The Kate Greenaway Medal, inaugurated in 1955, is awarded to the British artist who produced the most distinguished work in the illustration of children's books during the preceding year. The first winner was Edward Ardizzone, for his book, *Tim All Alone*.

Boys' Adventure Stories

The second half of the 19th century witnessed the birth of the adventure story specially written for boys of all ages. A debt is owed by many British writers in this field to their American counterparts, who had earlier helped blaze the trail. James Fenimore Cooper (1789–1851), had listened to the tales of the Indian wars told by his father Judge William Cooper, with much the same fervour that kept young Walter Scott silent and attentive while grey-bearded relatives recounted their personal adventures in the troubles of '45. As Scott used his first-hand knowledge of the Highlands and Borders of Scotland when writing the first historical novels, so Cooper added life and colour to his father's tales by his own exploring expeditions in the backwoods and prairies of North America. The result was a series of adventure stories that came to be known as *Leather-Stocking Tales*, starting with *The Pioneers*, 2 vols. New York 1823; and continuing with *The Last of the Mohicans*, 2 vols. Philadelphia, 1826; *The Prairie*, 1827; *The Pathfinder*, 2 vols. Philadelphia, 1840, and *The Deerslayer; or, The First War-Path*, 2 vols. Philadelphia, 1841; all of which were soon adopted by children all over the world. He wrote many other novels, the rarest of his first editions being *The Water Witch*, 3 vols. Dresden, Germany, 1830, a copy in the original boards, complete with all its half-titles, now being worth in the region of £750 ($1,800). Most of his stories and tales were published in England hard on the heels of their first appearance in the USA and were usually dated the same year. By the mid-1830s Cooper's name was internationally famous, and it was he, more than any other writer, who created the legend of the Redskin and Paleface that gave birth to the 'Cowboys and Indians' saga that continues in children's games, Western novels and films, and the elaborate television presentations of the present day.

It was left to Frederick Marryat (1792–1848), sea captain and novelist, to be the first to intentionally create plots and characters in his romances and adventure stories aimed specifically at a juvenile audience. Cooper's works had been discovered and read by at least one generation of children before the publishing profession awoke to the fact that here was a ready-made series of tales for which the teenage youth of the day was avidly waiting. Before long *The Last of the Mohicans* and several of his other novels and romances were reissued in single-volume form, dressed in a variety of brightly-gilt cloth bindings specially designed to attract the young. Marryat, however, made it quite clear on the title-pages of several of what proved to be his most popular works that it was children and young people he had in mind when he wrote these particular books. *Masterman Ready; or, The Wreck of the Pacific*, 3 vols. 1841, had the words 'Written for Young People' across its title-page; as did *The Settlers in Canada*, 2 vols. 1844; and *The Mission: or, Scenes in Africa*, 2 vols. 1845. His earlier works, such as *The Naval Officer*, 3 vols. 1829; *The King's Own*, 3 vols. 1830; *Peter Simple*, 3 vols. Philadelphia, 1833–4; *Jacob Faithful*, 3 vols. Philadelphia, 1834; *Japhet in Search of a Father*, first issued in four parts, New York, 1835–6; and *Mr. Midshipman Easy*,

A cover design by R. M. Ballantyne for one of the most difficult of his first editions to find in original state. It was published in 1881.
Size of cover: 17.5 cm × 12 cm.

3 vols. 1836, and several other titles, are all taken from personal experience during his naval career both ashore and afloat. They made an instant appeal to the minds of young readers, although the original format of several of these novels had been designed to attract an adult readership. With *The Children of the New Forest*, 2 vols. (1847), his publisher, H. Hurst, of Charing Cross, London, made concessions to attract young people to buy the work, or, what is more likely, have it purchased for them, by designing eye-catching title-pages brightly printed in glowing reds and greens. He did the same when *The Little Savage* was published in two volumes in 1848–9, this time having the words 'The Juvenile Library' blocked in gold on the front covers. The tentative beginnings of a specialised publishing industry channelled to provide books for teenagers rather than children in general could be discerned in this decade, although it was another thirty years or more before firms almost solely devoted to satisfying the needs of this age group flooded the Christmas counters of the bookshops with the vividly-bound pictorial-cloth-covers of adventure stories for the twelve- to eighteen-year-olds. A large and eager body of young readers at an age when reading was one of the primary and most absorbing pleasures in life, discovered that at last there were shelves and walls of freshly printed books that had been written and designed for their personal pleasure and enjoyment.

Edinburgh was the birthplace in 1825 of a Scot who was to be the first writer for boys to allow the youthful heroes of his tales a free hand to wander far from home in any upright and God-fearing manner they liked, un-restrained by the curbing hands and stifling platitudes of well-meaning accompanying adults. Robert Michael Ballantyne (1825–94), was appren-ticed as a clerk in the Hudson's Bay Company of Canada at the age of sixteen, returning to his native Scotland in 1847 to discover that his mother had carefully preserved all the long and intimate letters he had written to his family during the six years in the backwoods of Rupert's Land. These formed the basis of his first book, *Hudson's Bay; or Every-Day Life in the Wilds of North America*, 1848, the first edition privately printed and published at the author's expense, although it carried the imprint of William Blackwood, Edinburgh. The second (or first published) edition appeared dated the same year. The work was an autobiographical account of the youthful author's experiences in the Far North, but was far from being a financial success. Blackwoods were at fault in not preparing the volume in a style attractive to juvenile readers. Both editions were issued in an austere plain-grey cloth, unrelieved by any gold blocking on either cover. This was far too dignified a format to attract prospective young purchasers and the remainder of copies languished on the shelves until the end of 1853. Ballantyne's hopes of a career as an author received a set-back and it was not until some eight years after the first appear-ance of *Hudson's Bay* that his next book for young people appeared. *Snowflakes and Sunbeams; or, The Young Fur Traders*, 1856 (the first part of the title was dropped after three editions) was an immediate success and went far to establish the man who was to become the hero of Victorian youth and the first of the best-selling authors in the teenage market. But it was not until the appearance of the work with which the reading public will always associate his name, that he finally decided to make writing his future career. *The Coral Island: A Tale of the Pacific Ocean*, 1858, issued with a series of eight full-page coloured plates by T. Nelson & Sons, Edinburgh, at six shillings (72 cents) a copy, has been continually in print up to this present day. Despite this, Ballantyne received a total of only £90 ($216) from his publishers for writing a work which must have earned the company many thousands of pounds, having sold them the copyright for a mere fraction of its true value. Such was the fate of many an impecunious author in the mid-19th century, despite the protection which the Copyright Act of 1842 should, in theory, have provided.

Ballantyne set all his fictional tales against a factual and well-researched background, visiting whenever possible the regions and localities in which the action of his stories was supposed to take place. *Ungava: A Tale of Esquimaux-Land*, 1858; *The World of Ice*, 1860; *Silver Lake; or, Lost in the Snow*, 1867; *The Giant of the North*, 1882; *The Big Otter*, 1887; *The Buffalo Runners; A Tale of the Red River Plains*, 1891; and *The Walrus Hunters*, 1893, and several other titles, were written with the knowledge derived from his experiences in the service of the Hudson's Bay Company, as of course were *Hudson's Bay*, 1848, and *The Young Fur Traders*, 1856. *The Lifeboat*, 1864; *Freaks on the Fells*, 1865; *The Lighthouse*, 1865; *Fighting the Flames*, 1867; *Deep Down; A Tale of the Cornish Mines*, 1868; *The Floating Light of the Goodwin Sands*, 1870; *The Iron Horse; or, Life on the Line*, 1871: these titles and many others, were only written after the author had experienced weeks inside a lighthouse, worked as a crew-member of a fire-brigade, made a series of underground visits to Cornish tin and copper mines, trips on the footplate of an express train, among other adventures. But with *The Coral Island*, he was forced to rely on evidence that was secondhand and made several factual mistakes, notably in regarding cocoa-nuts growing on trees in exactly the same form as they are found in greengrocers' shops. Ballantyne had read up the subject of the South Seas and desert islands before he settled down to write what proved to be his most famous book. He obtained much of the background from *Recent Exploring Expeditions to the Pacific, and the South Seas*, 1853, by J. S. Jenkins; but his most fruitful source book was *The Island Home; or, The Young Cast-Aways*, by an American writer, James F. Bowman, first published in Boston, USA in 1851, although Ballantyne used the text of the edition of 1852, published by Nelson's of Edinburgh. Bowman was a Californian author who wrote under the pseudonym of 'Christopher Romaunt'. He was for many years the editor of the *San Francisco Chronicle*, a journalist rather than an author by profession, for the only separate publication of his that has survived in book form appears to be *The Island Home*. But he has more than earned his place in the annals of English literature by this one book, for it seems certain that Ballantyne lifted a great deal of his plot for *The Coral Island* from its pages and this work in its turn had a profound influence on the young Robert Louis Stevenson, ultimately leading to his introduction to the islands of the South Seas and his settling in Samoa in 1888. In 1883 that immortal classic

R. M. Ballantyne's inscription in the copy of *Shifting Winds; A Tough Yarn*, 1866, which he presented to his newly married wife.

Size of page: 17 cm × 11.5 cm.

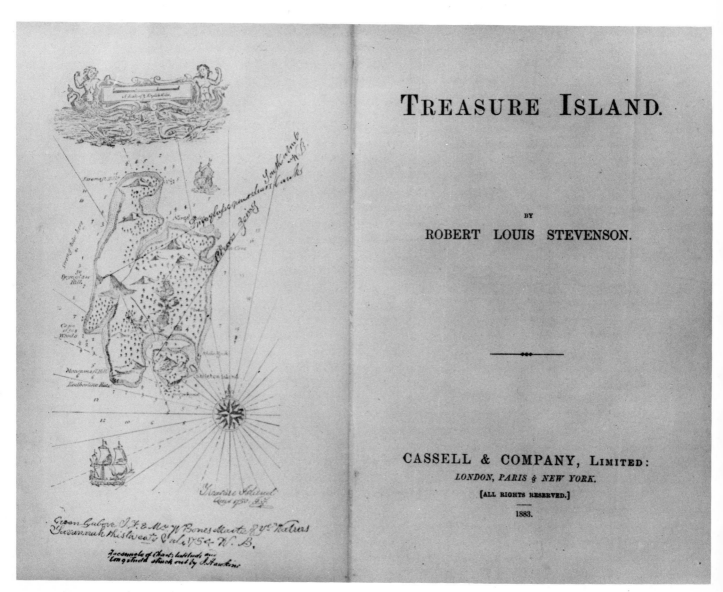

R. M. Ballantyne (1825–94), supplied illustrations for nearly all of his hundred or more books. This original drawing is a self-portrait of the author in the Botallack Tin Mine, Cornwall, made when he was writing *Deep Down: A Tale of the Cornish Mines*, 1868.

of romance and adventure for boys of all ages, *Treasure Island* was published. It had made a first appearance as a serial in *Young Folks* from late in 1881, under the title of 'The Sea Cook; or, Treasure Island'. From the time that the narrator, the lad Jim Hawkins, takes up the tale at the start of the book, until that plausible but likeable one-legged old schemer and double-dyed villain, Long John Silver, slips over the side of the 'Hispaniola' to safety, leaving the squire's party the vast bulk of the treasure, the tale grips and thrills each succeeding generation of young readers to a degree unequalled by almost any other adventure story of this or any other age. The story of the boy Stevenson's meeting with Ballantyne, a man he thought to be a giant in the world of literature and a hero on whose head it was impossible to bestow sufficient praise, may be read in *Ballantyne the Brave*, 1967, my biography of the author of *Coral Island*. Stevenson's passionate love of the romantic islands of the South Seas, to one of which he eventually retired, was first kindled by reading of the adventures of Ballantyne's three heroes Ralph, Jack and Peterkin, as they fought the cannibals and braved the dangers of their remote coral strand. *Treasure Island*, unsurpassed as a straightforward adventure story for boys, might never have been written had not *The Coral Island* stirred the young author-to-be's imagination to an extent that made it his favourite book in his formative teenage years. Ballantyne's own debt to James Bowman can be equated to some extent to Bowman's obligation to Daniel Defoe and Johann Wyss, the latter's *Swiss Family Robinson* having been first published in two parts in Zürich, 1812–3, with an English translation appearing a year later.

W. H. G. Kingston (1814–80) was a Londoner by birth, but spent many years in Oporto in his father's business, his frequent voyages between England and Portugal instilling a love of the sea that was later reflected in the many seafaring adventure stories he wrote. Unlike Ballantyne, who never attempted any fictional work for the adult market, Kingston started his literary career with the publication of several three-volume novels. *The Circassian Chief*, 3 vols. 1843; *The Prime Minister*, 3 vols. 1845; *The Albatross*, 3 vols. 1849; as well as several books of travel, such as *Lusitanian Sketches*, 2 vols. 1845; and *Western Wanderings; or, a Pleasure Tour in the Canadas*, 2 vols. 1856. The first of over a hundred books for young people appeared in 1851 with the publication of *Peter the Whaler*; and a second edition, this time with plates, was issued two years later. From that time onwards he devoted almost all his time to writing and editing books for boys and young people; among the better

Right
A harmonious combination of talent is shown in Charles Heath's engravings from the designs for *Robinson Crusoe* made by Thomas Stothard (1755–1834). The edition illustrated was issued in two volumes in paper-covered boards (and reissued ten years later in a cloth binding) at two guineas a copy, and contained 22 full-page engravings.

Size of title-page:
22 cm × 14 cm.

Left
The first edition of a classic among adventure stories for boys of all ages. The wording on the map frontispiece is printed in four contrasting colours.

Size of title-page:
19 cm × 12.2 cm.

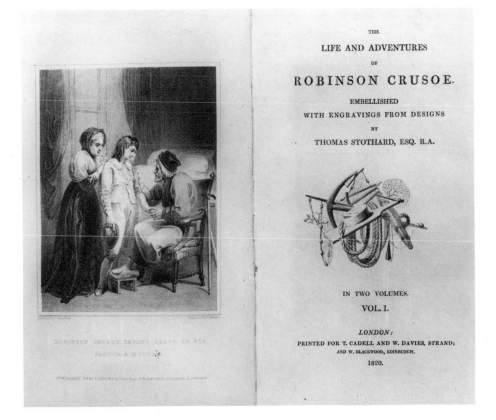

known of his stories are: *Adrift in a Boat*, 1869; *Ben Burton; or, Born and Bred at Sea*, 1872; *Cruise of the 'Frolic'*, 2 vols. 1860; *Digby Heathcote*, 1860; *Ernest Bracebridge*, 1860; *In the Rocky Mountains*, 1878; *In the Wilds of Florida*, 1882; *Manco; the Peruvian Chief*, 1853; *Old Jack: A Tale for Boys*, 1859; and scores of others to the end of the alphabet. He translated into English for the first time several of Jules Verne's futuristic stories, including *The Mysterious Island*, 1875; and *Michael Strogoff*, 1877. He was the editor of several magazines, including *Kingston's Magazine for Boys*, 5 vols. 1860–3 (the fifth volume was published in several monthly parts but not issued as a book); and *The Union Jack*, 4 vols. 1880–3, a magazine he founded as well as edited, handing over the chair to G. A. Henty after the appearance of the eighteenth number in April 1880, a few months before he died. Kingston was a prolific writer, churning out as many as five or six full-length books a year. His works occupy a full eight pages in the British Museum Library catalogue, but he never managed to achieve anything approaching the popular esteem or literary reputation of his contemporary, Ballantyne, in the eyes of 19th-century youth. He is remembered today almost solely for his first boy's book *Peter the Whaler*, yet the revival of interest in the minor writers of Victorian fiction means that several private collectors are attempting the all but impossible task of putting together a complete set of his 150 or so adult and juvenile romances and adventure stories in the original cloth-bound editions. Unlike Ballantyne and Henty, Kingston and many other writers in this field still lack reliable bibliographies, and the sifting of evidence regarding issue points, first edition dates and binding styles needs careful personal research.

Meanwhile, in the USA, the novelist and humorist 'Mark Twain', pseudonym of Samuel Langhorne Clemens (1835–1910), was writing some of his most famous books, notably that enduring favourite *The Adventures of Tom Sawyer*, 1876, followed later by *The Adventures of Huckleberry Finn*, the first edition of which appeared under a London imprint in 1884, with a New York edition dated 1885 shortly afterwards. *Tom Sawyer* in its original state is now a rare work and seldom appears on the market priced at less than £300 ($720). Clemens' later work is of uneven quality; *Pudd'nhead Wilson*, 1894, and *Personal Recollections of Joan of Arc*, 1896, ranking with the best of his writing; but his two later books for young people, *Tom Sawyer Abroad*, 1894, and *Tom Sawyer, Detective*, 1895, are only feeble shadows of the earlier classic that children throughout the world have come to love.

An Irish emigrant to the USA was Captain Mayne Reid, originally Thomas Mayne Reid (1818–83), who obtained a commission in the New York Volunteers in 1846 and was later wounded in the Mexican War, while attempting to storm Chapultepec. He put his experiences to good account when writing his first novel *The Rifle Rangers: or, Adventures of an Officer in Southern Mexico*, 2 vols. 1850; and from that time onwards devoted himself almost solely to writing adventure stories and romances. *The Scalp-Hunters*, 3 vols. 1851; *English Family Robinson*, 1851; *The Desert Home*, 1852; *The Boy Hunters*, 1852; *The Young Voyageurs*, 1853; *The White Chief*, 3 vols. 1855; were some of his early works, but novels and adventure stories continued to appear once or twice a year until his death in 1883, and even came out several years after as posthumous works were edited and published by his widow. Many of his three-volume novels now command high prices, such as *The Wood-Rangers*, 3 vols. 1860; *The Child Wife*, 3 vols. 1868; and *The Flag of Distress*, 3 vols. 1876; all of which fetch up to £40 ($96) in their original cloth bindings. *The Headless Horseman; a Strange Tale of Texas*, 2 vols. 1866, perhaps his most famous work, is difficult to find complete with all its twenty full-page plates and is catalogued at over £100 ($240). Mayne Reid's rarest work is a title quite out of the general run of his writing, and almost unobtainable in acceptable state in its original limp orange-cloth binding blocked in gold on the front-cover with the title and the author's name. *Croquet*, 1863, with a frontispiece of the lay-out of the game, contains a preface dated from The Ranche, Gerrard's Cross, Bucks., in which district the author ruined himself financially with building speculations that finally caused his departure for New York in 1867, where he founded and conducted *The Onward Magazine*. The slim, 46-page octavo *Croquet* was published by Skeet of Charing Cross, London, and not the author's usual publisher at this period, Routledge, Warne & Routledge. (His earlier works were issued by David Bogue, Fleet

Street.) There are many factors that play a part in ultimately deciding the rarity or otherwise of any particular issue of a title, and one of these is undoubtedly the publication of a single work by a publisher that does not normally handle the output of a well-read and relatively successful writer. One can cite many instances of the application of this rule: Ballantyne's *Life in the Red Brigade* (1873), published by George Routledge & Sons, at a time when James Nisbet was his regular publisher; or G. A. Henty's *The Young Colonists*, 1885, again published by Routledge, and not Henty's usual publisher Blackie & Son, thus making this latter title one of the rarest of his single-volume adventure stories for boys. The reason for the rarity of titles issued by houses other than the author's usual publisher is that an established outlet was built up over the years, often with a regular readership taking copies of each and every title as it appeared in the bookshops. Librarians, too, had their own particular ordering habits, and standing orders were given for the works of established authors as they were issued by his regular publishers. Any work issued outside the normal channels, or from amongst other than a publishing house's regular stable of writers, was handicapped from the start of its career, and it is well known among book-collectors that some of the most difficult titles to acquire are those that fall into the category given above. Many other factors weigh in the balance: the popularity of any given work, the number of copies originally issued, the type of binding, the physical make-up of the book (a thick and dumpy octavo in a fragile binding quickly falling to pieces – the first edition of Mrs Beeton's *Book of Household Management*, 1861, being a notorious example), even the paper on which the work is printed; all these and many other attributes play their part in the eventual survival or disappearance of copies in original condition. And with books produced for children and young people these factors weigh even more heavily, for the expectation of life of a juvenile work is very much shorter than those of adult counterparts.

Croquet, by Mayne Reid; and such titles as *Environs and Vicinity of Edinburgh*, 1859, or *Handbook to the New Goldfields . . . of the Fraser and Thompson River Gold Mines*, 1858, by R. M. Ballantyne; or *The March to Magdala*, 1868, by G. A. Henty, have no proper place in this chapter, or in a work purporting to deal exclusively with children's books. One is, however, faced with the difficulty that almost every collector of juvenilia, once he has become interested in a particular author, nearly always ends up by attempting to make a complete collection of his or her works, usually in first edition form. Very few writers were content to stick rigidly to a straight and undeviating literary path – poets wrote prose; novelists wrote verse; essays in political philosophy came from the pens of detective-story writers; historical novelists have been known to write science-fiction; and almost every writer of fairy stories, nursery rhymes, folk tales, and juvenile romances and adventure stories has made at least one attempt to break into the grown-up world of the circulating libraries and shelves reserved for belles-lettres, travel and topography, or the novel. Space can be found for no more than a passing mention of the more important works in the adult field by the better-known of the writers of children's books: those collectors seeking a complete set of any particular author's works in the original state must consult the relevant bibliographies or have the satisfaction of undertaking personal research. This fact is mentioned here as the writers of boys' adventure stories were particularly prone to stray from the narrow path by which they have since become well known to bibliographers and the reading public at large.

Friedrich Gerstäcker (1816–72), was a German writer and traveller in both America and Africa, whose subsequent narrative descriptions of his trials and tribulations in the wilds enjoyed considerable popularity, besides acting as source books for many English writers, notably W. H. G. Kingston. One of the most successful translations of his works was *The Little Whaler*, which appeared under a London imprint in 1857, with eight full-page illustrations by Harrison Weir. Anne Bowman was a rarity amongst writers, a lady novelist who specialised in adventure stories for boys. Most of her books were first issued by George Routledge & Sons, and comprised such titles as *The Castaways*, 1857; *The Kangaroo Hunters*, 1859; *The Boy Voyagers*, 1859; *Among the Tartar Tents*, 1861; *Clarissa*, 1864, described as 'A Book for Young Ladies'; *Tom and the Crocodiles*, 1867; *The Young Nile-Voyagers*, 1868; and a dozen or more titles in much the same vein. She also wrote several grammar and reading books; but little else is known about Miss (or Mrs) Bowman, except that she resided in Richmond, Surrey, and produced at least one book a year during the period 1855–75. Her work can be favourably compared with those of her masculine rivals in the same field.

George Alfred Henty (1832–1902), was ridiculed by his classmates for writing poetry while a pupil at Westminster School. Born at Trumpington, near Cambridge, the son of a wealthy mine-owner, he enlisted in the Hospital Commissariat soon after the outbreak of the Crimean War, and later represented the *Morning Advertiser* as one of the earliest war-correspondents. During the decade that followed, he was employed by *The Standard* and found himself in the thick of several minor European wars and almost a dozen colonial campaigns of varying degrees of bloodiness. The crushing of native tribes in revolt, and the flag-planting and empire building that went with it, stood him in good stead when he at last established himself as a historical novelist. His first attempts as a romantic writer of three-volume novels failed to make the slightest impact on the adult readership of the circulating libraries, *A Search for a Secret*, 3 vols. 1867; and *All But Lost*, 3 vols. 1869; faring as badly as his later work in the same field: *Rujub the Juggler*, 3 vols. 1893; *Dorothy's Double*, 3 vols. 1894; and *The Queen's Cup*, 3 vols. 1897. Autobiographical accounts of his experiences as a war-correspondent were given in *The March to Magdala*, 1868; and *The March to Coomassie*, 1874. But it is with his adventure stories for boys that Henty's reputation stands or falls. The first two, *Out on the Pampas*, 1871, and *The Young Franc-Tireurs*, 1872, apparently were only moderately successful in attracting young readers, and it was not until he took over the editorship of *The Union Jack* magazine from W. H. G. Kingston in May 1880, that he established himself as a popular writer of

The frontispiece of G. A. Henty's first book for boys, *Out on the Pampas; or, The Young Settlers*, 1871, published by Griffith & Farran. Size: 15 cm × 11 cm.

romances and historical novels for teenage readers. *The Union Jack*, a weekly magazine 'for British boys', cost a penny a week, or sixpence monthly, and was issued annually in four cloth-bound volumes during the period 1880–3. It contained stories by all the best-known writers for juveniles of the day, including Kingston, Ballantyne, Harry Collingwood, and of course Henty himself, six of whose full-length stories were serialised before their appearance in book form. From the time that *The Young Buglers*, 1880, made its appearance in the bookshops, until *With Kitchener in the Soudan*, 1903, issued after his death, hardly a year passed without at least two (sometimes as many as five) of his adventure stories being published for an eager young public. *The Cornet of Horse*, 1881; *Facing Death*, 1882; *With Clive in India*, 1884; *The Young Carthaginian*, 1887; *With Lee in Virginia*, 1890; *A Woman of the Commune*, 1895; *With Roberts to Pretoria*, 1902; are a few of his titles from a list of a hundred or so stories for boys. A complete check-list contains nearly 250 items for those collectors intent on tracking down each and every reference and contribution to magazines and periodicals.

Ballantyne and Henty had much in common. Both portrayed a world in which there were no shades, but black and white; the good invariably being terribly good and the bad acting in a totally un-British manner. Neither for a moment doubted the innate benevolence of British imperialism, coupled, as sooner or later it always was, with the blessings that Christianity would visit on the subject races of the Queen's vast dominions. Both suffered as writers from their inability to tell a straightforward adventure story that was free from the moralising of their puritanical predecessors in the same field, and youth had to wait for Stevenson's *Treasure Island* for a tale of adventure without sermons and unashamedly cheerful in tone. Ballantyne carefully researched a factual background before weaving his fictional plots against a realistic setting. A boy could smell the tar and taste the salt, duck at the twang of a bow-string, shovel coal on a swaying express, maroon himself on the Bell Rock lighthouse, play the part of detective in the underground cellars of the General Post Office, or choose any of a dozen different roles from a diversity of titles covering every aspect of adventurous, youthful endeavour. Henty, unlike Ballantyne, chose a historical background for his themes of dash and daring, and owed much to Scott. But both authors projected into lives that were often drab and humdrum a realistically coloured adventure image, mirroring their readers in the figures of their young heroes. They opened for the sons of middle- and working-class families an exciting new vista of a world spiced with danger and romance, which lay waiting for the young men of Britain to grow up and explore. Both supplied more self-education to willing and intelligent youth than years at school were able to instil; and, through the scrambling feet and inquisitive eyes of boyhood heroes whose exploits with Clive in India, with Buller in Natal, with Gascoyne, the sandal-wood trader, or Martin Rattler in the forests of Brazil, taught geography and history unobtrusively and persuasively. They revealed a world which generations of young men would never have known otherwise. Several of the best of Ballantyne's stories are still in print today. Henty has not worn so well; but his fellow member of the Savage Club, George Manville Fenn, a contemporary author of juvenile fiction, was correct in his assertion that a debt was owed to Henty for teaching 'more lasting history to boys than all the schoolmasters of his generation'.

Manville Fenn (1831–1909), was another of the prolific writers, publishing three or four titles a year, that the final decades of the 19th century produced so readily in the genre of juvenile fiction. He wrote well over a hundred full-length novels and adventure stories, including a number of three-volume fictional tales aimed at the adult market. His boys' books bear intriguing titles, such as *The Golden Magnet*, 1884; *Quicksilver; or, The Boy with no Skid to his Wheel*, 1889; *The Rajah of Dah*, 1891; *Walsh, The Wonder Worker*, 1903; and *Marcus: The Young Centurion* (1908), among a vast list of works. His first editions are not always easy to identify, for many appeared undated, under the Ernest Nister imprint, or that of the S.P.C.K. He is closer to Ballantyne than to Henty, and several of his titles, such as *Menhardoc: A Story of the Cornish Nets and Mines*, 1885, owe a considerable debt to his rival. *Hollowdell Grange; or, Holiday Hours in a Country House*, 1866, is one of the most difficult of his works to find in acceptable condition. William Gordon Stables

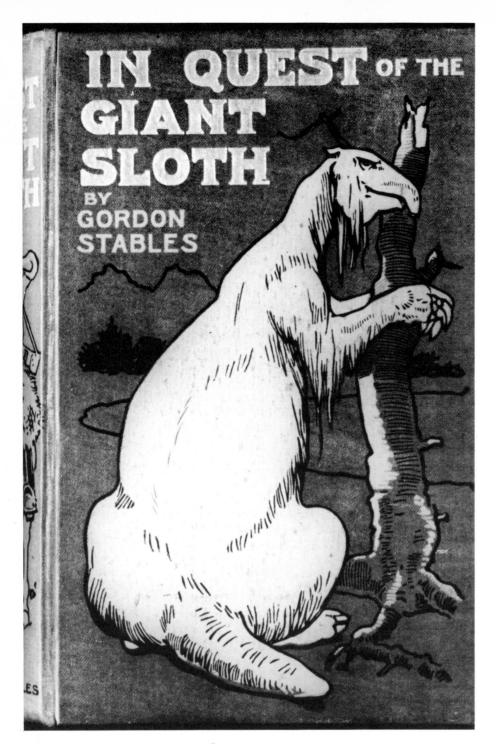

The cover of one of Gordon Stables' most stirring tales, published in 1902.

Opposite:
Top left
'Smooth cloth over bevelled boards, blocked pictorially in gilt and colours.' A typical Edwardian binding, dated 1908. The cover design and the eight full-page illustrations were by Harold C. Earnshaw.

Top right
Captain Frederick Sadleir Brereton (1872–1957), was a relative of G. A. Henty, whose influence can be discerned in the many historical adventure stories he wrote. The title shown was published by Blackie & Son in 1920.

Size of cover: 19.3 cm × 13 cm.

Bottom left
The cover design by E. S. Hardy for a work by W. J. C. Lancaster, published in 1908. He wrote all his tales under the pseudonym of 'Harry Collingwood'.

Height of spine: 19.3 cm.

Bottom right
A juvenile science-fiction tale, published by Cupples & Leon, New York, in 1910. Clarence Young was the author of a long series of popular *Motor Boys Books*, and of the *Jack Ranger Series* of tales for boys which ran for many years.

Size of front cover: 19.3 cm × 12.5 cm.

(1840–1910), had voyaged to the Arctic while still a medical student, later achieving the rank of naval surgeon. Soon after his retirement from the sea in 1871 he began to churn out story after story for boys, averaging close to four books a year for the next thirty years. *Wild Life in the Land of the Giants*, 1888; *Our Home in the Silver West* (1896) (this last published by the Religious Tract Society, who seldom, if ever, dated their publications, the same rule applying to the Society for Promoting Christian Knowledge; the two are known to collectors as the R.T.S. and the S.P.C.K.); *Remember the Maine*, 1899; and *Kidnapped by Cannibals*, 1900, are representative titles from a list that would all but fill this page. David Ker (1842–1914), specialised in adventure stories set in the wilder and unexplored regions of the earth: *On the Road to Khiva*, 1874; *The Boy Slave of Bokhara*, 1875; *Lost Amongst White Africans*, 1886, and *O'er Tartar Deserts*, 1898, number amongst his tales for youth. James F. Cobb (1829–c. 1895), is remembered for his *The Watchers on the Longships*, 1878, a tale which went through at least twenty editions before the turn of the century. *Silent Jim; A Cornish Story* (1871), and *Off to California* (1884) (the latter a free translation from the Dutch of Hendrik Conscience's *Het Goudland*, 1862), were less successful, and he wrote little else.

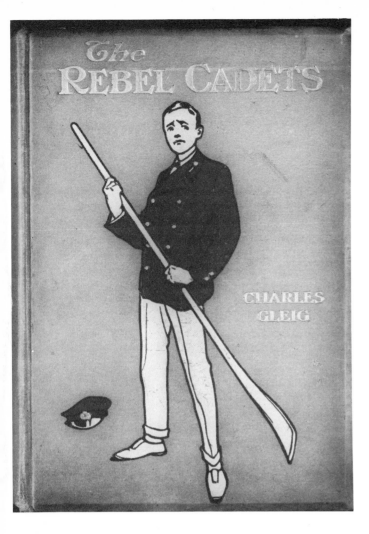

To enumerate every boy's author of note during a period in which writers jostled to crowd a rapidly expanding market is beyond the scope of this present work. Young people in their 'teens were not only literate, but were eager to devour with impartial vigour almost everything set before them – just for the sheer joy of being translated from the formalised surroundings and boring pomposity that characterised so much of late Victorian existence. Until the outbreak of the First World War in 1914, when children who could read were leaving school in their hundreds of thousands, those publishers who had made a speciality of issuing books for older children were sometimes hard put to it to cope with the incessant demand. A whole fresh crop of writers sprang up to occupy territory that was once the preserve of Ballantyne, Mayne Reid, Kingston, Manville Fenn, and G. A. Henty. W. J. C. Lancaster (1851–1922), who wrote under the pseudonym of 'Harry Collingwood', produced his first book for boys, *The Secret of the Sands*, in 1879. Although the majority of his tales were about the sea (he was an ex-naval officer) he produced some of the earliest adventure stories featuring aerial warfare and bombing attacks. Typical titles are *The Log of the "Flying Fish"*, 1887; *The Congo Rovers*, 1886; *With Airship and Submarine*, 1908, and *A Middy of the Slave Squadron*, 1911. Army and naval officers on retired pay crowded the publishers' lists: two in the Harry Collingwood vein were Captain F. S. Brereton (1872–1957), with his *Under the Spangled Banner; a Tale of the Spanish-American War*, 1903; *The Great Aeroplane*, 1911, and its sister volume, *The Great Airship*, 1914; as well as at least forty other titles; and also Captain Charles Gilson (1878–1943), who wrote *The Lost Column*, 1908; *The Lost Island*, 1910; *The Race Round the World*, 1914; *Submarine U-93*, 1916, and a string of other titles, publishing steadily until his death in 1943. One other notable author of the genre picked from a host of deserving names is 'Herbert Strang', the pseudonym of a partnership between George Herbert Ely (died 1958) and James L'Estrange (died 1947). Their first book *Tom Burnaby*, 1904, was the forerunner of fifty or more stories which included *The Cruise of the Gyro-Car*, 1911; *The Flying Boat*, 1912; *The Air Patrol*, 1913, containing the first coloured pictorial representation of a bombing attack by a conventional (as opposed to a science-fiction) aeroplane; and *With Haig on the Somme*, 1918, among several wartime titles. They achieved what is probably the unique distinction of having several of their adventure stories for boys issued in special limited editions as large-paper copies published simultaneously with the ordinary trade editions.

It is becoming increasingly difficult to obtain good copies of many of the titles listed above, and of the works of a host of other authors in the same field for which space could not be found. Few specialist book collections look better on the shelves than fine copies of first or early editions of adventure story books written during the period 1860–1910. We can allow a few years at either end of this time scale; but with the outbreak of World War I the glitter began to fade and the real gold blocking rapidly gave way to tinted aluminium substitutes which tarnished within a few months of purchase. The fiercely-coloured pictorial spines and covers of the earlier fifty-year period still display the gilded magnificence of gold lettering and startling eye-catching designs in the bright war-paint so beloved by the publishers of the 5s. (60 cents) or 3s. 6d. (42 cents) boys' adventure story books. Publishing houses vied with one another in their efforts to produce the most arresting styles, some of which can be seen in the illustrations to this present work. Many of the more progressive firms, such as Blackie & Son, who were amongst the first to use the varnished lure of olivine edges to attract prospective young purchasers, and T. Nelson & Sons, Edinburgh, who embellished their children's books with high-quality chromo-lithographed plates as early as the 1850s, were among the pioneers in the evolution of publishers' binding styles, and the volumes they issued found a shoal of imitators who were eager rivals in the same field. Most of the 5s. (60 cents) publications were issued in colour-printed dust-wrappers, which bore a totally different pictorial design from that found on the book itself.

It is only in the last few decades that the attention of book-collectors and literary historians has been switched to what was once almost unexplored territory in the field of English literature. First editions of Ballantyne, Henty, Mayne Reid, and W. H. G. Kingston, could be obtained in almost pristine

The first English edition, published in 1931, of Kästner's best-seller that was subsequently translated into nearly every European language. The first edition was published in Germany in 1929.

Height of spine: 20 cm.

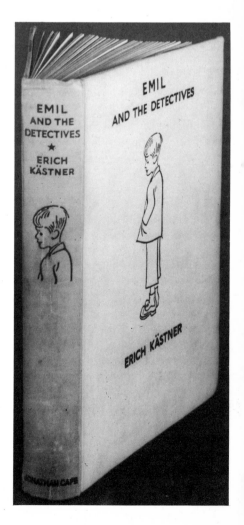

condition for a few shillings apiece, with the less well-known writers such as Edward S. Ellis, Herbert Hayens, Andrew Hilliard, Bertram Mitford, Kirk Munroe, J. Macdonald Oxley, S. Walkey, and Percy F. Westerman, hardly warranting shelf-room. Those days are gone forever, and the happy hunting ground of a handful of far-sighted and discerning collectors has now been invaded to an extent which sees the better known titles such as *The Coral Island* making up to £100 ($240) at auction. But there is still ample scope for collectors of only moderate means to acquire a representative collection of first editions of the works of writers whose vocation it was to produce the kind of book for boys that has been the subject of this chapter. Sisters often read them as well, and many a young lady learned a deal of her history from Henty, and as much geography and exotic natural history from Ballantyne as she obtained in years at school. The importance these authors had in moulding young minds at their most impressionable age has been emphasised by many modern investigators concerned with the influence which the reading of fictional romance and adventure stories has had on the teenage youth of the past and present. The young men who devoured the annual Christmas tales, with their too-good-to-be-true heroes and often threadbare plots, were the boys who, in their turn, became the soldiers and sailors, the explorers and trail-blazers, the merchant adventurers, the successes and the failures of the great British Empire on which the sun never set.

The first edition of *The History of Babar, the Little Elephant*, by Jean de Brunhoff, published in 1931. A slim, folio-sized, book of 48 pages, it is a 'modern' first edition to the collector of children's books, yet extremely difficult to find in acceptable condition. The illustration shows the title-page.

Size: 36 cm × 26.5 cm.

JEAN DE BRUNHOFF

HISTOIRE de BABAR le petit éléphant

Editions du Jardin des Modes
groupe des Publications Condé Nast
11 rue St Florentin - Paris

115

Periodicals, Annuals and Penny Dreadfuls

'Myself? Or the children?'. This illustration is not taken from a children's book, but is a full-page woodcut by Robert Barnes (1840–95) for the December 1872 issue of *The British Workman*. The attraction of magazines and annuals such as this is the intimate glimpses they give us of 19th-century working-class life.

Size of engraved surface: 38 cm × 28 cm.

The earliest magazines and annuals for young people took the form of weekly or monthly paper-wrapped pamphlets and tracts of a pious and evangelical nature. At the end of a year of issue there was usually a special Christmas number with which was given a specially-printed pictorial title-page showing the year of issue's date and the volume number. This, and the collected parts, were then bound up into a volume, but with the wrappers that protected the parts removed. One of the earliest of these periodicals for youth was *The Juvenile Magazine*, edited by Lucy Peacock. It ran for only twelve months, the last monthly number dated December 1788. In the fashion of the times it was illustrated with folding maps, engraved sheets of music, and numerous copperplate illustrations, and the contributors included several well-known writers of children's stories, including Dorothy and Mary Kilner. *The Youth's Magazine or Evangelical Miscellany*, 1816, which started what it described as its 'New Series' at the beginning of that year, was issued monthly as a 36-page periodical for children. In addition to a large woodcut illustration on the front page, each issue had a full-page engraving that took the form of a sheet of music, a map (usually folding), or a picture to illustrate an incident in the accompanying text. Mingled with the usual religious exhortations and moral platitudes were stories, tales of travel and adventure in foreign parts, potted biographies, poetry, songs and hymns, and numerous instructional articles with intriguing titles, such as: 'The Surprising Vigour of the Whale', 'Death at a Card Table', 'Scoresby's Account of the Arctic Regions', and 'The Depravity of the Morlachians'. The quality of many of the stories and articles was higher than one would expect to find in a children's magazine of that period and a number of well-known writers of the day can be identified by their intitials or pseudonyms. Jane Taylor of Ongar contributed some of her most successful juvenile tales during the period from February 1816, to the end of 1822, signing them with her pseudonym 'Q.Q.'. These were later collected by her brother Isaac and published in two volumes as *The Contributions of Q.Q. to a periodical work*, 1826.

The appearance of the first of the Christmas annuals for adults, *Forget Me Not*, 1823, was quickly followed by dozens of rival publications who vied with each other to catch the public's eye in a variety of novel bindings. The first annual that made any pretentions of having young people's welfare and entertainment at least partly in mind was issued in time to catch the Christmas

A selection of children's annuals in their original publisher's bindings, 1829–50.
Size of left-hand volume on shelf: 18 cm.

trade in October, 1824, although it was dated forward to the following year, as was commonly the custom. *Blossoms at Christmas and First Flowers of the New Year*, 1825, was published by J. Poole, Newgate Street, as a joint venture with Simkin & Marshall, Stationers Court, London. The proprietors stated in their preface to the work that they hoped it would rank with the 'tokens of affection to young persons, [which] have for some years been greeted with the strongest manifestations of public favour on the Continent'. The engraved title-page and the presentation leaf were both hand-coloured, and there were eight full-page copperplate engravings showing portraits of the famous, and views of cities or towns. The articles and tales made few concessions to the taste of young people however, but there were 'humorous anecdotes', fables, and instructional tit-bits on such subjects as 'The origin of duelling', which teenage children may have read with some measure of interest. The enterprise could not have been a commercial success, for the second annual volume, dated 1826, was the last to appear. In the meantime, *The Children's Friend* had been growing from strength to strength. It started as a penny monthly magazine in January 1824, and was published as an annual at the end of each year, complete with a specially-printed title-page and woodcut frontispiece, as well as the usual engravings which accompanied the text. This periodical continued without interruption until 1860, when a new and enlarged series commenced in 1861. Until 1850, it was edited by the Revd. William Carus Wilson, Rector of Whittington, who had the magazine printed at Kirkby

An illustration by Robert Barnes (1840–95), for the front of the monthly penny magazine *The Children's Friend*, 1876, published by S. W. Partridge & Co., London. It commenced publication in 1860 and was issued as an annual every year.

Size of page: 22 cm × 17 cm.

Lonsdale, Westmorland. It was here, at Cowan Bridge, that he founded the ill-omened Clergy Daughters' School, which the unfortunate Brönte sisters were forced to attend in 1824. Charlotte Brönte had her revenge by modelling Mr Brocklehurst in *Jane Eyre* on her late schoolmaster. The same year that Wilson's magazine appeared, saw the birth of *The Child's Companion; or, Sunday Scholar's reward*, which was published monthly from 1824 by the Religious Tract Society, with an annual volume at the end of each year. In January 1832 they issued a 'New Series' in a similar format; and a third series, this time enlarged, came out from 1838 to 1844. It was one of the longest-running children's periodicals, continuing as *The Child's Companion and Juvenile Instructor*, from 1846 to 1921, and then under a number of modern-sounding titles until it ceased publication in 1932. It has the distinction of being the first magazine for children to contain examples of the colour-printing of the famous George Baxter (1804–67), although it was issued at the price of only a penny a month. The first of these coloured plates was given with the December issue of 1846, and was used as a frontispiece in the annual volume for that year. Altogether a total of six of Baxter's pictures were used, and with the second, a view of 'Her Majesty's Marine Residence, Isle of Wight', which was a frontispiece to the 1847 volume, the inventor of the process was at pains to explain to his young readers how the plate was produced. 'At first sight it will be seen that it is a picture not like those commonly found in books', he pointed out. 'It is a new invention, and it is printed, not with ink, but with oil colours, the same

This copperplate engraving was one of eight plates to illustrate *The Juvenile Album*, first published by Ackermann & Co., 1841, and later by Thomas Holmes, *c.* 1845. The text was by Mrs R. Lee (Sarah Bowdich Lee, 1791–1856), but the interest lies in Thomas Woolnoth's fine engravings.

Total size of page:
24 cm × 20 cm.

as used in painting. It is done from ten different engravings, on steel plates, each of which prints a separate colour, and altogether they form the picture as it now appears.' From 1852 onwards the Religious Tract Society awarded the contract to J. M. Kronheim, a licensee of the process, probably on the grounds that a more competitive price was quoted. The first children's book, as opposed to a magazine, to contain colour-printed illustrations is discussed later in this chapter.

Another monthly publication for young people was *The Infant Scholar's Magazine*, which commenced in January 1827, published by John Stephens, London. With the third annual volume, dated 1829, the title was changed to read *The Child's Repository, and Infant Scholar's Magazine*. It lasted only as long as the earlier *National School Magazine*, which was issued fortnightly by C. & J.

119

Rivington, London, from April 1824, until December 1825. Another in much the same style was *The Nursery Infants' School Magazine*, a monthly edited by Mrs L. L. B. Cameron under the supervision of the pubishers, Houlston & Son, Wellington, Shropshire. It ran from 1829 until 1832, after which it was known as *The Nursery Magazine*.

The Boy's Own Book, 2 vols. 1827–28, published by Vizetelly, Branston & Co., sported a single-colour frontispiece printed in a bright shade of blue. The sub-title announced to its readers that it was 'A complete Encyclopedia of all the diversions, Athletic, Scientific, and Recreative, of Boyhood and Youth'. *The Christmas Box; an Annual Present for Children*, was more closely modelled on adult annuals than any of its predecessors, and was a more tasteful and sumptuous production than those that had gone before. Nevertheless, it survived for only two issues, in 1828 and 1829, despite the talents of its editor, Thomas Crofton Croker, whose collections of fairy and folk tales were well known. *The Juvenile Keepsake*, edited by Thomas Roscoe, fared no better, for the volumes dated 1829 and 1830, issued in a binding of pic-torially-printed paper-covered boards, were all that appeared. *The New Year's Gift, and Juvenile Souvenir*, 1829, was one of the first children's annuals to have a woman with full editorial powers, Mrs Alaric Watts, who was married to the editor of the long-running *The Literary Souvenir*, 1825–36, first of the annuals to be available in a large-paper edition, with the plates printed on India-paper, as well as the usual trade edition. Under her superintendence, *The New Year's Gift* completed a total of eight annual volumes during the years 1829–36. The earlier numbers were published in a binding of glazed paper-covered boards with a green morocco spine on which the title and the year of issue were blocked in gold. A distinguished list of contributors in both prose and verse included Mrs Hofland, Mary and William Howitt, Mrs Amelia Opie, Agnes Strickland, and Mrs Felicia Hemans, while the tissue-guarded engravings used to illus-trate the work were of a quality that compared very favourably with those found in the expensive adult annuals. It deserved its success, as did *The Juvenile Forget Me Not*, edited by the redoubtable Mrs S. C. Hall, which was issued in an almost exactly similar format (although an inch or so taller) and ran from 1829 to 1837. One other early annual that deserves a mention is *Marshall's Christmas Box*, published by William Marshall, London, whose pocket-books and almanacks found a ready sale. The first of the two volumes which appeared has the distinction of being the first fully cloth-bound book for children to be published. Marshall issued it in a binding of red watered-silk, with the title and year of issue, 1831, blocked in gold on the spine. The fabric proved itself too tender for youthful hands and the second, final volume, dated 1832, was published in a binding of full-morocco, blocked in gold and blind.

The publishers of annuals were nothing if not innovators, both as regards the binding styles they employed and the contents of their yearly volumes. In 1835, William Darton & Son published *The New Year's Token; or, Christmas Present,* a pretty little annual much in the general run of the several that were then available to children. It was with the next issue, published in October 1835, but dated forward to 1836, that we find the first colour-printed illustra-tions ever to appear in a children's book. The frontispiece shows a delicately tinted view of Virginia Water, Surrey, with George IV's fishing temple in the background, while the ornamental title-page has a colour-printed vignette of a little boy examining a bird's nest. Both these illustrations were printed in colours from wooden blocks by George Baxter, who invented the process of printing with oil-colours, after designs by the artist John Brown. The view of Virginia Water was later used in other books, but the picture of the little boy is one of the rarest of Baxter's prints. *The New Year's Token*, ran for only two years, so that the second volume is the target for several classes of collectors from the mid-19th century onwards. One other rarity that a few lucky children received as a Christmas present was the *Geographical Annual or Family Cabinet Atlas*, 1832, a choice and highly-finished work that was designed and engraved throughout by Thomas Starling. All the maps on the 96 engraved plates were coloured by hand. In their preface to the work the publishers expressed the hope that, 'on account of its enduring interest, the present publication may justly lay claim to the title of a Perennial rather than an Annual & be valued as a lasting Gift of Friendship rather than a Pastime offering'. The following year they published the *Biblical Annual or Scripture Cabinet Atlas*, 1833, again engraved

Right
A complete set of Kate Greenaway's *Alma-nacks*, 1883–97, there being no issue for the year 1896. The two shown at bottom right are reissues of the 1920s. Much the rarest is the leather-bound issue for 1897.

Over page
Books with 'pop-up' pictures appeal still to children of the present day, although the high cost of manufacture has caused them to all but disappear. The one shown is *Nister's Panorama* (1890), manufactured in Nuremberg for the British market, and contains five double-page panoramas that stand out in relief when the book is opened.

Size of double-page spread: 31 cm × 50 cm.

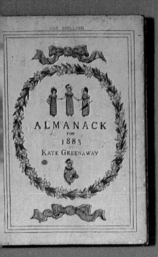

ONE SHILLING

ALMANACK
FOR
1883
KATE GREENAWAY

ALMANACK · FOR · 1884

BY
KATE GREENAWAY

ALMANACK

1885

BY KATE GREENAWAY

ALMANACK 1886

BY
KATE GREENAWAY

ALMANACK
FOR
1888

Kate Greenaway

ALMANACK FOR 1887

BY
KATE GREENAWAY

ALMANACK
FOR
1889
BY
KATE GREENAWAY

LONDON: GEORGE ROUTLEDGE & SONS
BROADWAY, LUDGATE HILL
GLASGOW AND NEW YORK

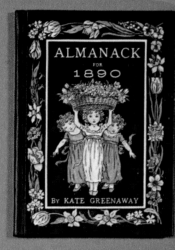

ALMANACK
FOR
1890

BY KATE GREENAWAY

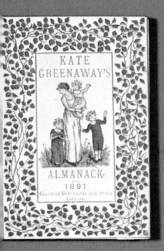

KATE
GREENAWAY'S

ALMANACK
1891
GEORGE ROUTLEDGE & SONS
LONDON

KATE GREENAWAY'S
ALMANACK
FOR
1892

KATE GREENAWAY'S
ALMANACK

FOR 1893.

KATE GREENAWAY'S
ALMANACK

for 1894

KATE GREENAWAY'S
ALMANACK

for 1895

KATE GREENAWAY'S

ALMANACK
FOR 1896

ALMANACK FOR 1924
BY KATE GREENAWAY

KATE
GREENAWAY'S

ALMANACK
FOR
1927.

ON THE BEACH.

A four-volume set, extremely rare in the original, printed paper-covered boards, dated 1822. The publisher, John Arliss, started one of the first juvenile libraries.

Height of book: 13 cm.

A musical toy that must have delighted the hearts of children in the 1870s. Disguised as a book, it opens as a series of eight full-page coloured illustrations. By gently pulling the ivory tassels on the side, the voices of a cockerel, a donkey, a lamb, a nestful of birds, a cow, a cuckoo, a goat, and a baby, are heard in succession, the sounds being reproduced by a series of miniature bellows.

Size: 32 cm × 24 cm.

throughout by Thomas Starling, and with all the maps hand-coloured. Both volumes were issued in bindings of full morocco, blocked in blind with the titles and year of publication in gold.

The first children's annual in the modern sense was *The Excitement*, 1830, published by Waugh & Innes, Edinburgh, in pictorial paper-covered boards with a morocco spine blocked in gold. It was first published in December 1829, dated forward to 1830, and was edited by Adam Keys, an Edinburgh schoolmaster. Whereas the children's annuals which had so far been published were usually scaled-down models of the volumes produced for the adult market, often using the same engravings and interspersed with prose and verse that was almost indistinguishable both in style and contents from that used in their more expensive counterparts, *The Excitement* set out with the avowed intention of printing adventure stories and romances solely for the interest and amusement of young people. According to the editor, there was the allied hope that, by so doing, children would be induced to read more than they did and take more interest in literature as a whole. Keys was a forward-thinking man, and he stated plainly in his preface to the first volume of the series that by printing adventure stories founded on fact the books would be read 'by boys particularly, with the greatest attention; and also narratives of such striking incidents as are fitted to rouse the most slothful mind – incidents in which the reader cannot fail to imagine himself identified, as it were, with the parties concerned, and to enter with the deepest interest into all their various feelings . . .'. This reference to reader identification with the characters and scenes depicted in the work is an interesting comment at so early a period; but Keys was later to run into serious opposition from some of the more evangelical Elders of the Scottish Kirk. Throughout the 418 pages of text there was almost no sermonising, and there were no moral aptitude tests set for its young readers, or for the heroes of the tales, except the test of courage and the ability to withstand trials and tribulations. The titles of the stories were as zestful as their contents, with no concessions made to the religious dogmas of the day: 'A Lion Hunt in Africa'; 'Boiling Springs of Iceland'; 'Whale Ship destroyed by a Whale', 'Sufferings endured in the Black-Hole of Calcutta'; 'An account of a Boa-Constrictor swallowing a Goat'; 'The Reign of Terror, and Fall of Robespierre'; 'The Lion Fight' and 'The Inquisition at Goa'; etc., being enough to stimulate the imagination of any boy lucky enough to possess a copy. Complaints from the more puritanically-minded of his critics caused Keys to insert a paragraph in the preface of the volume for 1837, and several of those that followed, to the effect that it had 'been hinted that it might be well to mingle more of pious sentiment with the details presented in the *Excitement*' ... 'But', he went on, 'it does not appear to us essential that *every* work put into the hands of the young should necessarily contain something of a religious nature...' The opposition eventually proved too strong; Waugh & Innes were taken over as a business, for unspecified reasons, by John Johnstone, of Hunters Square, Edinburgh, and Adam Keys was dismissed from the editorship of *The Excitement* in 1838. The new editor appointed that year was the Revd. Robert Jamieson, minister of Westruther, who considered it his duty to state in the preface that, in future, the annual's leading design would be 'to combine pleasure with instruction; and to give the mind a relish for truth, rather than to excite and vitiate its taste by the embellishment of fiction'. Adam Keys was determined to carry on and, with William Innes as publisher, started *The New Excitement*, 1838, on much the same lines as before. Both annuals ran side by side for a few years, the former turning more and more to the adventures of missionaries amongst the unconverted heathens, while Keys kept doggedly along his secular path, serving the young such tit-bits as 'Rat Eating'; 'The Dead Restored to Life'; 'Attempt to Steal the Regalia from the Tower'; 'A Combat between two Beetles'; 'Every Bullet has its Billet'; 'Funeral of a Dog', and so on, all of which, he told his readers, were strictly founded upon truth.

The Comic Annual, 1830, edited by Thomas Hood (1799–1845), although primarily aimed at the adult market, was very popular with the young. It was full of excruciating puns, comical stories in which one or other of the characters came to summary grief, and contained the sort of easy-to-understand humorous illustrations beloved by children of all ages. Hood wrote most of it himself, and the series continued until the ninth volume appeared dated 1839, all bound in pictorially-printed paper-covered boards with red morocco spines. There was no issue for 1840, and the next to appear (this time in a full-cloth binding) was dated 1841. This was reprinted, dated 1842, the following year. His son, Thomas Hood the younger (1835–74), known as Tom Hood, was later the editor of a comic paper *Fun*, 1865, and in 1867 began *Tom Hood's Comic Annual*, which was popular with older children and continued for some years after his death. To complete the period leading up to the appearance of the first *Peter Parley's Annual*, discussed in another chapter, mention must be made of *Fisher's Juvenile Scrap-Book*, 1836 to 1850, which survived for a total of fifteen yearly volumes under a succession of editors; and *My Own Annual*, edited by 'Mark Merriwell', an anonymous writer whose identity has remained undiscovered. This well-produced annual deserved a longer run than its two years 1847–8; it was larger in size than most of its predecessors, had hand-coloured title-pages and frontispieces, and was issued in a full-cloth binding blocked pictorially in gold.

By the 1860s there was a wide choice of juvenile annuals which were now issued as an integral part of children's magazines. Usually a full set of the weekly or monthly parts was issued by the publishers in December of the year as an annual volume, in a colourful full-cloth binding, bright with gold blocking. There were so many by the final quarter of the 19th century that only a selection can be mentioned here.

The Halfpenny Picture Magazine for Little Children, commenced publication in January 1854, and almost immediately changed its name to *The Pictorial Magazine for Little Children*, 1855–8, then to *The Little Child's Picture Magazine in Easy Words*, 1859–62, and finally to *The Picture Magazine*, 1863–5, all under the editorship of J. F. Winks. More important in the quality of its contributors, and for setting a standard that dozens of competitors later imitated, was one of the first of the boy's magazines issued in the size we know today, *The Boy's Own Magazine*, published monthly from 1855 to 1874. It was edited and published by S. O. Beeton, and in 1863 the circulation reached 40,000 copies a month. It was then enlarged and the price raised to sixpence. *The Boy's Penny Magazine* was started so that poorer children could still have a chance of affording a subscription. Contributors to the former publication included Austin Dobson, Thomas Hood, Mayne Reid, Mrs Harriet Beecher Stowe, W. H. G. Kingston, and many others. Gustave Doré, Harrison Weir, J. A. Pasquier, and J. B.

Opposite:
Top left
This weekly magazine was published at a penny a copy from November 1866 until June 1899, edited, after the first nine numbers, by E. J. Brett. The first *Jack Harkaway* stories appeared in July 1871.

Top right
One of the most difficult of the penny magazines to find in original condition, the first number of which is illustrated here. *Sixteen-String Jack* made his first appearance in September 1863.

Size of page: 24.5 cm × 17.5 cm.

Bottom left
The first issue of a magazine that continued publication until February 1967. It was also issued as a Christmas annual.

Size of page: 29.5 cm × 21.5 cm.

Bottom right
One of the dramatic woodcut illustrations for the front cover of a popular penny magazine for boys.

Size of page: 27 cm × 20 cm.

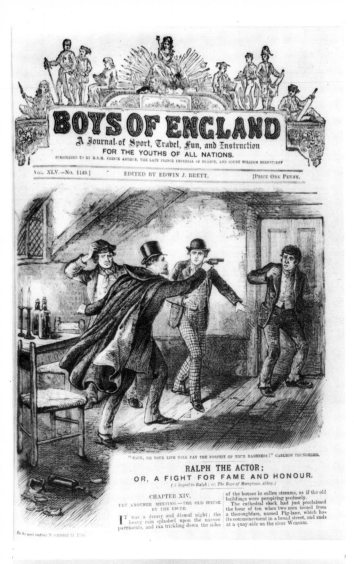

BOYS OF ENGLAND

A Journal of Sport, Travel, Fun, and Instruction
FOR THE YOUTHS OF ALL NATIONS.
SUBSCRIBED TO BY H.R.H. PRINCE ARTHUR, THE LATE PRINCE IMPERIAL OF FRANCE, AND COUNT WILLIAM BERNSTORFF.

Vol. XLV.—No. 1149.]   EDITED BY EDWIN J. BRETT.   [Price One Penny.

"NICK, OR YOUR LIFE WILL PAY THE FORFEIT OF YOUR RASHNESS!" CARLEON THUNDERED.

RALPH THE ACTOR;
OR, A FIGHT FOR FAME AND HONOUR.
(A Sequel to Ralph : or, The Boys of Merrytown Abbey.)

CHAPTER XIV.
YET ANOTHER MEETING.—THE OLD HOUSE BY THE RIVER.

IT was a dreary and dismal night; the heavy rain splashed upon the narrow pavements, and ran trickling down the sides of the houses in sullen streams, as if the old buildings were perspiring profusely.

The cathedral clock had just proclaimed the hour of ten when two men issued from a thoroughfare, named Pig-lane, which has its commencement in a broad street, and ends at a quay-side on the river Wensum.

THE BOY'S MISCELLANY

WEEKLY. ONE PENNY.

No. 1.]   SATURDAY, MARCH 7, 1863.

Contents:

THE WHALE KILLERS. *Illustrated.*
THE HORRORS OF THE WILDS. *Illustrated.*
HOW LITTLE BOYS BECAME GREAT MEN.
No. 1—GEORGE STEPHENSON, ENGLAND'S ENGINEER.
ON THE ORIGIN OF "OLD NICK."
A GHOST STORY.
CLIMBING WOMEN OF FLINDER'S ISLAND.
ENIGMATICAL EXERCISES.
FISH AND FISHING; OR, ADVENTURES WITH ROD AND LINE.
THE YOUNG CHEMIST.
COLUMN FOR THE CURIOUS.
MAGIC FOR THE MILLION. By THE WIZARD OF THE EAST.
OPEN-AIR SPORTS.

Among the Subjects introduced Weekly will be found the following:—

ARCHERY.	GAMES OF SKILL.	QUOITS.
BOATING.	GARDENING.	RACING.
CHARADES.	GYMNASTICS.	RIDING.
CHESS.	HUNTING.	ROWING.
COURSING.	MANAGEMENT OF	SAILING.
CRICKET.	ANIMALS.	SINGING.
DRAWING.	MODELLING.	SWIMMING.
FENCING.	PHOTOGRAPHY.	TENNIS.
FISHING.	POULTRY.	TURNING.
FOOTBALL.	PUZZLES.	

OFFICE: 135, SALISBURY SQUARE, FLEET STREET, LONDON.

THE BOY'S OWN PAPER

No. 1.—Vol. I.   SATURDAY, JANUARY 18, 1879.   Price One Penny.
[ALL RIGHTS RESERVED.]

MY FIRST FOOTBALL MATCH.
BY AN OLD BOY.

IT was a proud moment in my existence when Wright, captain of our football club, came up to me in school one Friday and said, "Adams, your name is down to play in the match against Craven to-morrow."

I could have knighted him on the spot. To be one of the picked "fifteen," whose glory it was to fight the battles of their school in the Great Close, had been the leading ambition of my life—I suppose I ought to be ashamed to confess it—ever since, as a little chap of ten, I entered Parkhurst six years ago. Not a winter Saturday but had seen me either looking on at some big match, or oftener still scrimmaging about with a score or so of other juniors in a scratch game. But for a long time, do what I would, I always

seemed as far as ever from the coveted goal, and was half despairing of ever rising to win my "first fifteen cap." Lately, however, I had noticed Wright and a few others of our best players more than once lounging about in the Little Close where we juniors used to play, evidently taking observations with an eye to business. Under the awful gaze of these heroes, need I say I exerted myself as I had never done before? What cared I for hacks or bruises, so only that I could distinguish myself in their eyes? And never was music sweeter

ONE PENNY PER WEEK
SIXPENCE MONTHLY

The UNION JACK
TALES FOR BRITISH BOYS.

Vol. I.—No. 14.]   Edited by W. H. G. KINGSTON.   [April 1, 1880.
[All rights reserved.]

Zwecker, were amongst the illustrators. At mid-summer and at Christmas, cloth-bound volumes were issued under titles whose names varied during the ensuing years: *The Boy's Own Volume*, and *Beeton's Annual*, had the longest run. A rival publication was *The Boy's Journal*, published by Henry Vickers and edited by C. P. Brown, which was published monthly from 1863 to 1871, before it was absorbed into *The Youth's Play-Hour*. *Every Boy's Magazine*, 1862–4, was incorporated into *Routledge's Magazine for Boy's* in January 1865, and issued as *Routledge's Every Boy's Annual* complete with a series of colour-printed plates by Leighton Brothers. The name changed to *The Young Gentleman's Magazine*, 1869–73, and to *Every Boy's Magazine*, 1874–89, when it was finally absorbed into *The Boy's Own Paper*. R. M. Ballantyne was a regular contributor at one stage in his career.

The most difficult of the early boy's magazines for a collector to find is *The Boy's Miscellany*, the first weekly issue appearing on Saturday 7 March 1863, priced at one penny a copy. Although it was never published as an annual it was possible to buy four of the weekly parts bound together in a colour-printed pictorial-wrapper at fourpence. It was originally owned and edited by E. Harrison of Salisbury Court, but was taken over by its printers, Maddick & Pottage, Crane Court, Fleet Street, as their account remained unpaid. It was in this magazine that *The Adventures of Sixteen-String Jack* were first recounted.

Good Words for the Young was published monthly from 1868 to 1872, and then continued as *Good Things for the Young of All Ages*, 1872–7. The standard of the woodcut illustrations was particularly high, derived in part from its adult counterpart *Good Words* which employed the talents of many of the foremost 'Sixties' artists of the day. From 1870 to 1872 the magazine was edited by

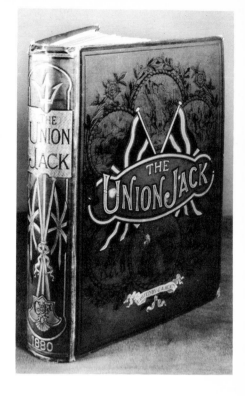

Above
Four cloth-bound annual volumes were issued during 1880–3, and none are easy to find in anything approaching original condition. W. H. G. Kingston was the first editor, followed by G. A. Henty.

Height of spine: 28 cm.

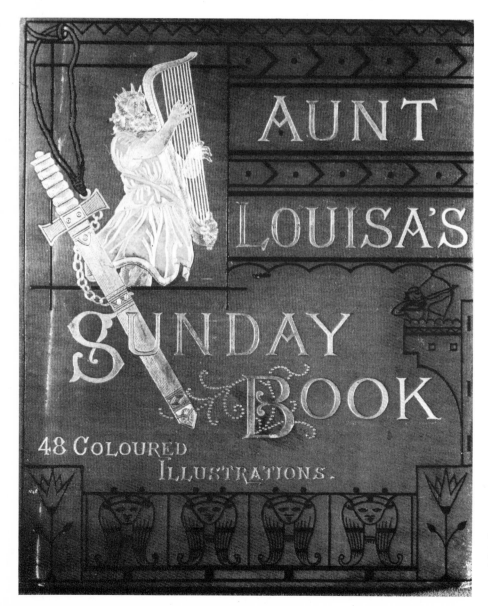

Left
'Aunt Louisa' was the pseudonym of Laura Valentine, the general editor of Frederick Warne & Company's juvenile publishing department. Her *Sunday Picture Book* was published *c.* 1870, with plates printed by Kronheim.

Size of front cover: 27 cm × 23 cm.

George MacDonald, and two of his stories appeared as serials: *At the Back of the North Wind*, and *Ranald Bannerman's Boyhood*, both with illustrations by Arthur Hughes.

The Boy's Own Paper survived without a change of name from the first issue published on Saturday, 18 January 1879, until its final appearance 88 years later in February 1967. *The Boy's Own Annual*, published in a pictorial cloth-binding at the end of each year, was issued regularly until the outbreak of World War II, but there was then a break of 26 years until it restarted at Christmas 1964. In its heyday it was the most popular boy's magazine, out-selling its many rivals by thousands of copies a week, and employing as regular contributors nearly every well-known writer for juveniles. The full-page colour-printed plates by Edmund Evans were a speciality. It was due to the popularity of this magazine that *The Union Jack* failed to command a similar market. It started in January 1880, as a penny weekly magazine (or sixpence a month, with a special photographic illustration of a well-known children's author). The first portion was edited by W. H. G. Kingston, but he was a dying man and G. A. Henty took over at the commencement of the 19th number, in May 1880. His tale, *Facing Death, a Tale of the Coal Mines*, had started as a serial the previous month. R. M. Ballantyne contributed *Fighting the Salmon in Norway*; Jules Verne *The Steam House*; and Manville Fenn *The Ensign and the Middy*, while several of Henty's best-known tales eventually found a place in its pages. Yet it managed to survive for only four volumes, and finished its life as a magazine with the issue dated 25 September 1883.

Magazines for girls and younger children were the province of women editors. *Aunt Judy's Magazine for Young People*, a monthly published from 1866 to 1885 in half-yearly, Christmas and mid-summer volumes, was established by Mrs Gatty, and included amongst its contributors such famous names as Lewis Carroll and Hans Andersen. The first periodical specially devised for teenage girls was *Every Girl's Magazine*, a monthly published from 1878 to 1888 and edited by Alicia Amy Leith. It appeared as *Every Girl's Annual* at the end of each year. Kate Greenaway contributed some of the colour-printed frontispieces, as she did for *Little Wide-Awake*, edited by Mrs Lucy Sale Barker, a monthly magazine that ran from 1875 to 1892, with an annual of the same name. The most famous of the magazines for girls was undoubtedly *The Girl's Own Paper*, which ran continuously (with various later changes of name) from 1880 to 1948. It appeared at the end of each year as *The Girl's Own Annual*, and in its time consumed the talents of nearly every female writer for schoolgirls in Britain. It was published by the proprietors of a successful adult magazine *The Leisure Hour*, 1852–1905, who were also responsible for *The Boy's Leisure Hour*, which commenced publication in January 1884, as a penny weekly magazine, but was also issued (from October 1887) in monthly parts, containing the previous four weekly numbers, and bound in illustrated colour-printed paper-wrappers at fourpence a copy. Annuals of this publication were not issued, but it is famous for having seen the appearance of such delights of Victorian boyhood as 'Three-Fingered Jack', 'Cheeky Charlie', 'Sweeney Todd the Demon Barber', 'Jack Sheppard', 'Broad Arrow Jack', 'Spring-Heeled Jack', and 'The Adventures of Ching Ching'. So popular did this little Chinese boy become that *Ching Ching's Own Magazine* came into being in June 1888, and continued until June 1893.

By this time the stationers and bookshops had their counters crowded with a bewildering array of children's magazines. *Comic Cuts* started in May 1890; *Comic Pictorial Nuggets*, in May 1892, continuing as *Nuggets* from November, 1892, until it ceased publication in March 1905; *The World's Comic*, 1892–1908, was followed by the famous *Chums* in September 1892; and from that time onwards we come into the age of the 'comics' of our own boyhood, with names like *The Magnet*, *The Gem*, *The Bulls-eye*, *Tiger Tim's Tales*, *The Champion*, *Chatterbox*, *Hotspur*, *The Jester*, *The Marvel*, *Merry and Bright*, *Pluck*, *The Rover*, *The Triumph*, and *The Wild West Weekly*.

One other class of paper-bound reading matter which children in their 'teens found irresistible were the 'penny dreadfuls', the 'bloods' of the period that extended from the 1840s to the 1900s. The earlier titles such as *The Royal Rake*, 1842, by Leman Rede (1802–47), who that same year had started the magazine *Judy* as a rival to *Punch* (only two numbers appeared), were satirical romances rather than true blood-and-thunder thrillers, although the vivid

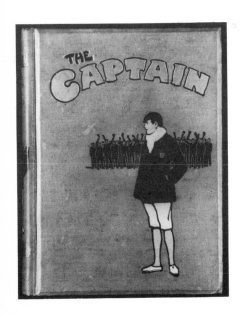

Typical of the 'public school' magazines of the early part of the 20th century, *The Captain* was issued monthly, and in book form twice a year, starting in 1899.

Height: 25 cm.

descriptions of such characters as John Rann, alias 'Sixteen-String Jack', and his henchman Kit Clayton, as well as the graphic woodcut illustrations of bloody deeds and highway robberies, pointed the way to the lurid sequels that were to follow from other hands. By the 1850s the publishers of 'penny parts', to be known all too soon as 'penny dreadfuls', had settled to their task of providing sorely needed escapism for those of the indigenous poor who had learned to read. Edward Lloyd (1818–90), founder of *Lloyd's Newspaper*, was one of the first to see the possibilities of this market, and during the 1840s he started to put out an increasingly wide range of penny-a-week gibbety horror-stories, using as *dramatis personae* the more accomplished of the upholders of the *laissez-faire* principle listed in the *Newgate Calendar, or Malefactors' Bloody Register*. Some of the tales he wrote himself, but he also gathered around him a stable of specialist hack-writers, of the calibre of Edward Viles and John Frederick Smith, who themselves employed threadbare and under-nourished minor hacks to help in churning out the hundreds of thousands of words needed weekly. *Gentleman Jack; or, Life on the Road*, 1852, was typical of the long-running serials issued at a penny a week, 'No's 2, 3, & 4, presented gratis with No. 1'. *Vileroy; or, The Horrors of Zindorf*; *The Black Monk; or, The Secret of the Grey Turret*; and *The Castle Fiend*; paved the way for one of Lloyd's most successful publications, *Varney the Vampire*, by James Malcolm Rymer. None of these titles was meant primarily for the juvenile market, but it did not take adolescents long to discover the blood-curdling excitements to be had for the price of a penny. Thomas Frost, in his *Forty Years' Recollections*, 1860, told how

A distinctive binding from the library of the late Barry Ono, Clapham Common, London, who described himself as 'The Penny Dreadful King'. *Gentleman Jack*, 1852, by Edward Viles, was published by Edward Lloyd, London, and regaled its readers with the bloodthirsty adventures of Claude Duval in a series of 205 weekly penny parts.

Height of spine: 22.5 cm.

he met Lloyd's manager, 'a stout gentleman of sleek costume and urbane manners', in the hope of selling him a story for publication in penny parts. It was admitted to him that:

Our publications circulate among a class so different in education and social position from the readers of three-volume novels that we sometimes distrust our own judgment and place the manuscript in the hands of an illiterate person – a servant, or machine boy, for instance. If they pronounce favourably upon it, we think it will do.

So children took as their own such stories as *Almira's Curse*; *The Ranger of the Tomb*; *The Maniac Father*; and *Geralda the Demon Nun*; these last two titles written by the indefatigable Thomas Peckett Prest, the creator of that undying favourite *Sweeney Todd*; *The Demon Barber of Fleet Street*, first published by Lloyd under the unlikely title of *The String of Pearls*.

Dick Turpin had been endowed by the writers of romantic fiction with the Robin Hood qualities we associate today with the protection racket, and Edward Viles made full use of these sentiments in his *Black Bess; or, The Knight of the Road*, a serial published by E. Harrison which ran to the astonishing total of 254 weekly parts. But even this paled into insignificance beside the series of 'Jack Harkaway' stories, written by Bracebridge Hemyng. The first of the Jack Harkaway stories appeared in *Boys of England Magazine*, published by Edwin J. Brett (1828–95), as a penny weekly which commenced publication in November 1866, and continued until June 1899. The youthful hero of ten thousand fights and several hundred hair's-breadth escapes from death made his bow in the issue for July 1871, and his subsequent exploits boosted the sales of the paper to the point where the proprietor named his newly acquired premises Harkaway House.

By 1890 the market was saturated with the paper-bound products of scores of printing and publishing firms which had mushroomed into prominence in attempts to satisfy the public appetite for blood-and-thunder. By this time there was a choice of fifty or more new titles to choose from each week. Such firms as the Aldine Publishing Company issued lists of four hundred available

Below left
Published in pictorial paper-wrappers in 1894 by the Parlour Car Publishing Company, the series *Old Sleuth's Own* finally comprised several hundred titles.

Size of cover: 18.2 cm × 12 cm.

Below right
The adventures of Pip and Squeak, and later, Wilfred the Rabbit, started as a newspaper strip-cartoon in 1920. This was the first of their many Christmas annuals, the *Wilfred Annual* first appearing in 1924.

Size of cover: 24.3 cm × 18 cm.

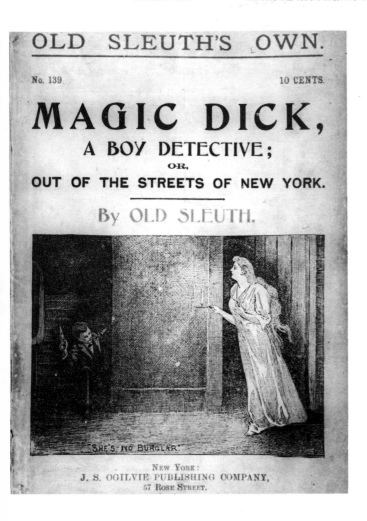

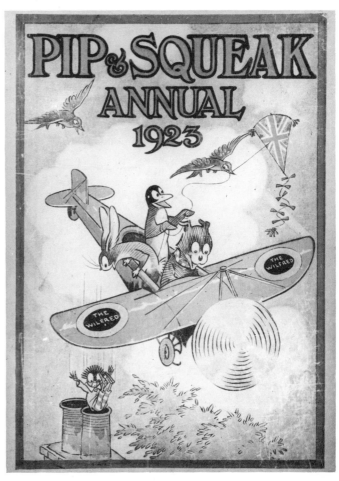

The long series of *Books for the Bairns* commenced publication in 1896. They were excellent value at a penny a copy.

Size of front cover 18.2 cm × 12 cm.

numbers from which their young readers could make their choice. Tales such as *The Wolf Demon*; *Tiger Dick*; *Fire-eye, the sea Hyena*; sometimes continued in weekly serials for as long as a year and seemed only to whet the appetite of their subscribers for more. Fortunes were made out of a single author's series of tales: Hogarth House, Bouverie Street, London, carried many of the successful George Emmett stories, and found a money-spinner in *The Blue Dwarf*, by Percy B. St. John (1821–89), a lurid and bloodstained tale of Dick Turpin's fictional hunchbacked friend. It was continuously reprinted, with variations, for over thirty years. By 1890 *The Quarterly Review* was complaining vigorously to its readers that such stories as *Broad-Arrow Jack*, by Edwin Burrage, were 'a class of literature which has done much to people our prisons, our reformatories, and our colonies with scapegraces and ne'er-do-wells'.

Fortunately not all the paper-bound juvenile periodicals were devoted to the interests of the blood-and-thunder school. In 1896 publication commenced of a monthly series of slim little booklets, each of 62 pages of text and pictures, which were issued in pictorially-printed pink-paper wrappers, at the price of a penny a copy. *Books for the Bairns*, edited by W. T. Stead, were an immediate and unqualified success. They were published at first by *The Review of Reviews* office, and later, when each printing of a new number ran into hundreds of thousands of copies, by Stead's Publishing House, an enterprise set up specially to cope with the demand. The first title to be issued was *Aesop's Fables*, with no less than 200 illustrations, and this set a standard that could only be maintained by selling up to and exceeding 50,000 copies a week. But the price of one penny a copy stayed constant throughout the life of the periodical. All the well-known fairy stories and folk tales were printed, and when these were exhausted the editor turned to historical tales, biographies, mythology, pictures and stories from foreign lands, digested versions of literary classics, and a host of other easy-to-read works that young people could enjoy. *Books for the Bairns* represented the first serious attempt to supply a cheap form of reading matter for the tens of thousands of poor children who could now, thanks to the passing of the Education Act, at last experience the long-denied pleasure of reading for their own entertainment.

Miscellanea, Toy Books and Moveable Books

18th-century booksellers commonly carried a stock of prints to attract their young customers. This is one of a set published in 1784. Total size of print: 26 cm × 16.5 cm.

Lodged safely in nearly every large collection of early children's books are a few examples of toy-books and knick-knacks which booksellers specialising in the sale of juvenile works displayed in their shops in the hope of tempting their young customers. John Newbery, far back in the 18th century, offered various little gifts to his young subscribers, such as fans, pincushions, spinning-tops, whips, and dolls. These were sold on the persuading principle of 'book alone – sixpence – book and pincushion together eightpence'; but there is no reason to suppose that the gifts could not be purchased separately if the client so desired.

When Robert Sayer became owner of a print and bookshop opposite Fetter Lane in Fleet Street, London, about 1765, he set about finding novel and attractive items that would sell side by side with his books and pictures.

Printed for & Sold by Carington Bowles. MODERN EXERCISE. No 69 in St Pauls Church Yard London.

Some of the leading theatres in the town featured pantomimes, then often termed 'harlequinades' after the part of the show in which the harlequin and clown play the principal rôles. Sayer had been experimenting with little 'turn-up' books, composed of single pictorially-printed sheets folded perpendicularly into four. Hinged to the head and foot of each fold was the picture, cut through horizontally across the centre to make two flaps that could be opened up or downwards. When raised they disclosed another hidden picture below, each having a few lines of verse to tell the story – finishing with the words 'Turn Up' or 'Turn Down', so that another picture came into view. These 'harliquinades' as they soon came to be called, for Sayer had featured the adventures of Harlequin in many of his titles, were one of the first toys in book form. Children referred to them as 'turn-up books'. By the end of 1770 Sayer published the first four, but they soon became a craze with children and by the turn of the century there was a choice of scores of titles. They were sold at sixpence plain, or one shilling with the illustrations hand-coloured, and rival booksellers, including Thomas Hughes, Ludgate Street, and George Martin, who published children's books at 6 Great St Thomas Apostle, Bow Lane, Cheapside, London, soon followed in the field. This latter publisher issued only coloured versions of his 'turn-up' books, and had brought the price down to sixpence. Typical of his titles were *The Woodman's Hut*; *Blue Beard*; *The Miller and His Men*; *Bertram*; and *Philip and his Dog*; all published undated about 1810. These fragile relics of a bygone age are now prized by collectors and fetch anything up to £20 ($48) each.

These little books were the forerunners of what is now termed the 'Juvenile Drama', a form of printed toy in sheet form that was probably invented by John Green, 121, Newgate Street, London, a publisher of children's books. The earliest sheets of the juvenile drama can be dated about 1810, and they have many affinities with the theatrical tinsel pictures of the same period. These were a favourite form of recreation for both young and old on wet afternoons and winter evenings. A printed sheet depicting the backdrop of a well-known play was purchased, together with an envelope or small box containing a variety of shaped and coloured tinsel and other materials, as well as the head and shoulders of the purchaser's favourite actor or actress of the day. The figure of the actor was gradually built up on the pictorial background by lightly gluing into place the bits of dress material, tinsel, feathers, beads, silver-paper, silk-scraps and velvet, that were shaped to make the body. The finished picture, with such wording as 'Mr Almar – as Steel Cap the Outlaw', or 'Mrs Egerton as Helen MacGregor', printed underneath, when framed and glazed made an extremely colourful exhibit for the drawing-room wall. Young people preferred the juvenile drama which rapidly became one of their most popular indoor pastimes. Sheets of scenery, flats, wings, and drop scenes, both interior and exterior, became available for children to construct their own miniature theatres. The proscenium arch itself, and the cardboard stage, were on sale in bookshops ready for young purchasers to construct and paint. By 1830 there were over fifty publishers who advertised *Juvenile Drama Sheets*, printed and ready for the scissors, and for sale in book-form portfolios to protect them from wear and tear.

From these theatrical sheets stemmed a new development that was promoted by the firm of S. & J. Fuller, at Rathbone Place, London, who intrigued children by calling their premises 'The Temple of Fancy'. Here they displayed an assortment of peepshows, panoramas, children's books and toys, and their novel and newly-invented paper-doll figures which were accompanied by stories in verse. A series of loosely inserted cut-out figures took the place of the conventional pictures in these little stories, which were sold in the form of printed boards tied with silk ribbons and issued in a board case to match. When the lucky child opened her present she discovered several hand-coloured paper-dolls representing the hero or heroine of the tale – but all were without their heads. A set of these heads, and an assortment of hats to put on them, accompanied the dolls, and they fitted into place on the bodies with paper tags. They were delightful toys to own, and a child could change the dress of the doll, and its face, by substituting new sets of clothes, heads and hats. But S. & J. Fuller catered only for the 'carriage trade'; their carefully hand-constructed wares were expensive purchases, selling in this instance at from five to eight shillings each. It seems that they could only have been playthings for children whose parents were in the upper income-bracket.

The History of Little Fanny, 1810, was Fuller's most successful venture in this field, and no less than four separate editions were called for in the first year of issue. Very few of the paper-doll books have survived complete, and it is usual to find that some of the separate heads and hats are missing. Complete examples can fetch anything up to £100 ($240) at auction. Other sought-after examples to enhance collections of early children's books are the *Toilet Books* of the 1820s and later. Stacey Grimaldi (1790–1863), son of the miniature-painter William Grimaldi (1751–1830), discovered a set of his father's drawings which the artist had made of a dressing-table and its contents. These depicted nine toilet articles, each hinged to a flap. As each flap was raised a suitable moral observation was found beneath it. A bottle marked 'A Wash to smooth' wrinkles' disclosed the word 'Contentment', and when the looking-glass above the table was lifted with the finger the word 'Humility' came into view. William had painted the little pictures and designed the flaps for the amusement of the younger members of his own family, but his second son, Stacey, then just over thirty years of age, decided to incorporate them into a book. He provided verses to go beneath each of the nine pictures, and wrote a preface to the work which made use of paraphrased quotations from *Visions in Verse*, by Nathaniel Cotton. *The Toilet; a book for Young Ladies*, was published at his own expense (dated 1821), and sold at the shop of William Sams, who had gained the distinction of being appointed bookseller to the Duke of York. A second edition was required the same year and Grimaldi was sufficiently pleased with the success of his enterprise to ask his father to design a similar work for children. He called this *A Suit of Armour for Youth*, 1824, and it was published by Ackermann, with the plates engraved by

The first known 'do-it-yourself' model of an aeroplane, dating from 1909. Printed in colours on a sheet of stiff cardboard, the cut-out model was glued together to complete the 'Antoinette' monoplane shown in the centre picture.

Size of sheet: 49.4 cm × 39 cm.

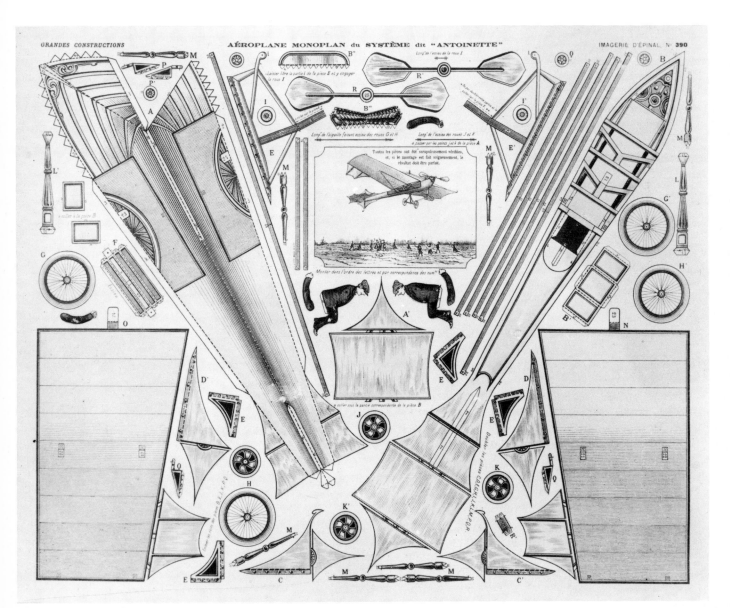

Armstrong after the designs of William Grimaldi. In this version the pieces of body-armour could be raised to reveal the maxims and morals. The one marked 'The Strongest Breastplate', when raised, disclosed George III addressing the House of Lords, with the word 'Virtue' printed beneath; and that of the 'Admirable Plume', the name attached to the Prince of Wales's feathers on the top of the helmet, was 'Loyalty', a reference to the future George IV who was Prince of Wales at that time.

Publishers who specialised in the publication of children's books had been an almost separate trade for many years; but even here there was division of enterprise into specific categories, some catering almost exclusively for younger children while others looked after the interests of teenagers or concentrated their attention on the provision of school text-books and primers. The firm of Thomas Dean, later Dean & Munday, of Threadneedle Street, London (after 1846, Dean & Son), turned their attention early to the toy-book trade, and were also one of the first publishers to make extensive use of lithography, and later chromo-lithography, for supplying the illustrations to their children's books. From about 1840 onwards they all but established a monopoly in the trade in all forms of movable and flap books. They set up a special department of skilled craftsmen to prepare the complicated and exacting systems of stiff-paper levers which made the pictures in their books dissolve into fresh and unexpected scenes at the pull of a tab. Many were extremely complex and could only have been marketed at prices the public could afford because at the time the skilled hand-labour needed was available cheaply. Some examples are shown in the illustrations to this present work. Typical of their ingenuity are *Dean's Moveable A.B.C.* (*c.* 1850), with the subtitle of *Prince Arthur's Alphabet*, each letter of the alphabet being accompanied by a hand-coloured illustration, the figures of which moved their heads or limbs when a tab at the bottom of the page was pulled; *Dean's New Moveable*

A page from *More Pleasant Surprises* (*c.* 1895), by F. E. Weatherly, a moveable book produced by Ernest Nister, Nuremberg, Germany. When a tab is pulled the first picture disappears and the other takes its place.

Size of pictorial area: 17.3 cm × 12.3 cm.

I don't think black suits him, do you? And soon a great change you will view.

I don't think black suits him, do you? And soon a great change you will view.

A GREEDY PIG.

One of the lithographic illustrations from *Shadows* (1856), by Charles H. Bennett (1829–67), the first of many similar works that were issued both plain and coloured.

Size of page: 18.6 cm × 13.3 cm.

Book of the Boy's Own Royal Acting Punch and Judy (c. 1860); *Dean's New Book of Dissolving Pictures* (1862), in which one picture slides over another at the pull of a tab to give a transformation scene; and *Dean's New Dress Book* (1860) telling of Rose Merton's adventures with the gipsies. The six hand-coloured pictures of Rose showed her clothed in actual dress materials of brightly coloured fabric. Then there was *Moveable Picture of our Four Footed Friends* (c. 1878), in which the animals in the six coloured pictures moved their heads and legs when the book's youthful owner operated the cardboard levers.

Shadow and silhouette, and books containing illusion pictures, have always been popular with young people. One of the finest exponents of the first of these arts was Charles Henry Bennett (1829–67), who brought a great deal of amusement to children with his numerous picture-books. The first of these proved to be one of the most successful, and copies of the first edition are now very hard to find. *Shadows* (1856), was published by D. Bogue, London, in a binding of pictorially-printed paper-covered boards, a fragile protection that does not appear to have withstood the test of time. The 24 leaves were printed by lithography on one side only with circular pictures depicting comical figures of the day, each casting shadows on the walls behind them. The shadows show no human likeness to their owners, as can be seen here in the illustration. Many of Bennett's children's books proved extremely popular and young people took such an interest in his unusual pictures, and handled his books so often, that copies in good condition are now very rare. *The Fables of Aesop and others Translated into Human Nature* (1857), was a slim quarto issued by Kent & Co., London, at a price of six shillings plain, or 10*s*. 6*d*. coloured. It contained some of his finest and most vigorous work. *Proverbs with Pictures*, 1859, Chapman and Hall, is a picture book he designed throughout, and the entire work was lithographed, with the text included with the pictures. In *Shadow and Substance*, 1860, he collaborated with Robert B. Brough who supplied the text. The 'shadows' are the best Bennett achieved in any of his books. *The Stories that Little Breeches Told*, 1863; *The Nine Lives of a Cat; a tale of wonder* (1863); *The Fairy Tales of Science* (1864), by J. C. Brough; *Fun and Earnest*, 1865, by Darcy W. Thompson; *Lightsome, and the Little Golden Lady*, 1867; and his satirical *London People: Sketched from Life*, 1868; are collected both by those interested in the history of book illustration and those adding to their library of children's books. Bennett also edited and illustrated *Old Nurse's Book of Rhymes, Jingles and Ditties*, 1858, with the hand-coloured illustrations engraved by Edmund Evans. Bennett supplied a remarkable set

First published in 1786, the *Adventures of Baron Munchausen*, by Rudolph Erich Raspe, contained exaggerations of the grossest and most improbable kind; but the tales of his exploits were beloved by generations of children and adults. This copy, dated 1819, is still in its original binding of paper-covered boards with uncut leaf edges.

Size of title-page: 19 cm × 11 cm.

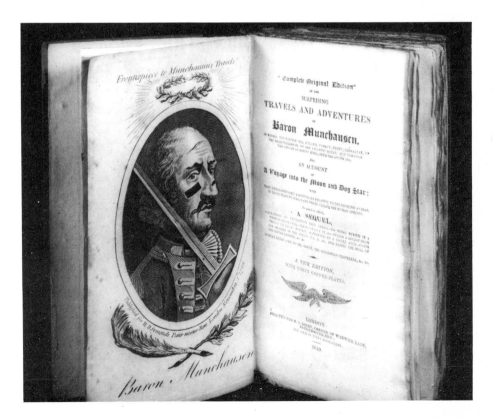

A silhouette illustration from *Karl Fröhlich's Frolicks with Scissors and Pen*, 1879, with translated verses by Clara de Chatelain.

Size of silhouette: 11.5 cm × 8.2 cm high.

A GREETING TO HIS READERS:

A second silhouette illustration from *Karl Fröhlich's Frolicks with Scissors and Pen*.

OUR COACH AND HORSES:

of portraits to illustrate Bunyan's *Pilgrim's Progress*, 1860, to which Charles Kingsley contributed the preface. A special favourite with children was *The Surprising, Unheard of and Never-to-be-surpassed Adventures of Young Munchausen*, 1865, which Bennett related and illustrated in twelve very tall stories. The book was published by Routledge, Warne & Routledge, and the hand-coloured plates were engraved by the Dalziel Brothers.

The best of the silhouette books was *Karl Frölich's Frolicks with Scissors and Pen*, 1879, translated from the German by Clara de Chatelain (1807–76), and published by R. Worthington, New York. Frölich had made a living for many years in his native Germany as an expert silhouettist, quickly cutting the sitter's protrait in profile with scissors from coloured paper. Before the advent of photography this was a cheap and speedy way of having one's likeness taken. Military men and travellers, embarking for overseas, often had a head and shoulders silhouette taken, then enclosed it in a letter home, complete with a lock of hair, as a token of remembrance for their families. The first of the Fröhlich silhouette books appeared in Germany in 1852, and others were published later. The example quoted above and illustrated on the page opposite contains some of the best of his work.

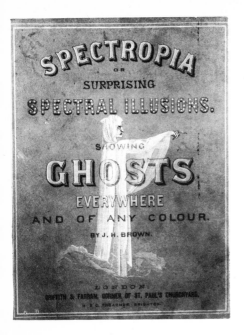

Illusion books were popular in the 1860s, and some of the best of the children's versions were produced by J. H. Brown of Brighton. *Spectropia; or, Surprising Spectral Illusions*, 1864, contained sixteen full-page plates of ghostly phenomena hand-painted in vivid colours. If the printed directions were followed, images were seen on ceilings and walls in complimentary colours. This was due, of course, to persistency of vision and the retention of the image on the retina of the eyes. It did not take children long to make their own 'ghosts', but *Spectropia* proved popular for many years and passed through several editions.

The best of the animated picture books were undoubtedly those devised by Lothar Meggendorfer in the 1880s and 1890s. Most of them were published by T. F. Schreiber, at Eklingen, near Stuttgart, Germany, or by Braun & Schneider, Munich. They were marvels of ingenuity a single tab at the side or bottom of the page making apes swing from trees, crocodiles swallow little boys, umbrellas open, boats roll, and houses collapse. Usually several movements took place at the same time on the same page: a horse rearing would throw its rider while his companion would successfully jump a fence. The 'works' which operated the various figures consisted of a series of interconnecting cardboard levers sandwiched between the coloured illustration on the front of the oblong leaf and the dummy pasted behind it. The animated limbs and heads were cut-out models on the front of the picture, and moving the tab set the whole scene in motion. Titles included *Reiseabenteuer des Malers Daumenlang und seines Deiners Damian* (c. 1885), with little Damian displaying a startling likeness to the classical figure of Little Lord Fauntleroy created by the artist Reginald Birch; *Schau mich an!* (c. 1886), a series of comic indoor and outdoor scenes; *Kasperl – puppenspiele für Jung und Alt*, by 'Dr Fidel Fidelius', (c. 1885), a German version of Punch and Judy; and Meggandorfer's *pièce-de-résistance*: his magnificent *Internationaler Zirkus* (c. 1888) containing more

An illusion book by J. H. Brown, of 1864. The sixteen full-page plates are hand-painted in vivid colours. Ghostly images are seen (if the directions are followed) on ceilings and walls in complimentary colours, with persistent vision, due to the retention of the image on the retina of the eyes. The book was a great favourite with children and went through several editions.   25 cm × 19.5 cm.

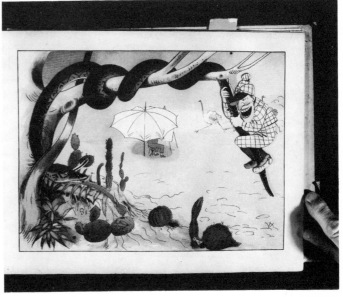

Most of the moveable and toy books of the 19th century were manufactured in Germany. *Daumenland und seines Dieners Damian*, by Lothar Meggendorfer, an oblong toy book of the 1890s, was produced by T. F. Schreiber, Stuttgart. The eight dramatically coloured scenes change position when the protruding tabs are moved.

Size of page: 33 cm × 25.5 cm.

than 450 separate pieces in the form of performers and animals, and issued complete with a circus ring tableau beneath which were the tabs to bring the circus to life. It sold at 7 marks 50 pfennig as against the usual 5 marks for the more conventional animated books. Many of these German toy-books were issued with the verses and stories in English, such as *Comic Actors* (c. 1891), described as 'a new movable toybook by Lothar Meggendorfer', and published by H. Grevel & Co., the London agents of the Munich firm. There are Meggendorfer collectors who snap up every example of his ingenuity that comes on the market. Very high prices are paid, for children inevitably tugged a little too hard, or tried to adjust a figure that had obstinately stuck and refused to perform its antics, with catastrophic results for Meggendorfer's hidden machinery. Providing all the bits are still in place repairs can be carried out, but finding these intriguing relics of the master showman is another matter. The expectation of life of an animated book must be considerably lower than its literary counterpart, and once broken down its probable fate was consignment to the dustbin at the next spring-clean.

Ernest Nister, London, represented the Nuremberg firm of Nister in the English market; but all the books they issued started life in Germany. The English versions were imported, but the text was not added to the German designed pictures without careful research into what would and would not sell in Britain. Nister specialised in 'dissolving picture-books', and 'stand-up' books, as well as more conventional but beautifully produced picture books for children, examples of which are given in this present work. Most of their transformation scenes were contrived by means of sliding slats, so that one

Books with shaped covers are still with us today; but the earlier models, such as these two of the 1890s, are difficult to find. Both were produced by Ernest Nister, Nuremberg, although the text and illustrations were first prepared in Great Britain.

Size of the little girl' book: 25.5 cm high.

picture was replaced by another as the colour-printed slats moved into place at the pull of a tab. *Pleasant Pastime Pictures* (c. 1895); and *More Pleasant Surprises*, were typical of the slim, folio-sized books that told a story in verse, while the extremely well executed oil-colour-printed illustrations dissolved from the heat of a summer's day to a snow-covered Christmas scene in the twinkling of an eye. Sometimes the slats were arranged to operate by a circular movement, as in *Magic Moments* (c. 1892); or in *Twinkling Pictures*, of about the same date, with verses by L. L. Weedon. One of the finest of their three-dimensional 'stand-up' books was *Peeps into Fairyland* (c. 1895), a panorama picture book of fairy stories, including an English text devised by F. E. Weatherly (1849–1929), a writer and versifier extensively employed by Nister. This oblong folio operated its three-dimensional grottos and fairy-tale scenes as the leaves were opened and the book laid flat. Linen slips pulled the integrated pictures upright, with as many as four different levels of scenery to give the pictures the desired depth. *The Land of Long Ago*, was a similar production of about the same date. All these early examples were carefully made, artistically designed, and printed in harmonious selections of colours that blended with the colour-printed backgrounds. Those that have survived intact are treasured by collectors, for they call to mind that more leisurely age in which they were so painstakingly designed and produced by the craftsmen of Nuremberg. Later versions, produced in Britain and the USA were called 'pop-up' books. The pictures automatically erected themselves into fairy-castles or woodland scenes when the volume was opened at the correct section. Those of the 1920s and 1930s were mass-produced to sell cheaply in the bookshops, and the pop-up models were printed in the most garish of contrasting colours. Nevertheless, they supplied a need and were no doubt treasured in equal degree by the children who received them at birthday or Christmas time. Similar models are obtainable to this day, and another age will be happy to find shelf room for the percentage that survive into the 21st century.

Pride of place in my own collection of toy-books has been given to *The Speaking Picture Book* (c. 1875), a musical toy in the form of a book that has fascinated young visitors (and my own children when younger) whenever they have been allowed to hear it in action. It consists of a folio-sized box (32 cm × 24 cm), that outwardly looks very much like a large, thick, children's book. Where the edges of the leaves would normally be is a carved facia of gold-coloured wood made to resemble the gilt edges of the leaves of a book. On the fore-edge there is a series of nine little ivory tassels attached to strings that disappear into the interior of the volume. The front cover is blocked pictorially in colours, showing a little girl reading a book, surrounded by various birds of the fields and watched attentively by her dog and doll. The spine has the title blocked in gold, and in the bookcase would be indistinguishable from a real folio-size volume. When the 'book' is opened the first eight leaves are much like those of any other children's picture book, except that they are printed on very stiff paper, with the text in verse form on one side and each picture on the other. But in each outer margin is a printed arrow pointing to a different ivory tassel as each leaf is turned. The title-page announces that this is *The Speaking Picture Book* and that it will reproduce 'the voices of the cock, the donkey, the lamb, the birds, the cow, the cuckoo, the goat, and the baby', if the reader will gently pull out and release the appropriate tassel opposite each picture in the book. The sounds reproduced are extremely lifelike, almost startlingly so, each picture having a different 'voice' that issues from between the carved wooden top and bottom edges of the 'leaves' of the book. The cords operate a system of miniature bellows concealed in the interior of the book and my own copy is still in perfect working order. The final two tassels cause the two children in the accompanying picture to call out 'Mama!' 'Papa!' as they wait at the lakeside for their parents to reach the shore in their boat. Copies of *The Speaking Picture Book* are occasionally offered for sale at about £100 ($240). The toy was manufactured in Nuremberg and originally sold with a German text. The English versions were imported into Great Britain by H. Grevel & Co., London, and into the USA by F. A. O. Schwarz, New York. A London example similar in format was titled *The Speaking Toybook*, and was published in 1893. The 15th edition of *The Speaking Picture Book* appeared undated about 1898, but the sub-title was changed to read: 'With Pictures, Rhyme, & Sound for Little People'.

Bibliography

The bibliographical works listed below form a selective reference background that a collector of early children's books needs to consult. Specialist collections and some of the best-known writers for juveniles have their own individual bibliographies which can be bought and consulted separately as your interest dictates, and these are not included in this general list.

Annals of English Literature, 1475–1950. Oxford University Press, 1961.

Book-Auction Records – 1902 to present day. 65 annual vols, London and New York, Henry Stevens.

Boys will be Boys, by E. S. Turner (magazines and penny dreadfuls). Toronto, Collins, 1948.

Cambridge Bibliography of English Literature, edited by F. W. Bateson. 5 vols. Cambridge University Press, 1940–57 (under revision).

Cambridge History of English Literature, edited by A. W. Ward and A. R. Waller. 15 vols revised. Cambridge University Press, 1907–33 (also issued in single volume concise form, 1970).

Cassell's Encyclopaedia of Literature, edited by S. H. Steinberg. 2 vols. London, Cassell, 1953.

Children's Books in England, by F. H. Darton. Cambridge University Press, 1932.

Children's Books of Yesterday, by P. James. London, published by 'Studio' periodical, Sept. 1933.

Children's Books of Yesterday, by P. H. Muir. London, published for the National Book League, 1946.

Children's Toys of Yesterday, by C. Geoffrey Holme. London, 'Studio', Nov. 1932.

Dictionary of Anonymous and Pseudonymous English Literature, by S. Halkett and J. Laing. 9 vols, Edinburgh, Oliver and Boyd, 1926–62 (also known as 'Halkett and Laing').

Dictionary of National Biography, edited by L. Stephen and S. Lee. London, Smith Elder, reprinted 1950; 28 vols to date.

Early American Children's Books, by A. S. W. Rosenbach. Limited edition, USA, Portland, Me., Southworth Press, 1933.

English Children's Books, by P. Muir. London, Batsford, 1954.

Key Books of British Authors, by A. Block. London, Archer, 1933.

Les Livres de L'Enfance. 2 vols. Gumuchian & Cie, Paris (1930).

Newbery, Carnan, Power, by S. Roscoe. London, Dawsons of Pall Mall, 1966.

Nineteenth-Century Children, by G. Avery. London, Hodder & Stoughton, 1965.

Osborne Collection of Early Children's Books, 1566–1910, edited by J. St. John. Canada, Toronto Public Library, 1958.

Oxford Dictionary of Nursery Rhymes, by I. and P. Opie. Oxford, Clarendon Press, 1951.

Pages and Pictures from Forgotten Children's Books, by A. W. Tuer. London, Leadenhall Press, 2 vols, 1898–1900.

The 'Studio' Special Winter Number 1897–98, edited by Gleeson White.

The Who's Who of Children's Literature, by Brian Doyle. London, Evelyn, 1968.

Written for Children, by J. R. Townsend. London, Miller, 1965.

XIX Century Fiction, by M. Sadleir. London, Constable, 2 vols. 1951.

Index

Numbers in *italic* denote captions and/or illustrations